The Challenge of Racism in Therapeutic Practice

The Challenge of Racism in Therapeutic Practice

Engaging with oppression in practice and supervision

Dr Isha Mckenzie-Mavinga

First published 2016 by
PALGRAVE

Palgrave in the UK is an imprint of Macmillan Publishers Limited, registered in England, company number 785998, of 4 Crinan Street, London, N1 9XW.

Palgrave Macmillan in the US is a division of St Martin's Press LLC, 175 Fifth Avenue, New York, NY 10010.

Palgrave is a global imprint of the above companies and is represented throughout the world.

Palgrave® and Macmillan® are registered trademarks in the United States, the United Kingdom, Europe and other countries.

ISBN 978-1-137-39702-7   ISBN 978-1-137-39703-4 (eBook)
DOI 10.1007/978-1-137-39703-4

This book is printed on paper suitable for recycling and made from fully managed and sustained forest sources. Logging, pulping and manufacturing processes are expected to conform to the environmental regulations of the country of origin.

A catalogue record for this book is available from the British Library.

A catalog record for this book is available from the Library of Congress.

Contents

Foreword

I first became acquainted with Dr Isha Mckenzie-Mavinga and her work at the Stephen Lawrence Centre whilst attending her training seminars. The teachings and experiential exercises were derived from her pioneering first book: *Black Issues in the Therapeutic Process*. This work sought to address the lack of material on training courses tackling the subject of racism in society and psychotherapy training courses and also found a language with key concepts to discuss and explore subjects such as: a black empathic approach; recognition trauma; healing ancestral baggage; and the black western archetypes.

This seminar was unlike any other training on 'Difference and Diversity' I had previously attended. Isha's approach was honest, open and uncompromising in exposing racism in society. She teaches that we as therapists run the risk of perpetuating oppression of our clients if we have not processed our own issues around race and thus have an ethical responsibility not to re-traumatise our clients who have come to us for help.

The book quite early on addresses the myth that institutions and the wider society posit the argument that we now live in a post-racist multicultural society. This avoidance is a convenient distraction and engenders complacency in not having to engage with what is a difficult history. Britain as a nation has obviously made great strides in race relations and equality. However, hundreds of years of Imperial power aligned with a white supremacist ideology where the racism is embedded in the history, culture, media and psyche cannot be eradicated overnight.

Black people as a minority group within a larger dominant white culture are still disproportionately over-represented in the mental health institutions and are more likely to be given higher doses of medication. This societal crisis is also reflected in other areas such as education, health, unemployment, low-income, incarceration rates.

An apt quote from a client at the beginning of the book states: 'When will I be able to live my life without having to think about being black?'

Expanding on her earlier work, this new book focuses on the dynamic within the therapeutic and supervisory setting. Isha asks us as counsellors and supervisors to look again at our practice. Using a transcultural model of therapy, she presents rich case studies to highlight and teach from her many years working in this field.

She examines the dynamic between a white therapist and a black client and how recognition trauma and guilt or defensiveness can create a rupture in the therapeutic relationship and create a silencing of the client.

She also focuses her lens and hones in on the black therapist's supervisory relationship and how this space of support, learning and ethical practice can become a space of being gagged if the supervisor has had limited training, inadequate engagement and lack of empathy, or her unprocessed issues around racism could hamper an opportunity for personal growth of the therapist and effective support for the client.

Further along the author reflects on her own Eurocentric training and assimilation into a model of therapy and because of holding rigid boundaries with black clients how this could have contributed to them not returning. Western theoretical conceptions on therapy have been primarily formulated by white middle-class men and these theories portray an incomplete model in regards to understanding and working with oppression and multidimensional oppression from societal forces such as sexism, classism and racism.

Isha challenges orthodoxy and yet, where necessary, draws on what resonates with her experience and research, such as the Jungian concept of Archetypes, etc. She is a breath of fresh air, introducing new ways of thinking and being in a sometimes staid and rigid academic environment regarding psychotherapeutic theories.

As practitioners we all sign up to an ethical code of conduct, which emphasises an anti-oppressive approach to working with difference and diversity. To be a reflective practitioner is to acknowledge our shortcomings and take action; anything else is to fall short of what is expected.

I hope this book will serve the counselling and supervision community in the way that I received it, which is to instil a sense of urgency in creating a healing environment for our clients so that we may all live more fulfilled lives free of discrimination.

Phoenix Gentles
Counsellor

Acknowledgements

Giving thanks:

To those who inspire my thinking and encourage me in my writing. My peers, colleagues, clients, supervisees and students. My ancestors and those who have gone before me and alongside me. My children and Gran children. Thanks especially to Thelma Perkins, Anthony Dowling. Patricia Gonsalves. Furlan Dick, Kris Black, Anita Mckenzie. BAATN. My Sista writers Wendy Francis, Hyacinth Fraser. My Sista friends and Tanya, Liz, Wendy, Gilly, Margaret.

Thanks to those who have contributed with their voices:

Carlana, Sadie, Nicky Bowler, Jenny Harrison, Ian Simpson, Mrs. Barua, Aileen Alleyne, Dom Powel, Samuel Ocheing, Pearl, Eugene Ellis, Phoenix Gentles.

Introduction

'When will I be able to live my life without having to think about being black?'

This powerful quote from a client moves me to take action against racism. I feel the pain of racism with her as she shares with me her rage and passion for moving out of this shared stuck place to a future where 'no one will be judged by the color of her or his skin' (Martin Luther King, Jr, 28 August 1963). This is the challenge of racism in therapeutic practice.

My experience of counselling and psychotherapy training courses has revealed a layer of institutional racism that initiated this work. I believe that the idea of post-racism is a mythology, because the work is not yet done. There is a risk of coasting along on multiculturalism and equal opportunity training, yet what has been started will not be finished until the social psychology of the people has healed. Fear of consequences such as being judged, mocked, branded, shamed and rejected as anti-racist campaigners, politically correct morons, and the idea that racism is happening in reverse creates numbness and inactivity.

Equal rights are everyone's right. Equal rights are intergenerational, and this book comes from a perspective that equal rights are fundamental to the psychological well-being of every nation. Thus there is no real blueprint for this work. Several attempts have been made to address the need for political direction in therapeutic discourses. Tuckwell (2002), Moodley et al. (2003), Fernando (1995), Eleftheriadou (1994), Dhillon-Stevens (2005), Dalal (2002), Fanon (1986), Lago (2006), Davids (2011), Fletchman Smith (2000) and DeGruy (2005), to name but a few, have provided the field with pointers that lead into a greater reflective approach to working with oppressions such as racism.

In support of Fanon's drive to end the traumatizing impact of racism on human psychology, it is time to carry this further and process the ways that racism can damage individual psychology if left unattended to. The experience of trauma and recovery from racism should not be underestimated. There is not much documented about healing our past and the impact of slavery on black people's psyche, and few attempts

1

have been made to address the challenge of racism in therapeutic practice and supervision.

Music, poetry, spirituality and art were always used to heal the mind and spirit, and as a method of self-expression, but hurts that became hardened due to slavery and the ongoing trauma of racism also need healing. Lack of attention to this aspect of past pain has caused disassociation as a means of survival in black individuals and families. Internalizing racism equals self-hatred, and black people have experienced limitations on support to exorcise their internalized negative stereotypes.

This book will expand on the themes and concepts previously addressed in *Black Issues in The Therapeutic Process* (Mckenzie-Mavinga, 2009). In that book, I referred to the term 'black issues' that embraced the life experiences of black and Asian people and their experiences of racism. I may also refer to the term 'person of colour', sometimes used for those who may not subscribe to the identity of black, yet who by virtue of their skin colour are inevitably targeted by racism.

My motivation to write comes from a lack of literature that specifically focuses on black issues and the impact of racism in practice. It is therefore my aim to assist ways of working with these areas in both therapeutic practice and clinical supervision. This will incorporate ways of utilizing a transcultural framework to assist understanding and attention to the process of engaging with black issues and, essentially, the challenge of racism.

One particular concern is the comment from some supervisees that they cannot take their work with black clients to their white supervisors. This shows that the impact of racism ripples through to the supervisory triad or group and affects the interrelationship between therapist and supervisor.

Supervision is a critical area of trainees' and professionals' personal development; therefore, this type of comment must be attended to. Whether the therapist or supervisor identifies as black, white, or a person of colour, it is clear that there is a need for a less inhibited dialogue and greater communication about black issues and the impact of racism on therapeutic practice. In the study presented in book one, student placements were the main area in which this gap was apparent. This gap in clinical support has appeared because of sensitivity about racism. This book will support an approach that encourages attention to this area of clinical work for supervisors and practitioners, particularly in relation to responses to the volatile and often silencing theme of racism.

Responses from both black and white professionals have been very positive since the publication of my previous book and subsequent seminars on the concepts presented in the book. Individuals find the use of concepts to create a framework for working with black issues useful. This revealed a need for further elucidation and ways to apply the concepts. The question frequently asked in the UK is, how do we open a dialogue about black issues, given the sensitive nature of racism?

I have heard from white therapists that sometimes their interventions are impacted by concern about being racist to a client, or being called racist by a client. This is usually where the issue of guilt comes into play and can silence individuals. Black therapists have also expressed concern about opening up the guilty feelings of a white therapist, peer or client, and this dilemma can inhibit immediacy and congruence. Whether the situation is perceived as a negative transference, lack of congruence or silence, this may be considered as a rupture. These practice concerns demonstrate a need for strategies to create safety to address racism. This book will address some of the complexities that underlie fear and guilt factors and engage with both the causes and outcomes.

This book is about developing black self-love and a positive black gaze, and celebrating the developmental processes of individuals impacted by racism based on skin colour. It is about moving beyond shame, denial and debilitating assimilation processes. I want readers to know that if I speak of 'we', I mean 'us', the parents, leaders, facilitators, educators, friends, clients, learning community and survivors, oppressed and oppressors of our time. We are both them and us because we are all oppressors and we are all survivors of oppression. We are the one nation of humanity, with the ability to influence change for future generations and create greater notions of equality.

Let us engage on a deeper level with the dreams of Rosa Parks, Angela Davis, Claudia Jones, Martin Luther King Jr, Gandhi and Mandela, and the creativity of Maya Angelou, Oprah Winfrey, Iyanla Vanzant, Toni Morrison, bell hooks and Audre Lorde, who were all about making their dreams of giving voice to the oppression of racism and making equal rights a reality.

This book is for those who want change in therapeutic practice. It is for individuals incarcerated in the mental health system, and for their families. It is for those who have lost their lives from racist attack and for black and Asian children who have suffered the multidimensional oppression of sexual abuse, racism and being silenced. It is for those who have experienced domestic violence and institutional racism and for the perpetrators and survivors of racism and oppression. It is, essentially, for those seeking to facilitate recovery from the impact of oppression, grief and trauma from multidimensional oppressions including racism.

How does one write about racism without invoking re-traumatization or feeling overwhelmed by fear? How do therapists work with the impact of racism without re-traumatization? Feelings of rage, guilt and numbness might make this appear to be impossible, but nobody died from feelings about racism. Genocide is a current phenomenon; human massacre continues on an international scale. Men control weapons of mass destruction. Women and minority groups continue to suffer heinous exploitation and domination. Males and females suffer physical and sexual abuse. Rape and misogyny are rife, and the institutional perpetuation of racism contributes to death of the spirit and slow, tortuous degeneration of the soul.

The intergenerational context of institutional racism is rooted in the training of white universities and mainstream institutions. This means that therapists seeking to be accredited by organizations set up by elders in the field may not have received training in anti-oppressive practice and the challenge of racism. Anti-oppressive practice encourages therapists to be aware of where they might perpetuate oppression in their responses to clients (Dhillon–Stevens, 2005).

The therapist's job is to listen and support individuals connected to these social processes. We must therefore consider what constitutes good practice and how therapists and supervisors deliver a service that is inclusive and culturally sound or unbiased. This book will offer an opportunity to think ethically about how this theme may affect the therapeutic and supervisory dynamic. As I reflect, poetry enables my process and hope for change:

A powerful state
Micro classifications
In monochrome

Reality
A third eye
In Technicolor

Exposing
Intrinsic bias
And maybe

Compassion
May evolve

Maybe!!!!!!!!
Maybe!!!!!!!!!

Isha Mckenzie-Mavinga, 2014

This book will concentrate on ways of working therapeutically with the impact of racism, internalized oppression, multidimensional oppressions and the intergenerational impact of sociocultural history on African, Caribbean and Asian people in the UK. Ideas and experience will be drawn from clients and professionals in the UK, since this is my area of expertise. It will include aspects of intra-cultural process and ways of understanding the therapeutic process when both therapist and client have a similar or different background. These areas will be explained using concepts that have evolved from research, training, life experience and practice.

Concepts such as a 'black empathic approach', 'recognition trauma', 'black Western archetypes' and 'ancestral baggage' (presented in my previous book) will be used in the context of therapeutic practice and clinical supervision, creating a model for therapists and care workers of today. Whilst empathic attunement is a key transtheoretical factor in many therapeutic disciplines, and in particular the person-centred approach, therapists and supervisors cannot take it for granted that empathy will be utilized in the context of black issues and racism in the therapeutic process. A black empathic approach specifically offers a response that relates sensitively to the client's racial and cultural experiences as they express them, and as the therapist intuitively recognizes them, and this will be presented as an element of the therapeutic and supervisory process. This approach associates the concept of 'holding' with knowing and remaining aware that racism in one way or the other will influence the developmental process of people who may benefit less in a majority white population and assimilation process. In less overt ways, racism also impacts on the perpetrator group, so a black empathic approach embraces all individuals involved with and concerned with the ways that racism impacts therapeutic practice.

This book promotes cultural connection and dialogue that offer an opportunity to explore identity in the context of racialization and racism. Opportunities to explore and contradict the impact of racism and internalized racism on African and Asian identities will be provided. The terminology used may imply a sense of homogeneity. This is not intended, but it is difficult to avoid given that contractual commitment and word limits confine me to what I am more familiar with and have more experience of, in using the term black, when discussing the challenge of racism.

Ultimately, my aim is to counteract the impact of Eurocentric dominance in theories that purport to assist psychological support.

Therapists will be encouraged to explore perspectives on African/ Caribbean/Asian and mixed-heritage experiences and include them in their approach to therapy and supervision. The concept of recognition trauma will be discussed in relation to both clients' and therapists' responses to themes such as racism, race-related guilt and the impact of history on individuals. The term recognition trauma portrays the experience of powerful feelings that occur when an individual becomes aware that they have been a victim of racism or that they are a member of the perpetrator group. These feelings can block the individual from self-expression, causing self-doubt, depression and low self-esteem.

Relative trust issues when dialoguing about the challenge of racism will be explored in the context of facilitating clients and therapists during clinical supervision. This is where the concept of black Western archetypes, denoting the collective perpetuation of racism and ancestral baggage, identifying an intergenerational context, will be put to use. These two concepts are useful when examining relational discourses and therapy where unconscious processes and relational ruptures need to be considered. The use of these concepts supports a black empathic approach and can enhance the therapeutic tools of therapists from all cultural backgrounds.

I shall talk about listening specifically to the challenge of racism in the therapeutic triad and ways to influence related practice. I want readers to be saying these are good ideas and we can look at this in terms of our practice, we could use this, we could pay attention to what she is saying here in that we need to take risks and need to work through the consequences in our own process and responses to racism and be actively working with these challenges in the therapeutic process. At the end of each chapter I shall present pointers for training and supervision.

This book has four parts. A brief introduction to these is below.

Part I: Ungagging: Denial, Silence, Rage

Part I concentrates on ways of breaking the silence that often evolves when black issues are being explored. Finding a language to address emotions linked to racism without further perpetuating racism is one of the biggest challenges. A twentieth-century challenge that has slowed down progress in working with the impact of racism is the mythology of a post-racism period. This assumption has caused institutional lockdown on efforts to continue supporting those experiencing racism. The resulting silence that has occurred can be linked to personal or institutional denial of racism because it is not always overt and blatantly in your face. It is generally seen as happening on the football pitch or when there is a threat to public safety, or a riot.

I have named this perceived negative transference, lack of mindfulness, disconnection, and silence due to racist content a 'psychological gagging'. Practices that run into gagging are likely to perpetuate oppression and therefore create a need for strategies to recover safety and empathy. Empathy between client and therapist and therapist and supervisor can be interrupted when there is stuckness in processing racism.

This section will address the complexity and cause of these challenges and explore how these concerns can be supported in therapeutic practice and clinical supervision. A question that often arises for the supervisee is, 'how safe is it to raise the issue of racism with my supervisor?' In response to this question, I shall address causes and outcomes of denial and silencing in the therapeutic relationship and clinical supervision. Black rage is the term that I have given to the eruption of powerful feelings of anger that black and Asian people often associate with racism. This considerably underestimated phenomenon and its associated challenges will be given attention. The question of rupture in the supportive or therapeutic relationship will be addressed in this context.

Chapter 1: Denial and the Myth of Post-Racism

This chapter will challenge ideas about the existence of a post-racism period that proposes racism no longer exists. The challenge of facing the reality of how this perspective can silence individuals and inhibit proactive engagement with the theme of racism in therapy and clinical supervision will be addressed.

Chapter 2: Silencing and Taboo Subjects

This chapter explores the consequences of silencing and ways of empowering individuals who experience intersecting oppressions. Relationship taboos are a common feature for people of African and

Asian heritage. Being in a sexual minority and being subject to racism is a also complex issue. In addition, the combination of taboo and intra-cultural influences on survivors of incest, rape and violence within the family and intergenerationally can have a particular impact on the way individuals cope and the ways they are responded to by professionals.

Chapter 3: The Process of Black Rage

Individuals and oppressed groups hold a tremendous amount of pow-erful feelings and rage that can remain unprocessed and unsupported due to fear, inhibition and concerns about mental health. In this chap-ter, suppressed and expressed rage and outrage will be addressed in the context of working with psychological material and mental health. Challenges presented in the role and responsibility of the therapist and supervisor to create a safe supportive space for rage to be explored in the context of ethnicity, assimilation and mental health will be discussed. Assumptions based on stereotypes of Asian passivity and lack of con-sideration for cultural heritage and expression of feelings drawn from empirical material will also be addressed in this chapter.

Part II: Identity, Shadism and Internalized Oppression

The challenge of racism and developmental processes has to be sensi-tively negotiated when working therapeutically in the context of cul-tural diversity, assimilation, family fragmentation and mental health. When the psychological challenges of living with diversity are not taken into account, a client's whole experience can become denied or split off from their experience of being black, Caribbean, African, Asian or immigrant and belonging to a group whose origins differ from the host population. In this section, problems of personal and institu-tional disassociation, and the process and healing of internalized nega-tive cultural messages and racism that come from within the family and from the environment will be addressed. I have framed this as the concept of ancestral baggage. The term 'shadism' is used to describe prejudice based on diversity between light skinned and dark skinned black people. The cultural origins of the black and Asian family are integral to individual personal development processes. With this comes association with mixed-heritage experiences and specific gender influences that intersect with racism. Part II will address some of these experiences and support ways that therapists can be more inclusive of these areas.

Chapter 4: The Melting Pot

This chapter will address concerns about homogeneity and perspectives that include diversity within African/Caribbean and Asian families. I shall take a look at the problems of tarring everyone with the same brush, so to speak, and how the therapist can use diversity and sameness to get to know the client's cultural background. I will address ways that assimilation can compound the expression of hurt related to racism and responses to this distress. The chapter also addresses the challenge of racism and aculturalization as a feature of the client's personal development and ongoing life experience.

Chapter 5: African Heritage, Asian Heritage, Mixed Heritage

This chapter will unpack the mysteries and nuances of African/Caribbean family influences, Asian family influences and mixed-heritage experiences. The challenge of sociocultural stigmas and assumptions about being black enough, white enough or mixed culturally and racially will be explored. Using empirical material of the supervisor, therapist and client, the role of a racialized identity in self-esteem and psychological development and support will be addressed.

Chapter 6: Gender Influences and Racism

This chapter will consider the role and designation of black men and black women in terms of coping with racism. Ways that therapists and supervisors can reflectively contradict the harmful process of stereotypes and their influence on the therapeutic triad will be considered. Racism and gender often feature in one-dimensional ways, and it is rare that the spotlight gets focused on how individuals cope with intersecting oppressions, so this chapter will take a look at the challenges of working therapeutically with this multidimensional context. The challenge of parallels between interracial and intra-racial dynamics, and gender discourses, will be addressed.

Part III: The Traumatic Effects of Slavery and Colonialism

Racism continues to cause and compound trauma and depression. It is often forgotten that slavery was damaging for both the perpetrators and the enslaved and that both parties have played a significant role in moving on from this atrocity. Silences about the impact of slavery and colonialism within therapeutic discourses often mean that black clients may not receive appropriate support for the intergenerational impact of this collective trauma. This section will offer some insights about ways that therapists and supervisors can process the post-slavery traumatic impact and the intergenerational duality of contemporary coping mechanisms. The concept of black Western Archetype and ancestral baggage will be expanded to support these challenges.

Chapter 7: The Intergenerational Context of Internalized Racism

In this chapter, the intergenerational and internalized context of how racism has impacted black, Asian and white people will be explored. Attention will be given to the way that the hurt of racism gets taken into the psyche and re-enacted in the daily lives of black peoples, for example hair straightening, skin whitening and negative mirroring of identity and appearance. This exploration will inform and support the challenge of engaging with the impact of intergenerational and social racism on the developmental process of black people.

Chapter 8: Working with Trauma and Recognition Trauma

I have previously introduced the concept of 'recognition trauma' to identify responses to black issues in my study with trainee counsellors. In this chapter, I explore the use of this concept in the client, therapist and supervisor experience. I suggest ways of supporting an open dialogue about these feelings to ultimately support the client through this kind of trauma that may often lay dormant in their lives.

Chapter 9: Emerging from Recognition Trauma

This chapter will explore ways of working with the conscious and unconscious impact of racism. Identifying and working through recognition trauma will be explored. Working with the apparent but unspoken and the therapist/supervisor dialogue and relational context of the theme will be supported. The impact of silencing and negative emotions related to revealing and acknowledging racism in the therapeutic triad will be discussed.

Chapter 10: An Ethical Context

In this chapter, I will outline some ethical challenges that arise from proposing this discourse and from reflection on the written text. Ethical contradictions relating to ideas and suggestions about practice and supervision will be explored and supported. The chapter will also encourage readers to try different approaches to acknowledging and addressing black issues and racism in the context of their discipline, service provision, and supervisee settings.

Jackson (1996) states: 'If we have any hope of putting our house in order, we have to accept that racism exists and that it festers in every aspect of life' (p. 9).

Part I

Ungagging: Denial, Silence, Rage

Racism plays a huge role in how black issues are defined and experienced. As a black student expressed, 'black issues are also white issues'. An example of this manifests in the difficulties of addressing racial diversity in the therapeutic relationship.

In terms of the black–white dyad, there is a tendency to focus on the therapist's responsibility to open this diversity issue. We often forget that this issue can be influenced by assimilative processes – ways that racism plays out between individuals. I, myself, must own that I have been more likely to attend to racism in the therapeutic dynamic when counselling black clients. My internalized process of fear when confronting white people about racism kicks in and can create denial of the diversity between us. This is how my own assimilation into Eurocentric ways of being has influenced my therapeutic practice.

What is denial but a defence against strong emotion? In the world of psychotherapy, denial is a defence to be taken seriously. Suppression of powerful feelings can cause emotional and physical disease, leading to depression. Therefore, denial is a behaviour that needs some reflective evaluation. In the early chapters of this book, the courtship between denial, silence and rage will be observed, and their collusive relationship on an institutional, personal and therapeutic level will be addressed.

Denial and the Myth of Post-Racism

This chapter takes a look at the myth that the work on racism is finished and how this functions as denial in the context of racism, thus inducing a silence that inhibits the explicit engagement of black issues in the therapeutic process. Howitt and Owusu-Bempah (1994) describe this occurrence as racism having 'changed its clothes' (p. 9).

It is generally assumed that institutions in the UK are in a discourse of post-racism – a neo-colonial period of acceptance, tolerance, understanding and living in harmony with our differences. Therefore, the assumption is that racism is no longer relevant to healthy psychology. This assumption is far from the truth. Things appear to be OK on the surface, until we hear of a racist incident in the media. Multiculturalism is doing its job of integrating diverse cultures and experiences into employment and social institutions. The media portrays more affirming images of brown-skinned people. The art and music world is edging its way past tokenism. The education system takes bullying and racial abuse more seriously, and there are laws to curb overt racist abuse.

However, the mythology of a post-racism period (Mckenzie-Mavinga, 2010) has created a denial of where psychological therapies stand in the process of supporting awareness and change in this area. As a result, hesitation to address racism, based on the belief of a post-racism period, serves to stagnate challenges to institutional racism and the growth of anti-oppressive practice. Any progress is then relegated to individual therapists and students, who soldier on, often with little support. This important concern raises the question of what gets bypassed or passed on in the client therapist–supervisor triad? Racism has permeated the psyche and continues to be a fearful, guilt-ridden theme that may be addressed by its victims and rarely acknowledged by its perpetrators. This oppression, in all its guises, needs to be an ongoing concern in order to preserve the integrity of therapeutic work and client welfare.

The women's movement was accused of whitewashing women of colour. Sexism and homophobia permeated the black power movement, and racism and sexism impact gay and lesbian communities. Multiculturalism has thus arisen out of a need to understand and eliminate oppressions within and between different ethnic and minority groups and their respective individual intersecting identities. Intersecting identities is a conceptual model of ways that individual and socially constructed identities such as gender, race, sexuality and spirituality influence individual personal development processes. Therefore, by considering a person's ethnicity, place of origin, cultural background, spirituality, gender and sexual orientation, a greater understanding of their identity development and experiences of oppression can be gained.

In this respect, internalized oppression, a term given to destructive attitudes and behaviours that result from the distress caused by oppressions such as racism, must be considered. Lack of opportunity to express hurt caused by oppression contributes to internalized oppression. The oppression is sometimes re-enacted against the self and others causing low self-concept and feelings of powerlessness.

Attempts to understand denial as a response to these discourses have thus become a feature of ongoing efforts to process how the hurt of prejudice impacts on the unconscious psyche; however, learning about the impact of racism and oppressions does not give licence to assume the work is done. A stuckness that prevents active involvement in addressing racism and cultural oppressions underpins the mythology of a post-racism period.

A greater understanding of diversities has led to equality legislation and more challenge to institutional oppressions. These are the outward, more observable, signs that contribute to the myth of post-racism. The unconscious and internal effects of oppression and intra-cultural dynamics have been addressed to a lesser degree and usually within specialist agencies such as PACE LGBT+ mental health charity, Nafsiyat Intercultural Therapy Centre, the Refugee Therapy Centre, the Asian Family Counselling Service, the Women's Therapy Centre, and One in Four therapy for sexual abuse survivors. These agencies grew out of a need for marginalized voices to be heard.

The challenge is upon us to unpick this mythology in an ethically sensitive way that supports individuals and institutions. Below I have listed some pointers relevant to this transitional process.

- Individuals and institutions must recognize and work towards anti-oppressive practice in therapeutic relationships and supervision.
- It is important to raise issues of 'difference' in a sensitive, therapeutically supportive manner.
- Remember that all of us, no matter how well trained, have difficulties with issues of difference, including black issues. Individuals need acknowledgement of the different levels of awareness and experience that they may be at with this.
- White therapists and supervisors have an ethical obligation to be non-defensive about the impact of racism.
- Black and Asian therapists and supervisors must be aware of over-identifying with black issues and work with the diversity within black and Asian communities.
- Flexibility is important, as black issues often challenge our theoretical commitments – for example, our understanding of transference and counter-transference dynamics, or using a strictly person-centred approach.

Choosing to be silent plays into the mythology of post-racism. White tutors, quoted below, evaluating a black issues workshop on a training course explain how they can choose to be silent or choose to have a voice because they may not be directly impacted by racism.

Tutor 1:   I remember that training day and I think that that was quite a moment for me. There have also been other moments that have been challenging for me in the teaching of this course ever since it started. I am aware of how I am often reluctant to speak. It isn't that I am not thinking about things; it is that I am often reluctant to speak. There are times when we are reminded by Isha to think about things and I say, 'Yes it is another thing on my list to do.' I don't know that I feel any bolder. I feel more secure in myself and in my thinking about where I am, but I don't think I am any braver than ten years ago about confronting racism or addressing black Issues. There is sometimes a borderline between those two things. I like the way that white students have become bolder and braver. I suppose that I was saying that knowing that black people have to deal with things that I never have to deal with from the minute you set out side of your house and there are things that I can pretend are not happening.

Tutor 2:   I am thinking about speaking, about having a voice, and as two white tutors leading a workshop, the fear that came with that. Also one of the things that I felt about the continuous input of black

issues through the postgraduate training and all the discussions that go with that outside of the teaching time have made me slightly more able to speak. I was thinking about one of the things that both white and black students from a different perspective, is being able to continue my voice despite my anxiety. But I still censor myself even after all this time. I don't know, in terms of evaluation, how that influences the students, if I am doing that. The other thing is, there still seems somehow, not to have been picking up when two white people are working together. It doesn't seem to be translated across to other oppressions. At the end of all of this, I have learnt masses, and I still find it a struggle and it's still difficult and it still causes me anxiety and it's still painful.

Tutor 1 clearly demonstrates how slow change can be, in that she has 'not felt much braver approaching black issues in ten years'. Tutor 2's evaluation shows that she continues to 'censor herself'. It is important to observe the consequences of this behaviour, as censoring can translate into the student's perception of therapeutic behaviour and, indeed, into the therapeutic relationship, subsequently perpetuating denial of racism.

Both these voices dispel the myth of post-racism. Tutor 1 uses the concept of bravery in situating an experience that many black people face on a daily basis; however, I am aware that black people also have ways of coping with their powerful feelings about racism. Here denial can happen from a survivor perspective. Each individual has his or her own ways of coping with racism, whether from the survivor or perpetrator perspective. We are where we are, and you are where you are on this challenging theme. However, as a therapist it is not enough to just acknowledge where you are, because this stuckness and silencing can contribute to the mythology of post-racism. I want to encourage therapists to consider the importance of deciding to work through the ongoing challenge of racism and its imposition on the psyche.

When observing students responding to racialized concerns, I found that although non-intentional, the needs of the white students became prioritized over the learning of black students and subsequently black students become their facilitators. This is where the mythology of post-racism becomes operative, because in this situation racism gets transferred into an unconscious dynamic that perpetuates a subservient, less-educated position of the black student. Tutors, therapists and supervisors are positioned in an educative role and have a responsibility to challenge this aspect of institutional racism, otherwise the mythology of a post-racism phase can be perpetuated.

Hussain and Bagguley's study (2007) supports this concern. They interviewed 114 young female students of Indian, Pakistani and Bangladeshi background (p. 24) and asked them about their experiences of learning. The study concluded that

> Insufficient attention to the impact of isolation, racism and Islamophobia was a primary concern. In addition, 'racism and homophobia in universities have all too often been brushed aside'. (p. 144)

You may be wondering why this has become an important concern, or you may be thinking why am I making an issue of something that is not really apparent. These concerns echo familiar questions asked by trainees. Samples of these questions are presented below.

- Do we focus too much on the colour of each other's skin and consequently generate unnecessary barriers?
- Is this a class issue rather than a race issue?
- If I haven't got an issue with racism, is it that I am not aware?
- Do I compensate in my behaviour when I deal with black issues, to hide my prejudice?

These questions indicate that the challenge of racism is not just about being politically correct. There are deeper, more fundamental, concerns that may need to be resolved. For example: saying the right thing about racism in the right way, or not saying in case of causing offence. I shall attempt to address some of these questions and their relevance as we journey through the book. The challenges identified require a particular type of empathic approach. I have called this 'a black empathic approach' (Mckenzie-Mavinga, 2009, p. 58). A black empathic approach offers a response that specifically and sensitively relates to a client's racial and cultural experiences as they express them and as the therapist intuitively recognizes them as an element of identity and psychology.

I encourage readers to ask questions, but don't stop there or confuse the question as the answer. Defensiveness that arises from trying to cope with the emotions associated with racism causes the mythology of a post-racism period that I am addressing. It is therefore important to reflect on your personal response to both the questions and possible solutions. One solution is to seek peers, supervisors and supportive individuals to voice your fears and concerns to, with a view to gaining insights that will support your practice.

Wheeler (2006) supports Tuckwell's (2002) suggestion that 'the attitudes and beliefs about race and culture are thus implicit in the inter-psychic world of both the counsellor and client, and these impact on counselling interactions in various ways, whether in homogenous dyads or racially culturally mixed dyads. In view of deeply held assumptions about race and culture with the intra-psychic life and interpersonal functioning, it is essential that counsellors be alert to racial and cultural dynamics that arise in the counselling process' (p. 149), and that 'unless counsellors have come to an awareness of themselves as racial and cultural beings, their capacity to work effectively with these dynamics will be considered impeded' (p. 150).

This is the work of unpacking the mythology of post-racism, and I want readers to join with me in addressing this challenge to institutions that train in therapeutic practice. The way to start is by taking on board the voices of black and Asian trainee therapists and actively developing a multicultural anti-oppressive curriculum. Below are some examples of those voices. We must consider whether they get heard and responded to in training and clinical supervision.

- I am wondering why, as a black woman, up to now, I have not thought of bringing black issues into my relationships with white clients?
- What if a client rejects me when I am a counsellor, because of my African Caribbean heritage?
- Why is it that I don't feel as good as white contemporaries? Most of the theory and models are from non-black backgrounds, and this has an impact on black culture. It does not fit into the way we think. How can we work with this?
- What if this is an issue with racism in the counselling process, and every time I reflect on it the client changes the subject? Then, when I address that, the client says 'That is not what I am trying to say' and I still feel something is not quite right? Considering this resistance on the client's behalf, should I address my fear and uncertainty of dealing with black issues with my client?

It is important to listen to these questions in the context of the experience and process of these individuals, because the development of their therapeutic ability also relies on their self-concept as subjects of racism.

In this whole challenge of racism in therapeutic practice, I frequently feel gagged, yet the irons that muzzle me are a feature of the past. How do you feel when you are intuitively aware that racism is functioning in a situation? Being aware but not attending to the oppression causes racism to become internalized because ideas about post-racism set in and can cause low institutional esteem and low self-esteem. I use the concept of 'black Western archetypes' to describe the collective unconsciousness of this process (Mckenzie-Mavinga, 2009). These are inherited psychological patterns influenced by racist images, behaviour and attitudes. They are carried in the unconscious life of individuals and recognizable in outer behaviour. They are also portrayed in family structures, perpetuated by the collective unconscious, within social structures, throughout history and reinforced by tradition and culture.

The human psyche processes cultural concepts and internalizes both the positive and negative elements of prejudice and oppression that individuals and communities inhabit. Racism is a prejudice that in its extreme has created hostile and dangerous discourses. It doesn't take much to recognize the damaging influence of groups such as the Ku Klux Klan, the British National Party and the Nazi regime, all products that developed out of negative, hateful archetypes. Uninterrupted, these harmful insights are passed intergenerationally and instilled into the early life and developmental processes of both survivors and perpetrators of racism. Individuals are not born with these oppressions, but they easily become influenced by outward manifestations of them, if parents and carers are not aware of the damage they can cause.

We learn to manage these harmful influences by projecting them onto others or suppressing them into the shadow part of our psyche. Jung (1972) explains 'the shadow' of the inferior traits of others perpetrated in a trickster style. This is where denial, silencing and gagging become functional.

Humans are steeped in archetypes that collectively uphold oppressions. These archetypes are harboured within families, educational institutes and organizations. They are brought to light by insights about challenge and change that become training elements and can transform attitudes and the behaviour of individuals. Surely this means that the human psyche needs ways to therapeutically heal its path from the intergenerational processes of racism.

The black Western archetype is one aspect of what gets passed on intergenerationally. Black Western archetypes have fuelled social discourses such as the underachievement of black boys in the UK educational system and over-representation of black people in prisons and the mental health system. The proposition of 'drapetomania', which an American physician, Samuel A. Cartwright, in 1851 attributed to African slaves who attempted to flee captivity, can be seen to have fuelled misdiagnosis and over-representation of black people in the mental health system. A greater emphasis on the historical consequences of this injustice may provoke ways of coping with multidimensional oppressions, and intergenerational trauma caused by racism.

It could be said that the mythology of post-racism is exacerbated by the internalization of white archetypes. It is a painful and difficult battle to stay awake and present enough to challenge the idea of a post-racism mythology; yet, not attended to as an aspect of denial, this schism can create an unconscious defence against supporting clients who experience racism.

This process can be associated with the defence of splitting, a coping mechanism where individuals transfer bad feelings into some other place (Klein, 1946). The mythology of post-racism may, indeed, fundamentally be caused by splitting, which invokes silence due to the prospect of really getting into the underbelly of racism and addressing it.

Tuckwell (2002) suggests that the silence occurring in the face of racism is damaging to the therapeutic relationship. Left unattended, this silence can result in the client leaving their therapy (p. 138). I have first-hand experience of how Eurocentric influences can drive clients away. The Rasta man whom I refused to give advice to did not return. The black woman who walked out and never returned seemed furious with me because I kept rigid boundaries about time and money. Of course, there were other reasons why these clients had difficulty conforming to what might look like my assimilative behaviour, but I am also pretty sure that my training and initial silence about the cultural dynamics of forming a therapeutic attachment were relevant to these situations. Looking back, I can see how the theories of counselling that I was taught and my own silence were provoked by naivety or fear of upsetting the apple cart by addressing our diversities as black people.

This most crucial silence that suggests numbness and lack of connection led to inactivity about cultural dynamics and assimilation. I am sure that both clients were already familiar with the response and looking for more culturally appropriate support. As I recall, in terms of intra-cultural dynamics it was a learning curve for me. I came face-to-face once again with past loss of my black heritage, and I had to process my rejection issues as a black, mixed-heritage woman, abandoned by black clients. Whilst attending to the domestics of setting up a contract, I was buying into the mythology of post-racism, because the meetings lacked attention to the likely reason these clients had sought after me as a black therapist.

I suggest that the idea of post-racism is a figment of recognition trauma, and this mythology is built on denial, probably evoked by a fear of the magnitude of racism and other intersecting oppressions. Recognition trauma is a developmental process to be worked through, a phase, like Klein's depressive phase (Klein, 1975). Having gone into the phase and explored its symptoms and hurts, it is generally possible to move through it into a more empowered and liberated position. This process can be supported by building what is known by Byfield (2008) as 'cultural capital'. In the case of young black scholars, the term cultural capital was used to identify levels of support derived from family, peers and educators. A high level was seen to build and maintain a confident, black identity. Those with lower cultural capital achieved lower results in school. Therapists can reinforce this by offering cultural empathy, which places an emphasis on connecting and engaging with the cultural elements of the therapeutic process on a deeper more meaningful level.

Transculturalists such as d'Ardenne and Mahtani (1989); Eleftheriadou (1994) highlighted the cultural elements of the relational process between therapist and client and the impact of the therapist's attitude to diversity in the therapeutic space. Their approach emphasized an expectation of the therapist to re-evaluate their own prejudices and experiences of oppression in order to be with the client's experiences of diversity and oppression. Upholding a mythology of post-racism can inhibit this responsibility, if not attended to, upholding a mythology of post-racism can inhibit this responsibility.

In the first place, trainers have a responsibility to re-evaluate their attitude and approach to teaching anti-oppressive practice and unlearning silences about racism. Dhillon-Stevens (2004) specifies that:

> We need to be extremely questioning of ourselves and our own assumptions and being very patient and not punitive with supervisees who may be beginning to think about these issues. (p. 155)

She advocates that we must be aware of the dangers of perpetuating oppression within the therapeutic relationship. From this perspective, I have devised some key areas for therapists and supervisors to consider when addressing racism.

Key areas for therapists and supervisors

- Therapists and supervisors must acknowledge and understand the nature and impact of difference and similarity, identity, racism, culture and belief systems in the therapeutic relationship.
- Supervisors and therapists must accept that clients may experience specific or intersecting oppressions in addition to racism.

- Therapists and supervisors must examine the impact of racism and other oppressions on their own personal development process and the client's developmental process.
- Therapists and supervisors must develop ways of being present in the client's process of cultural identity development, racism and other oppressions.
- Most importantly, therapists and supervisors must find ways to engage with each other and clients in anti-oppressive, empowering ways that support intercultural and intra-cultural experiences and the challenge of racism.

Unconscious racist stereotypes passed on intergenerationally and through sociocultural processes can be explored using the concept of the black Western archetype. Unconscious racist stereotypes perpetrate homogeneity and create a mindset that brands all black people as one and all Asian people as one. This stereotype uses features such as skin tone, class and immigration status to undermine the client's specific racialized identity development and individual life experience.

Asian people, for example, are subject to the impact of colonization and the effect of collective cultural practices. These practices are sometimes experienced as restrictive, when confused ideas are taken on. Forced marriage, for example, as opposed to arranged marriage, is oppressive and tantamount to heterosexism, and individuals outside of this cultural context often view both in the same bag, as though they are one and the same and therefore both negative. Confused perspectives of the multicultural aspects of Asian communities can create exoticism, ill-informed approaches that do not fit the Asian clients' real experiences. In the same way, connections and differences between Africans and African Caribbean and Asian Caribbean people can become confused and homogenized.

Homogeneity pervades assumptions that uphold a post-racism mythology like a kind of monochrome mask. Combined with assimilation, whether involuntary or imposed via immigration processes, it can contribute to oppression. We are all affected by and feel cultural assimilation at some level throughout our lives, so consideration of this feature of human development is important. A client's assimilation process can influence their levels of engagement with a therapist and may cause hesitation to discuss cultural experiences, racism or abuse. Assimilative processes may support racist attitudes when levels of personal assimilation are viewed by a therapist as an indicator.

This is a vital area for consideration. Pro-assimilation attitudes can create ruptures in the therapeutic process and appear problematic if not processed in supervision. One student asked the question:

> What do we make of the world out there, which is still stuck in the collective unconsciousness of inequality/colonization/slavery/denial of heritage and history, that denies a psychologically secure base within which both client and therapist have to engage?

The above question shows concern about the frameworks that underpin cultural assimilation. As individuals, we are in that world, coping with the collective unconscious every day. This ongoing dilemma is coupled with the mythology of post-racism and denial. The student quoted above is drawing attention to how trauma and attachment issues link to the impact of racism and its intergenerational causes.

I had a client who came to see me because she had become aware that she was a descendant of black relatives. She was very light-skinned and she had been passing as a white person. Her fiancé became aware of her black heritage and he broke off the engagement. Understandably, the client was distraught. She was disappointed at the thought of coming to terms with her newly discovered identity and the racism she was facing. I was disappointed that she did not return after the third session, because as a black, mixed-heritage woman, I was prepared to offer her some support for her situation. I felt that my own disposition would have helped to provide a secure base from which she could re-evaluate her identity and recognition trauma, but this was not so.

A Ghanaian man seeing a white female therapist was deeply hurt about the racist behaviour he was receiving from colleagues. His white counsellor was empathetic and seemed aware that he was suffering from overt and covert racism at work. He described how a toy monkey had been placed on his desk. He was beside himself with frustration and hurt, and very concerned that this had caused him to revert to smoking and drinking and the intergenerational cause of letting his father down if he left the job. The therapist became distracted and began to focus on the addictive behaviour rather than the hurt from racism. She may have deferred to her denial of the main concern – racism – resulting in collusion with institutional racism and the mythology of racism (Alleyne, Tuckwell, Shears and Wheeler, 2008). Layers of shame associated with experiences of racism need to be considered: the internalized shame from the racism, the client's shame at their experiences, the therapist's shame at their inadequacy and the supervisor's shame at their denial or low level of support. These are all elements of attending to the challenge of racism and denial.

Whatever happens at the point when racism is disclosed is crucial to the client's assimilation process. This is subsequently influenced by the therapist's level of conformity to Eurocentric theory and their experience of supervision.

Freedom and support to develop the therapist's own style and antioppressive practice is important to the supervision process. This process must include ways of addressing racism. Defensiveness and denial about racism should not be an option for trained therapists. If the supervisor is embroiled in a post-racism mindset, the therapist may not receive adequate support to face their defensiveness and denial about racism. This pattern can be viewed as part of a therapeutic process.

I am fully aware of the many times I have felt defensive about the material I am addressing and my fears of further oppressing a client or supervisee. Alongside my fears about defensive attitudes, I am willing to face the challenges of transparency and disclosure that need to accompany this process, lest I contribute to the maintenance of a collusive institutional pecking order.

The following reflective questions about the challenge of racism in therapeutic practice may help therapists to unravel denial and the mythology of post-racism.

---

1. As a psychotherapist/counsellor:

  a. What therapeutic discipline/s inform your practice?

  b. In thinking about the challenge of racism in therapeutic practice, can you share your experience of and some of the challenges that have arisen for you during your practice and clinical supervision?

  c. Do you feel able to take these challenges to your supervision?

  d. If yes, what makes it safe for you to do so?

  d. If no, what limitations, blocks or difficulties get in the way?

2. In your own therapy and supervision:

  a. What are the challenges of racism in your own therapy and supervision?

  b. What works well when the challenge of racism is present?

  c. What limitations, blocks or difficulties get in the way?

3. **With supervisees:**

   a. How do you approach the challenge of racism in the client/therapist dyad?

   b. What works well in your approach? What are the challenges?

4. **How did you feel whilst reflecting on these questions?**

For the sake of transparency I want to share my own responses to these questions.

The therapeutic disciplines that I am influenced by have accumulated through a heuristic integrative journey as a therapist. I trained in psychodynamic therapy. The experience was not a very happy one when I realized that I felt marginalized as the only black trainee and there were no black tutors. I felt that no one really understood my situation as a black woman in a minority training situation. Very little support was offered when I attempted to raise these issues.

My first therapist was a white man who appeared to light up a cigarette whenever I raised challenging material. One day I challenged him about this, and after that he no longer smoked in my sessions. That was the era when smoking was allowed anywhere, and I felt respected by his action. We never touched on the issue of racism. After that, my therapist, supervisor and tutors were all white women. They all claimed that because they had no experience of being black, I was a challenge to them. Their naivety acted as a get-out clause for lack of response to my concerns about racism. Consequently, I was stuck in a mire of confusion and I did not feel sufficiently supported to explore my black issues and the impact of racism on my development as a counsellor.

I muddled through with the support of my homegirls and the one gay man on the course, who experienced similar marginalization. My first client was a white, gay man and using my experience and knowledge of an anti-oppressive approach, we achieved some important steps. We also discussed our limitations given the differences between us. In the supervision group, I shared the impact of my client's racist phantasies, but it fell on deaf ears.

After my training I was unable to locate a black supervisor, who I thought might be more empathic to my situation. I selected another white female. My internalized racism kicked in, and although I had expressed my need for attention to the impact of black issues and racism on my clinical disposition, I found it very difficult to follow this through. Her approach was psychodynamic and to a degree I felt supported, but I also felt overpowered by her approach and eventually found the courage to raise my concerns with her. I told her that I had wanted her to support me to develop my own therapeutic style and I had felt stifled and dismissed by her interpretations.

She accepted my challenge and we began to work out a way of allowing my voice rather than her dominating my approach with Eurocentric theory. That was a landmark for me because I was challenged to assert myself against her white power and her imposing Eurocentric theory on my work with black clients. On reflection, I would have been better helped if she had been able to challenge me and support me with the ethnic and racialized elements of my client work.

Along the way, I have been greatly encouraged by groups such as the Association of Black Counsellors (ABC) and a growing plethora of writing on racism and oppression in the therapeutic arena. My involvement with the Black and Asian Therapists Network (BAATN) has also been supportive. I am sure that without these groups I would have remained isolated.

I now have a better understanding about how racism permeates the psychological development of individuals. I work with this in a variety of ways. My approach stems from the knowledge that to be silent can perpetuate oppressions. I have found my voice, and although there are times when I am not sure what to say, I am aware that individuals may experience a whole gamut of oppressions throughout their lifetime. If the individual happens to be black/African/Caribbean or Asian, I am aware that it is highly likely that whatever cultural oppressions they may experience, these are likely to be compounded by racism. I do believe that therapists should hold this reality and be willing to address and explore the impact of racism on individual process. I may therefore acknowledge my level of cultural awareness and decide to use what I have named as a black empathic approach.

Some clients register with me because they specifically want a black woman to empathize with them, making the process less traumatic than having to explain and justify their experience of racism to a therapist who may be in denial. Taking into account how racism often creates silence and internalized hurt, I pay attention to signs of repression. This can show up when a client is sharing concerns about other oppressions such as sexism or homophobia, but they may ignore the impact of racism. I look for signs of denial that they may also be experiencing racism. Racism has a way of fixating onto other oppressions, and because it does not always show up in an overt way, it can cause clients to trivialize this oppression. One way of opening a dialogue about racism is to take a history of possible oppressions at the initial stages of the therapy. This can be viewed as essential to the client's developmental process.

Sometimes when clients approach me specifically because they are black and want to explore experiences of racism, I will ask them what they expect to receive from a black woman. This helps to open a space for the impact of internalized racism, which can create a rift in the therapeutic relationship if not addressed. This became apparent when a black woman whose skin tone was much darker than mine shared that at her workplace she had been hurt by a light-skinned manager. I noted the information as an operative pre-transference and that an area of our work together might be unpacking where racism is played out in shadism and the harmful nature of the internal oppressor. Pointing out my awareness of our diversity as black women, and my lighter skin, seemed to encourage her that I was willing to go to that awkward, painful place of shadism as a facet of racism within her experience.

I have now developed a peer-supervision relationship with a black colleague to support my own black empathic approach. This need arose due to the number of black clients and supervisees that I was attracting because of my outspokenness about black issues in the therapeutic process. This setup allows me the freedom to explore the impact of my own internal oppression on the therapeutic relationship. I also have the privilege of supporting my colleague with his challenges about racism, and we engage in the mutual challenge about the dynamic of racism and intersecting oppressions within our professional relationship. For example, there are sometimes blind spots and possible collusion. My co-supervisor is male, and I am challenged to notice and address the inter-gender dynamics in addition to racism. Due to my past issues with men, this is an area that I continue to work on.

I take my concerns about racism to my own therapy and supervision. This is not always easy, because racism can impact in such a way that it sometimes makes me feel like I am losing my mind, or perhaps over-emphasizing it where it may not exist. I sometimes feel overwhelmed by powerful feelings such as anger. Sometimes internal messages create denial, so although I have made a decision to bring it to these support forums, I sometimes forget and focus on something less important. I sometimes find it difficult to take ownership of areas where I may be oppressing a client and maintaining a silence, so my ignorance goes unnoticed. As someone who basically had to raise myself, I can also find it difficult to ask for help when I feel stuck, and then the reflective process goes out of the window. In short, I do not believe in a post-racism period. Being party to this idea reinforces denial and there is evidence all around to dispel this mythology.

Summary

In this chapter I have outlined the challenges of attitudes that perpetuate a post-racism status quo and the pitfalls of believing this discourse. There are several ways to approach this dilemma. Therapeutic practice and clinical supervision must provide a space to unpack the impact of this discourse. Therapists and supervisors must take responsibility for the gaps created when a post-racism approach is taken. Silences must be unpacked. Perpetuation of racism and the powerful feelings that create denial are a main concern. Homogeneity, assimilation, internalized negative cultural messages and oppression have been identified as important areas for consideration. I want to impress the importance of remaining aware that racism intersects with other oppressions, but has significant impact on both survivor and oppressor. Clients who are both survivors and oppressors should be facilitated to explore their projections and hurts.

Humiliation, guilt, naivety and hostility contribute to denial as a form of psychological gagging and create one of the biggest challenges to racism in therapeutic practice. Institutional and individual responsibility to address the impact of racism on the psyche is key to the progress of therapy training and practice. The impact of racism and oppression on the psyche is not a new phenomenon for psychotherapy, counselling and other therapeutic approaches; however, therapeutic disciplines have generally relied on traditional theories, rigidly binding them to steer away from the challenge of racism. Unlike when traditional models are applied, therapists and supervisors may struggle with the cultural aspects of integrating transcultural therapies, and their supervisory support must be appropriate.

The challenges of Eurocentric theory dominating practice and the need for therapists to create an integrative, culturally aware, anti-oppressive practice are paramount in this chapter about the mythology of post-racism. I have reiterated concepts such as gagging, black Western archetypes, a black empathic approach, cultural empathy and recognition trauma. I want readers to use these concepts and reflect on the ethical context of how they approach the challenge of racism in therapeutic practice. I am keen that this should also be reflected in how they cope with the silencing nature of racism. If this particular knowledge and understanding is not transferred into practice, it will be of little use. Therapists need to feel competent to address complex issues such as racism in their practice and be supported by their supervisors and respective organizations.

The remaining chapters will support therapists and supervisors faced with particular challenges about racism, denial and mythology in their practice. It is my greatest wish that readers will use the information and the exercises as a supportive framework for their own personal challenges about racism in therapeutic practice and develop supervision for personal support in this area.

Pointers:

- Therapists, supervisors, and training groups can invest in time to reflect on the impact of a mythology of post-racism on their work and supportive relationships.
- Reflecting on silence and denial in the therapeutic triad is key to understanding where the mythology of post-racism may uphold or interrupt the relational process.
- Regular re-evaluation of the use of traditional therapeutic approaches and their application to the challenge of racism is important.
- Racism has an impact on white people as members of the perpetrator group and on the personal development and whole lives of black and Asian people. It is important to remember that racism can also be an unconscious process.
- Ask your peers to engage in a dialogue about the challenges of racism in therapeutic practice.

2

Silencing and Taboo Subjects

This chapter explores the consequences of silencing and considers the impact of the past and empowering individuals who experience multidimensional oppressions. Taboo subjects usually evolve from the silencing aspect of social and cultural relations. These taboos can create personal disempowerment, and in some situations they can perpetuate trauma. Silence about sexual abuse is a prime example of this.

Relationship taboos are also a common feature for people of African and Asian heritage. Traditional and colonial nuances uphold taboos that affect intra-cultural relationships, such as relationships between people of different African communities. Interracial relationships between black people and white people can be affected by racism due to divisions based on skin colour and intercultural relationships. The term 'intercultural' is generally used to support understanding between different cultures.

Being in a sexual minority or same-sex relationship and subject to racism can also be a complex intersecting identity issue shrouded in taboo and affected by prejudices and sexual stereotyping. These multiple influences can cause underlying trauma. Trauma exacerbated by taboo in black and Asian groups is no different to that of other groups, but the consequences of multiple stressors, including racism, create difference.

The intention of this chapter is to open dialogue where clients, therapists and supervisors have felt silenced and to unpack therapeutic taboos that inhibit clients experiencing some of these concerns. For this purpose, I shall specifically focus on sexuality and sexual abuse. Gender and development of sexual identity for black and Asian individuals is an important area for consideration when intersecting identities become part of the therapeutic process. Constantine-Simms (2001) proposes that 'Taboos are unreflective customs accepted by a given community. These taboos change often and create conflict in individuals. For example: Preserving one's virginity until marriage has changed to couples living together for several years before marriage.' In addition,

'The influence of HIV and AIDS has placed an emphasis on promiscuity and safer sex' (p. 84). Hurtful experiences of prejudice towards HIV status and homophobia can also blight close relationships. They reinforce taboo and perpetuate multidimensional oppressions, pushing individuals into isolation. I invite therapists and supervisors to check whether they are willing to unpack taboos and whether the multidimensional impact of racism and culture is being considered in their work with clients presenting these silences.

There are particular challenges when an individual is a member of more than one oppressed group, for example a black woman whose identities intersect with being a Muslim and having a disability. This may not necessarily mean that she feels oppressed by any one or all of these identities, but the therapist must be aware of the potential for experiencing more than one oppression at a time, or at different times throughout life.

When engaging with a process of multidimensional oppressions, therapists must be aware how their responses may be influenced by homogeneity. An example of this would be responding to the hurt of racism by assuming that experiences of sexism or homophobia create the same level of hurt and therefore require similar empathic attunement. We cannot take for granted that we know or feel similar feelings to a client's feelings, no matter how similar the situation may seem.

Oppressions do not act independently of one another; they can interrelate and mitigate towards specific identities in negative, demeaning ways. Therefore, if the hurt of racism is present, a client may also reexperience feelings related to sexism. In situations where an individual has intersecting identities, confusion and depression can be created. There may be no way of extricating one oppression from the other, but therapists and supervisors must be aware that attention to one hurt may cancel out attention to the other. The feelings are not mutually exclusive, and both concerns are valid.

The complexities of holding an open dialogue about some of these issues in black communities are compounded by social norms and taboos about disclosure and the impact of racism. It is inevitable that if either therapist or client mention race, racism will be present. I want to explore how we talk about these issues and support the relevant conflicts without either ignoring or exacerbating oppressions such as racism within the therapeutic process. A student asks this question:

> How do we hold the stereotypes of the black/Asian family in abeyance and work with the here and now?

There is no single answer to this question. Yet if it is possible to be unbiased and work with an awareness of how negative stereotypes affect black and Asian families, we are on the road to providing congruent and empathic support in the here and now, when we are faced with social stereotypes, racism and intergenerational influences. Therapists therefore need to be ready to hold these important key areas of black and Asian identity development. Below I have listed some stereotyping features that contribute to taboo in the developmental process of black and Asian peoples. Levels to which these components may influence individuals may differ, due to diversity within different groups. They are all, in various ways, manifested intergenerationally, in child and adult self-concept. By the very nature of their intrusion into the mirroring of black identities, the following perceptions can create distortion of the real self:

- Stereotyping genitalia
- Black matriarchy, emasculation and power
- Black sexual identity – black homophobia
- Asian belief systems, gender and sexuality
- Myth of sacred white womanhood
- Sexual abuse

This list is not exhaustive, and it will be impossible to cover all themes in one chapter. Responses to these components from both the therapist and client can sometimes create anxiety, fear, silence and rupture in the relationship culminating in disassociation. Not attending to the therapists' and supervisors' emerging responses to these emotions is likely to create clinical taboo, and it is these elements that I wish to examine. First, I shall present some background information.

Sexuality

Black Western archetypes have created some indelible images of black sexuality. Many of these images arose from the eighteenth-century era of scientific objectification when African people were viewed as cargo and saleable goods and categorized by brain size, physical ability and genitalia. Due to this, white enslavers created a perceived disassociation between the body and mind of the African. The violent treatment of slaves and colonized peoples was built on the back of this perception and created numbness and lack of empathy towards victims.

With the onset of colonization and slavery, archetypes of black sexuality based on labour and subjugation became prominent. Treatments of enslaved Africans based on negative archetypes were reinforced by the moral codes of Christianity. Gilman (1985) reports on the nineteenth-century European stereotyping of black sexuality being perceived as diseased yet mythical attractive sexual objects, 'coupled with a sense of danger', aligned with the sexuality of prostitutes and Jews (p. 110). This gave overseers and slave masters licence to abuse, rape and mutilate African bodies. This stereotype permeated European minds to the extent of pathologizing black sexuality.

Objectifying body parts such as size of penis, buttocks, breasts, and differences as to whether African women held their skirts in front or behind to urinate, stereotyped them as the other and pathologically different to whites. These ideas were inculcated via cultural norms, symbolic representation and art, and black Africans were perceived as not having a normal sexuality.

Some contemporary African sexualities are based on patriarchal ideas and sacrosanct concepts of bodies, promoting circumcision, female genital mutilation and virginity fantasies that commercialize vagina tightening and ritualized sexual practice. The emotional impact of these practices is virtually hidden and held in place by taboo.

Asian sexuality has been perceived on the basis of exoticism and religious mythology. Sensuality and ceremony within patriarchal perceptions of dominant and subservient heterosexuality perpetuate particular taboos about sexual activity. This serves to silence and disempower individuals who identify as LGBTQ (lesbian, gay, bisexual, transgender, queer or transsexual). Although romanticized, this cultural dimension of sexuality has not been spared objectification. Objectification creates taboos about reality, taboos such as those about breast cancer being contagious, a punishment or a curse jeopardizing marriage and stigmatizing families. In some communities under Sharia law, taboos about the virgin bride have led to death.

Whilst abstinence and 'purity' among women are emphasized, sexual discussions and being sexually active before marriage are taboo. Rape, incest and sexual violence are kept silent due to a culture of censorship and fear of repercussions. Hypocritical standards about sexual purity reinforce male domination. Shame, or 'sharam', perpetuates the fear and silencing that uphold sexual taboos. Damaged marriage prospects, self-esteem and mental health issues manifest from secrecy and pressure to conform to cultural taboos. Due to cultural taboos, there may be a thread of secrecy that weaves itself around the client and therapist supervisory triad, maintaining silence about sexuality development and orientation in Asian communities. So, consideration of this silence is vital to the provision of therapeutic support to individuals in these communities.

Extended family relations are a central feature of support in many African, Caribbean and Asian families. However, this aspect of family life has its intrinsic pressures to conform to cultural norms in the family and community. Taboos held within these families are perpetuated by fear of gossip causing family exposure. Spirituality or religion plays a significant role in the enforcement of cultural norms. This can evoke shame and isolation for individuals who break rigid boundaries and transgress the cultural divide between African, Caribbean and Asian standards of moral behaviour and European cultural norms of sexual behaviour. Many Asian families uphold taboos about virginity and sex before marriage, common law relationships, intermarrying someone outside of the cultural norm, and traditional laws. Enforced or arranged marriages also contribute to taboos about challenging the status quo.

Social and traditional stigmas arise from taboo, and some customs have legislation that enforce stigma; therefore, breaking a taboo can involve family rejection, punishment, public shame, imprisonment or legitimized death, for example stoning of women under Sharia law and imprisonment for homosexuality in some African and Caribbean countries, causing mental ill health and suicide.

Hasan Mahmud (2008, in Basu, 2013) stated the following:

> Shame in Asian family systems is often a provokator of extreme violence or murder in families. According to statistics from the United Nations, one in five cases of honor killing internationally every year comes from India. Of the 5000 cases reported internationally, 1000 are from India. Non-governmental organizations put the number at four times this figure. They claim it is around 20,000 cases globally every year.

For a young woman raised within a Muslim family that adheres to orthodox Muslim rules, assimilation can cause emotional conflict. The teaching of her religion may clash with what she observes in the behaviour of young white British women. If, for example, she is discovered having sexual relations out of wedlock, or if she is unfortunate enough to be raped, punishment can be severe. Her physical safety and conflicting cultural messages may be a priority for the therapist.

The Quran does not mention rape. It severely prohibits 'Zina', which means sexual relations between a man and woman not married to each other. It can be translated as 'adultery' for married persons and 'fornication' for the unmarried. Muslim jurists included rape under Zina because, even though forced on the victim, sexual relations 'between a man and woman not married to each other' have taken place (Mahmud, 2008).

In some areas of the world there are no laws to avert racial, sexist or homophobic attack. This produces a minority within a minority – an unsupported, often stigmatized minority.

Black matriarchy, emasculation and power

I want to acknowledge the importance of addressing the background to how black males and females are perceived in the light of ongoing racism today. Plantation slavery undermined the role of black males and paternity, and it recognized maternity as the primary role of black females. Male slaves were prevented from fully claiming their masculine identity. On the other hand, Berger (1993) writes that 'Slavery precluded the black women from conforming to models of feminine sexuality and maternity' (p. 110). Female slaves were taken from their normative role as wives and mothers, to serve the sexual needs of their masters. Their bodies were mutilated and pillaged, and they were the sole property of their owners, for the purpose of procreating light-skinned children for sale, as sexual objects and slaves. Slaves were often separated from their own babies who were, if they survived, sold and raised as slaves on different plantations. Nevertheless, the black woman cooked, scrubbed, sang, minded the master's children and carried on.

Deserving some recognition is the intergenerational context and harshness of slavery, perceived as a precursor to serial monogamy and fatherless families. Legislation in Africa and the Caribbean did not recognize enslaved African marriages; this has contributed to the intergenerational impact on black families. So, the chain of heterosexual relationships was jeopardized. On one hand, the African and Caribbean extended family network is a traditional and essential feature of black family life. On the other hand, cementing relationships between black males and females would upset the social and political construction of the plantation polity (Scully, 1997, pp. 19–30 in Ocheing and Hylton, 2010).

The black woman carries the intergenerational scars of the mutilated slave. This historical influence has created a compromised relational legacy that the black man may never see her as whole. She carries the mark of the strong warrior matriarch, she is seen as difficult to dominate, she is often driven in her domestic chores, and her work and her love may not be taken seriously. Instead, she may be expected to carry the burdens of the extended family and develop behaviours emanating from a black Western archetype that I have called 'Aunt Jemima'. This archetype manifests in self-sacrificing emotional patterns. Part of the therapist's task would therefore be to unravel the intergenerational context of these patterns.

Mythology exists about the size of a black man's penis, along with the white man's envy, and so castration became a feature of lynching during slavery and was maintained as a hate crime in southern America until 1968. Although penis size has been mythologized, it could also be said that this is a prime example of Freud's penis envy.

Breaking this taboo means understanding that the size of a man's penis does not equate to how manly he is, just as the number of children he has produced does not equate to how many children he may have 'fathered', in the true sense of the word. (By this I mean that men adopt, foster and take up a stepfather role with children they have not made. They also produce children who may not have experienced them in the role of father.) This predicament is not confined to black men. Stereotypes stigmatizing the black man as socially irresponsible fuel the black Western archetype of the black sire as opposed to the 'father'. This perception perpetuates ideas that black men have many children that they do not recognize or offer fathering to. These confused images of black machismo can confuse ill-informed therapists.

Concepts of aggression, built on stereotypes, fear and lack of dialogue, create divisions between black men and between black men and women. The cooperative black man who doesn't challenge racism or emasculation may be viewed as superior to the black man who is struggling. This can evoke suspicion between black men because aggression is viewed as good and manly, yet it fits the bad, social stereotype of the highly aggressive, threatening black man. So where does the black man express his confusion, disappointment and rejection? Taboos that hold in place negative concepts of black machismo and lack of space for the black man to share his experiences and express his concerns can lead to hopelessness and mental health issues.

The following is an excerpt from an interview with Byron, a Trinidadian man trying to portray himself through masculine eyes (Mckenzie-Mavinga, 2009, pp. 169, 171).

Isha: So let's progress into the area of men and how you feel about Caribbean men especially.

Byron: This is a very complex issue. First of all, for the record, I am straight. I am a hot-blooded heterosexual male, who has had a few homosexual encounters when I was younger and in my teens, and I look back with a smile. I was born through the womb and I may die inside the woman. I always say this with a sense of humour. I was taught how to be a man from a female perspective; it does not work. I find myself having to be masculinist to get my point across. I saw my situation as a challenge. I was the result of a quick fuck. I saw the men in my family as confused, not aware of their sisters being abused by men, alcoholic fathers, and women being abused. I am very proud of my family and I believe in equality of women, and I want to be the best family man I can be. There are a lot of things that we have to unlearn. I cry in front of women, I cuss and I scream, I don't fix things, I don't drive a car. I still believe in the sanctity of marriage, but from a different perspective.

Listening to Byron helped me to consider the role that women play in raising men and my role as a black mother of sons. Similarly, in my role as a therapist, I have a responsibility to listen to the stories of the men in my family and my male clients. I must listen with acceptance and notice where it is hard to empathize, because we are different and whether he is gay or straight, I can never know what it is like to be a black man. The listening must be from an unbiased perspective whilst stepping out of my internalized racism, my homophobia and my internalized stereotypes of men, particularly black men and Asian men. Remaining fully aware of the taboos that black men experience and contribute to is key to being fully connected to them in the therapeutic process. Having said this, it is rare in my experience to have these discussions in therapeutic forums. I am also aware of the painful feelings evoked when attempts to dialogue between black men and women take place. The benefits in recognizing this may become a resource for the empowerment of black people.

Homophobia

Social and cultural discourses including homophobia within the black community must be considered when understanding the impact of intersecting identities and racism on sexuality and the identity development of black peoples. Living in a racist society, and the historical influences of slavery and colonialism, will inevitably influence the sexual identity of black and Asian people. From these cultural conditions come stereotypes and mythology about black sexuality.

Safety to process intersecting identities that embrace sexuality, colour and gender is a key concern for therapists and supervisors. This may require therapists to consider an appropriate level of disclosure. We cannot take for granted that everyone is heterosexual, and, therefore, in order to create safety, clients associating with minority sexualities may benefit from knowledge of the therapist's sexual orientation. As a black woman, I have been fearful about disclosing aspects of my sexuality, yet I have worked with many clients experiencing concerns related to their experience of gay or lesbian sexuality. I believe that my ability to create safety with these clients was located in my willingness to answer their questions about my own sexuality. Taboos about disclosure are upheld by heterosexist and homophobic attitudes and within a therapeutic relationship could be considered as an ethical concern. Social pressure creates a particular pull to label sexualities, and labelling is bound to homogenize individuals as this poem describes.

> *What am I?*
> *In love with a woman.*
> *I don't want a label*
> *Cos that's too common*
> *And I don't call myself lesbian,*
>
> *I am a woman's woman*
> *Maybe a Zami or a Dyke,*
> *But not a 'Lesbian'*
> *Cos 'Lesbians' are white*
>
> Isha Mckenzie-Mavinga, 2013

Considering a trilogy of oppression, mythology and stereotyping can feel overwhelming to both therapist and client. This is where adequate supervision must be held in place. I call this process that creates taboo and silence 'Gagging'. I consider that a language to express minority sexuality is a priority, and that therapists and supervisors must be aware how Eurocentric labelling can impact black and Asian members of the LGBTQ communities, as the following student question suggests.

> How are black lesbian/gay/bisexual/transgender people treated in their own community?

It is important to recognize that some black and Asian individuals who identify as LGBTQ may experience the stigma and oppression of hidden identity or closeting, due to taboos about their sexual orientation that arise from family, from the wider community and from within the black and Asian communities. A range of limiting sexual taboos such as masturbation, adultery, premarital sex, polygamy, sexual intercourse during menstruation and homosexuality are upheld by spiritual and cultural beliefs. So it is important not to allow our judgements to become essentialist, as we may be party to perpetuating taboo. This statement by Hemphill (in Constantine-Simms, 2001, p. 36) portrays the experience of taboo in the multidimensional context: 'I entered my final year of senior high school. By that time, I had arrived at a very clear understanding of how dangerous it was to be a homosexual in my black neighborhood and in society ... Facing this then limited perception of homosexual life, I could only wonder where did I fit in.' Topher Campbell (2011) also challenges intra-cultural homophobia when he states, 'It's time for black communities to wake up – and stop ostracizing those of us who happen to be homosexual.'

Heterosexism is the foundation of anti-gay attitudes and encourages men to feel they have to keep proving they are men, so they are not seen as breaking the sexual taboos held in place by homophobia and homophobic legislation in their countries of origin and peer groups. Black-on-black killings are prolific in the West, Africa and the Caribbean, and it seems there may be a correlation between the emasculated black man and his attempts to prove his masculinity, lest he be seen as gay by his black brothers. Whilst some black gay men are confident about their sexuality, many feel hopeless and suicide is sometimes chosen as an alternative to attack, imprisonment or rejection from loved ones.

Mason-John and Khambatta (1993) described the hiddenness of black lesbians and confirmed:

> The impact of racism on black lesbians was profound. On the whole black lesbians remained silent and isolated, we were required to break our identities into unacceptable fragments: we were black in black groups women in the women's movement and lesbians on the lesbian scene. There was no space to be whole, to be a black lesbian. (p. 18)

hooks (in Constantine-Simms, 2001) supports this observation. She says, 'Often we hear more about gay people who have chosen to live in predominantly white communities, whose choices may have been affected by undue harassment in black communities. We hear hardly anything from black gay people who lived contentedly in black communities' (p. 24). These gaps fuel misunderstanding and stereotyping about black gay folks.

Mason-John and Khambatta (1993) go on to say that

> some black communities have viewed lesbianism as a white disease. The implication is that the arrival of homosexuality in black communities is the fault of white people and colonization. This notion is reinforced by the absence of physical black lesbians and gay men. Black communities fear adding to the discrimination they already experience based on race color and language and therefore the black heterosexual population finds it difficult to admit to the existence of homosexuality and lesbianism in the black community. 'To call homosexuality a white disease is like saying' we don't want to discuss this, we don't want to deal with it, it has nothing to do with us. These views are perpetuated and reinforced by homophobia in churches and religious groups. (p. 21)

A plethora of names to describe black-woman-centred relationships have arisen (Mason-John and Khambatta, 1993). 'The term Zami is particular to the Caribbean island of Carriacou ... The term Khush is an Urdu word which came originally from Indian culture where it means gay and happy' (Mason-John and Khambatta, 1993, p. 39). Lesbian is English terminology and predominantly Eurocentric, and some women in Britain use the term black lesbian. Dyke appears in American slang dictionaries; it is a term used for women who adopt masculine or butch roles. Although this is a sexual stereotype, black lesbians often get viewed as butch due to the intergenerational context of being forced to take on masculine roles during slavery and having their femininity denied (Mason-John and Khambatta, 1993, p. 41).

One consideration in the discourse of being black and gay is that outness is sometimes weighed up against blackness. Some black people feel that their black identities are more important than a visible gay or lesbian sexual orientation, which therefore they may prefer to hide. Hiddenness about sexual identities and ideas about who is black are diminishing to black people and create taboo. So it is not surprising that racism becomes a primary challenge in identity development.

Many black gay or lesbian individuals experience conflict between both these identities due to racism within gay communities and homophobia within black communities. And that is not all. Some heinous stories of rape, imprisonment, death sentences and suicide of black lesbians and gay men, from those who have managed to flee from African and Caribbean societies and are grappling with their immigration status, have been revealed. Multidimensional oppressions such as legitimized homophobia and trauma from the threat of punishment and the addition of racism once in the UK compound these dilemmas. These situations place an emphasis on the therapist's and supervisor's abilities to hold intersecting identities, such as nationality and assimilation issues.

Conerly (in Constantine-Simms, 2001) reiterates the hidden nuances that need to be taken into account. There are silences that influence black lesbian and gay sexuality, and they create a challenge in versions of blackness depending on whether relationships are interracial or black-on-black (p. 20). This challenge can also be seen in black heterosexual relationships. This author cautions readers not to mythologize the link between interracial relationships and black self-hatred. Therapists must be aware of their responses and interpretations of what an interracial relationship may mean to a black or Asian client.

Sexual abuse

We know that throughout history, rape has been used as a war weapon and tool of domination. I wonder about the war that happens within, when denial or disassociation of feelings about rape, sexual abuse and violence are being silenced. Internalization of the strong black woman archetype can play a role in behaviour patterns that suppress the pain of these experiences. Some black mothers who have suffered sexual abuse, or whose children have suffered sexual abuse, feel they must show they are strong and coping. These women have silenced their emotional responses but continue to suffer confusion, isolation and deep hurt coupled with fear of being seen as weak if they disclose their feelings. This behaviour can create depression and a role model of silencing for the abused child. Sexual abuse and racism within the family can impact in multidimensional ways on minority groups, in particular women and men of African/ Caribbean and Asian background. Taboo, silence, incest, rape and violence perpetrated within the family and intergenerationally are discourses that impact on the way women of African/Caribbean and Asian heritage respond and are responded to when domestic and sexual violence are present in their lives. Although the hidden nature of the abuse is acknowledged, areas of particular concern need deeper consideration. Even when some awareness of the sexual abuse begins to surface, the pain of racism and cultural taboo can create a struggle to keep the silence in place. Although professionals acknowledge the hidden nature of sexual abuse, some particular blind spots need to be considered. Beatings, stigma, family honour and religion act as silencers. Race and gender dynamics also play an important role in whether or how sexual abuse is disclosed and the ways in which the survivor is supported. Female survivors and their mothers often get blamed, rather than a male perpetrator. Such attitudes create discourses that perpetuate occluded trauma and inhibit the healing and recovery process.

Barnard's (2001) study presents excerpts from black mothers carrying the multidimensional oppressions of racism and sexism. These oppressions are inevitably influenced by black Western archetypes. This mother's awareness of institutional oppression created a response coupled with internalized racism and the mammy archetype:

> On discovering that my daughter had been abused I had no one to talk to. It dawned on me that everyone turned to me when there was a problem to sort out. I was the primary nurturer and provider of emotional support for the family and friends. I felt I had no one to turn to at the time and had to rely on my own emotional resources to help my child come to terms with what had happened. I felt I had to conceal my own hurt and pain from my family. It was a difficult and stressful time. (Barnard, p. 49)

> Talking about an experience which was black on black with white professionals was very difficult to do. I kept thinking they must have been thinking this is typical of black families. It felt as if something like that is happening in your family it maybe a justification for how the white society sees you in the first place. (Barnard, p. 45)

> There was a pressure – not only from white society, but from within your own society, like a lot of covering up. The pressure is there to cover up. (Barnard, p. 45)

The mothers referred to in Barnard's study silenced themselves on their emotional responses to sexual abuse. The familiar experience of a black woman holding the fort alone and being the sole emotional provider, with little or no support for herself, is a common one in the UK.

This fits the intergenerational impact of slavery transferred via a black Western archetype of the black mammy, fighting for the survival of her children. I have worked with black women who are fiercely independent and give the appearance that they are strong women able to cope with whatever comes at them from family, work and society. Social responses to this type of demeanour generally provoke further isolation and lessen offers of support. The black woman may even refuse support because she has internalized these responses as not being good enough, or, because of racism, people are not willing to get in there with her and help her hold up the world or let go of it for a while. Ultimately, she may feel bad when her efforts fail or her children are having difficulties coping.

In Barnard's study, mothers were concerned whether their children would internalize the abusive experience as part of their black identity. She suggests that it is important to be aware that black children may internalize the experience as part of their black identity and believe that abuse happened because they are black, or that this only happens in black families. The statement below from a young survivor of sexual abuse bears this out:

> I thought it was my fault because of my color. I wished I was white so it wouldn't happen.

Anyone coping with racism and being abused by someone from their own cultural background is likely to suffer double trauma. Mothers of abused children may be subject to social assumptions about black motherhood, such as that their mothering does not match up to their white middle-class contemporaries. This situation can raise memories of the mothers' own childhood experiences embroiled in cultural taboos and powerful feelings about ethnicity.

Incest and sexual abuse are as equally prevalent in the black family as in white families; therefore, assumptions about motherhood in addition to the dual trauma of sexual abuse and racism need to be considered. This is particularly important when the abuse comes from within the black family and the silence is upheld. Silence about abuse within the black family is often upheld by intergenerational taboos, like a child or parent being afraid of receiving a violent response from the perpetrator, or the person reporting the abuse being threatened with murder.

Secrets are kept within small communities as well as within the family, and due to fear of breaking the taboo, victims of abuse often take sole responsibility for the silence. Barnard's study corroborated that professionals sometimes blame closed cultures for maintaining abusive behaviour. For example, the bogeyman in the village or the uncle or cousin in the family who instils fear into the victim is never confronted. This example of religion as a silencer shows how a terrible twist can sometimes go unattended.

A man who identified as a senior Muslim priest was jailed for eleven years for raping a schoolgirl and two other women. When he was charged he persuaded the schoolgirl's family that the girl was sick, and the girl lost trust in her parents, as they did not believe her initially. Her parents were devastated by the betrayal of the holy man (Barnard, 2001). It is therefore important to be aware of betrayal as an aspect of trauma, and of silencing linked to sexual abuse and taboos upheld within black and Asian families. If not attended to, associated buried feelings can cause depression, addictions and self-harm, especially for the abused individual.

The impact of these attitudes and intra-cultural oppression create discourses that perpetuate occluded trauma and inhibit the healing process, resulting in disassociation if it is not picked up. Then the whole experience of multidimensional oppression becomes taboo.

In my practice, black and Asian adult female survivors of sexual abuse have felt blamed or blame themselves. They sometimes blame the men in their current relationships or the women in their early lives rather than process their feelings about male perpetrators and the cultural taboos about incest, violence and sexual abuse in their family heritage. Black women have come to therapy because they are overworked, tired and feeling hopeless about their current relationship. In many of these cases, latent trauma and taboo about their experiences of sexual abuse have been revealed. Holding secrets within the family and a threat of violence if they disclose is often the cause of their depression, tiredness and relationship problems. Parents who are unforgiving of the blame they have foisted on a child for the abuse perpetuate the trauma of the abuse and may create cultural confusion about ways of loving for the abused individual. These experiences can be viewed in the light of black Western archetypes and ancestral baggage, a concept that I use to describe aspects of what gets passed on intergenerationally, usually an unconscious psychological process, where silence and taboo were common features of predecessors and their family life. This can be influenced by upbringing, education and cultural frameworks.

In some situations, the silence may be a feature of individual disassociation due to a combination of early sexual abuse and the impact of racism. Women caught in a web of ancestral baggage and silence often present symptoms of drivenness, compulsive independence, lack of holding and isolation. Through the reflection of an attentive 'black gaze' (hooks, 1992), they may come to realize that they are masking the impact of the multiple traumas they have experienced. Therapists and supervisors have a duty to facilitate confusion and trauma caused by sexual abuse, racism and cultural taboos. Accurate and respectful mirroring of the individual experience and oppressions are key to the healing process.

Alarming facts and figures on mental health patients support evidence of the link between experiences of sexual abuse in the UK and taboo. Sewell (2009) states that 'Sixty four per cent of women who use in-patient mental health services have suffered physical or sexual abuse (Fifty percent child sexual abuse specifically)' (p. 167). This means that repression of abuse-related trauma should be given attention in therapy and supervision. It is significant that a large proportion of detainees under the mental health act are BME (black minority ethnic) individuals. The trauma is no different for BME groups, but the consequences of multiple stressors and oppressions such as racism in addition to the offence are different and may push an individual over the edge. A black child or adult may feel bad or dirty, or an affront to their race or culture, even if they have not acknowledged these feelings. Associating abuse with your cultural environment can mean that there is nowhere safe to retreat to. Therefore, negative or biased responses that may exacerbate the trauma or occlusion need to be considered. These are the key areas when challenging taboo surrounding the black child/adult and sexual abuse.

Barnard (2001) observed that black mothers of abused children had to present themselves as strong and coping (p. 48), internalizing the strong black woman image and perpetrating this black Western archetype. Barnard supports the work of listening to black mothers and consideration of the strong black woman image, and affirms the importance of being aware of cognitive dissonance that creates silences and taboo about discussions related to sexual abuse within the black family.

So what can we take from this? The Barnard study concluded that:

- Closed cultures are often blamed for maintaining abusive behaviour.
- Beatings, stigma, family honour and religion act as silencers.
- Female survivors and their mothers fear the impact of racism when sexual abuse is being disclosed and often get blamed for the abuse.

Using Barnard's conclusions, I will now present some factors that influence the combined challenge of racism and sexual abuse.

- Priorities for black mothers and survivors are often marginalized or excluded.
- Sexual abuse is not just a female issue. Boys and men are also sexually abused. Incidence of black men being abused and raped in prison is high.
- Therapists and supervisors must be aware of history, mythology and racism that silence individuals and perpetuate taboo.
- Myths about black females being able to cope with anything are probably a direct result of intergenerational distress and having to face such traumas alone.
- Black and Asian people do love their children, and it is not true that black people don't abuse their children.
- Stereotyping families is not helpful, because sexual abuse is not necessarily a cultural or subcultural experience. It is a human problem created by power imbalance, and it is influenced by culture.
- It is important not to blame closed cultures for abuse; it can happen anywhere.
- Black children are often doubly confused by the dilemma of coping with their experiences of racism and being abused by someone who may be from their own family, culture or a different cultural group.

Summary

Consideration of history, mythology and the dynamics of racism and other oppressions in the process of service provision to already marginalized groups is key to challenging some of the culturally embedded assumptions that normalize taboos and exacerbate the trauma of multidimensional oppressions. Silence due to loyalty, shame and fear of a racist backlash creates stress and perpetuates taboo.

Gender, race and sexuality are inexplicably linked. Therefore, these intersections need interrogation to help understanding and openness. Mythology and taboos about the sexual orientation and development of black and Asian people fuel a negative gaze. This denotes the harmful way that stereotypes influence the reflective process. These stereotypes permeate the psyche and demean self-esteem. Greater awareness of their impact deters homogeneity and further oppression.

Therapists must remain aware that there is no single black sexuality. Being of black or Asian extraction does not mean we can assume cultural imprints when considering sexuality. The conflicts of intersecting identities need to be considered. It is inevitable that gender and sexual identity will be influenced by the sociocultural community of the individual and, in the West, the impact of living in a racist

society. Historical influences of slavery and colonialism, and traditional and culturally specific approaches to sexual relationships, are
bound to create a multidimensional effect on the development of these
identities.

Racism compounded by taboos about black and Asian sexualities
makes it difficult to emerge and be visible; therefore, we cannot take it
for granted that being freed from slavery, apartheid or the imposition of
partition constitutes personal freedom. Silence and inability to address
cultural identity and racism add to the hurt caused by negative historical influences, sexual stereotyping, sexual abuse, domestic violence and
the oppression of sexual minorities. Barnard (2001) identifies several
reasons that uphold taboos and lack of engagement about sexual abuse
and racism. We must be aware that these concerns may also affect therapists and supervisors, but we have a responsibility to take ownership of
them and prepare ourselves for working with others.

The challenge of racism is closely connected to sexual abuse and
must be considered by therapist and supervisor. It is not enough to
bear witness and avoid this duality and other related oppressions such
as sexism. Institutional racism influences the level at which training
of care workers and therapists takes on these challenges and addresses
them. Interrelational dynamics and racism are important and should
be considered as a key element of training. These subjects were not
included in my own training, and as a result I have had to learn to be
open-minded about them. Being open-minded is not enough because
it takes a good deal of confidence and personal experience to hold a
dialogue about issues that have become taboo. The therapist's fears,
concerns and silences can add to elements of internalized oppression
that may uphold taboos. Supported by Barnard's findings, the list below
indicates areas that uphold taboo about sexual abuse in the black family.

- Non-reporting and lack of attention by professionals.
- Feeling alienated from the notion of law enforcement, particularly given
  the nature of deaths of black people in police custody and the mental
  health system.
- Fear of exposing the black community to statutory agencies.
- Particular difficulties for black children to disclose, due to being cushioned
  from racism within the black family, feeling they are betraying the black
  family and their networks and therefore fearing exclusion.
- The taboo of washing dirty linen in public.
- Demonization of black men, that is, portrayal of black men as wanton and
  bestial, feckless and absent as fathers.

Barnard also emphasizes the importance of remembering the black family as a source of strengthening gender and power relations.

Pointers:

- Working through the challenge of racism as part of multidimensional oppressions such as homophobia, sexism, ableism and cultural taboos is essential to the development of intersecting identities.
- There may be unique empathic ties between black men and black women due to the experience of racism; therefore, this may also cause collusion.
- Be aware that when a black man is accused of rape or sexual abuse, racist stereotyping can attribute the problem to black culture, whereas if a white man is accused of rape or sexual abuse it is seldom constructed as a problem afflicting the white race.
- Be prepared to work with 'don't discharge' messages and shame about tarnishing the name of the family, which cause secrets and taboo.
- Know that the black and Asian child needs to be offered support to build their esteem, as being black or Asian did not cause the abuse.
- Be aware of the layered nature of responses, for example occlusion, self-blame and internalized racism.
- Talk about difficulties to disclose experiences because of shame on account of being black/Asian, as this compounds the experience of being abused.
- Explore the relationship between feelings of disloyalty about disclosure within and outside of the black/Asian family.

3

The Process of Black Rage

It seems appropriate that addressing rage should follow Chapter 2. Underneath the suppression of feelings caused by various taboos there lies a simmering pot of powerful feelings. Rage about racism is one such powerful feeling likely to be unveiled in the therapeutic process. Feelings about repression of any oppressive experiences are also likely to be included in the simmering pot.

Individuals and oppressed groups hold a tremendous amount of powerful feelings and rage that can remain unprocessed and unsupported due to fear, inhibition and concerns about mental health. In this chapter, suppressed and expressed rage and outrage will be addressed in the context of working with psychological material and mental health. Challenges presented in the role and responsibility of the therapist and supervisor to create a safe, supportive space for rage to be explored in the context of ethnicity, assimilation and mental health will be discussed. Assumptions based on stereotypes of Asian passivity and lack of consideration for Asian cultural heritage and expression of feelings drawn from empirical material will also be considered in this chapter.

Black rage is the term that I have given to the eruption of anger that can more often than not be associated with racism. There are several challenges associated with this phenomenon. On one hand, black rage gets trivialized, misinterpreted and underestimated due to the nature of racism. On the other hand, fear of black rage causes irrational beliefs about black mental health and confuses perspectives about sadness and madness. It is as if black rage is a taboo. Disconnection and rupture in supportive and therapeutic relationships can be caused by lack of attention to these responses. The challenge of unveiling these areas will be addressed in this chapter. I set aside black rage because of its association with racism. It is one of the biggest challenges, yet appears least attended to in therapeutic practice. Responses to racism vary, and there is no doubt that rage about racism invokes particular responses that sometimes force hurt about racism back inside individuals. This phenomenon is borne out in reviews about the mental health system in the UK.

The following figures infuriate me.

There were 3,628 deaths in mental health detention (501 self-inflicted) between 2000 and 2010, accounting for 61% of all deaths in state custody. The proportion of deaths recorded from 'natural causes' is also exceptionally high (Roberts, 2012).

The story of Orvile Blackwood, a young black man in Broadmoor high security hospital, is tantamount to Andrew Solomon's (2014, p. 41) suggestion that numbers indicate trends, while stories acknowledge chaos. He shared some of his story with me and we discussed his need to be listened to. At the case conference, he was criticized as having 'a problem with authority'. It was clear that the white psychiatrists expected him to agree with this opinion of him. I was aware at the time that he was not being listened to; he was being stereotyped, although he may not have been any safer in jail. He was in the wrong place after having used a toy gun to rob a betting shop. A few weeks after my visit, I was informed that he had died from over-medication and asphyxiation whilst being restrained. It was clear that had he been appropriately facilitated to work through his black rage, rather than being forcibly shut down, he might have survived.

Evidence shows there is huge risk for individuals entering the mental health system, as they may never come out. As a parent, I understand the powerlessness of carers and how useless I felt when trying to get the right care for my daughter when she was sectioned. I can also remember trying to silence my son's rage and his expressions of fear about police harassment, in case his words led professionals to deem him to be mad. This begs a huge question of how therapists contain and facilitate black rage.

The concept of black rage offers an opportunity to explore emotions that have a greater meaning than irritation, frustration, annoyance and anger. These terms are often used to downplay rage, and for a variety of reasons these emotions are often not fully attended to in therapy. Those who stuff the pain down and repress their powerful feelings often become rageful. Black rage is specifically linked to experiences of racism and a history of systemized violence, abuse and psychological influences on black people's feelings of worthiness. Naming this concept means recognizing the rage within us stirred by everyday experiences of racism, backed up by historical and intergenerational contexts of racism and current-day interrelational dynamics – in other words, rage as a pure emotion coloured in by racism.

Some people say that the African holocaust is in the past and we should move on; however, black psychiatrists Grier and Cobbs (1992) suggest that bringing together fragmented families that have been denied an equal status in the communities built on their heritage will be a lengthy process. They confirm the inevitability that people of African heritage will participate in returning the resentment of the majority. This view sits with the ways that internalized racism gets played out between individuals and within groups. Gang fighting, street killings and high levels of black citizens in the mental health system and prisons are manifestations of how this resentment gets re-enacted and how much unattended rage is about. Exploring internalized racism is therefore a key element of exploring black rage in the therapeutic process. Rage may be expressed in a variety of ways, but I am mainly concerned with the internalization of rage due to inability to challenge racism or experiences of disbelief that racism exists.

I am pretty sure that the term black rage will evoke strong reactions, as racism is an intense, sometimes internalized phenomenon. It is a good thing that powerful historical events such as slavery, holocausts and ethnic cleansing provoke powerful responses that keep alive the promise of healing. Deadened, numb feelings may indicate that the struggle for justice and liberation may be over, leaving death and destruction in its path. It is clear that the music and rhythm produced over centuries expressing powerful feelings about the treatment of black people shows that black rage is alive and kicking.

The wounds of the past must be acknowledged, and we must grasp every opportunity to heal the historical impact of slavery and colonialism, and other heinous crimes against humanity. This is the very substance of psychotherapy and counselling, and those involved in therapeutic work must know their part in the past and future of healing this blight on our history and psychology. The conditioning of personal development, intersecting identities and multidimensional oppressions therefore depends on how therapists and supervisors approach the delicate yet volatile subject of black rage.

hooks (1995), when addressing the perpetuation and maintenance of white supremacy, suggests that 'white folks have colonized black Americans, and a part of that colonizing process has been teaching us to repress our rage to never make them the targets of any anger we feel about racism' (p. 14). She goes on to say that 'most black people internalize this message well and though many of us were taught the repression of our rage was necessary to stay alive in the days before racial integration, we now know that one can be exiled for ever from the promise of economic well-being if that rage is not permanently silenced'. We also know that we can end up in prison or the mental health system if we express that rage too loudly. The impact of colonialism on the expression of rage is very clear. Suppressed rage results in obesity, stress-related disease, violence in the home and, ultimately, in an overloaded mental health system or increase in the murder rate.

The murder rate in Trinidad and Tobago, my second home, currently stands at one life every day. I am talking about a predominantly black society. So, black rage is not confined to white societies, although white societies have played a role in the evolution of class and economic systems that underpin black rage. Therefore, this dilemma cannot be solely blamed on everyday racism. There is a historical backdrop to black rage.

The provocative Willie Lynch (1712) statement 'Let's make a slave', as reported, prescribed how this rage would play itself out:

Don't forget, you must pitch the **OLD black male vs. the YOUNG black male, and the YOUNG black male against the OLD black male. You must use the DARK skin slaves vs. the LIGHT skin slaves, and the LIGHT skin slaves vs. the DARK skin slaves. You must use the FEMALE vs. the MALE, and the MALE vs. the FEMALE. You must also have white servants and overseers [who] distrust all Blacks. But it is NECESSARY THAT YOUR SLAVES TRUST AND DEPEND ON US. THEY MUST LOVE, RESPECT AND TRUST ONLY US. Gentlemen, these kits are your keys to control. Use them. Have your wives and children use them, never miss an opportunity. IF USED INTENSELY FOR ONE YEAR, THE SLAVES THEMSELVES WILL REMAIN PERPETUALLY DISTRUSTFUL. Thank you gentlemen.**

On top of my list is 'AGE', but it's there only because it starts with an 'a.' The second is 'COLOR' or shade. There is **INTELLIGENCE, SIZE, SEX, SIZES OF PLANTATIONS, STATUS** on plantations, **ATTITUDE** of owners, whether the slaves live in the valley, on a hill, East, West, North, South, have fine hair, coarse hair, or is tall or short. Now that you have a list of differences, I shall give you an outline of action, but before that, I shall assure you that **DISTRUST IS STRONGER THAN TRUST AND ENVY STRONGER THAN ADULATION, RESPECT OR ADMIRATION.**

Almost three centuries later, hooks (1984) sums up black rage:

Every black woman in America lives her life somewhere along a wide curve of ancient unexpressed anger. My black woman's anger is a molten pot at the core of me – a boiling hot spring likely to erupt at any point, leaping out of my consciousness like a fire on the landscape. How to train that anger rather than deny it has been our major task of life.

And Lauryn Hill (2012) symbolically represents black rage in our contemporary society in a song. She suggests that black rage is founded on draining and threatening our freedom and that to stop the complaining they poison our water and say it's raining, 'then call you mad for complaining'.

To corroborate ideas about black rage, I asked some individuals what it meant to them. These discussions took place in 2013:

Black mixed-heritage female, age 60:

I EXPERIENCED RACISM WHILE IN CARE. My sexual abuse was because of racism. The responses that I got were racist. This enraged me.

Wyn, age 52, of Grenadian origin:

Deep rage/isolation. Rageful around white middle class people. The only black in social situations. The silent way they respond. You are invisible. Watching a white film produced by a white industry. We don't exist. 'Mandela'. Auditorium empty. Physical impact. Silence attitude seems to say, 'don't touch me, I am afraid'. My son speaks about the same thing. Not being accepted as human. My son says he doesn't trust white people. SUS laws, supermarkets, work, his peer group. I don't think they will succeed in the UK. I did not raise him expressing my rage about the system, yet he knows white spaces. I.e. festival hall and science museum. Serving white people first. When out dancing, the black guys not asking black women to dance, white guys not asking us to dance. I am aware that white people have their own spaces and you feel like an intruder.

Andy, age 74, of Trinidadian and Bermudian origin:

Black rage conjures up racism. My first black rage was age 15 when I left school, in 1955. My grandmother told me I must learn a trade. I was taken around a cabinet-making factory owned by Jews. The workers were asked if they minded working with a black boy. **The boss let me work there, and because of the overt taunting from white gentiles, I began to hate white people. Although I had experienced racism at primary school, it was a shock. The teacher had called black Africans 'savages', but I did not associate with the Africans. I knew I was black and my rage came from being bullied. When I went to secondary school, I stamped out racism towards me when I beat up the first guy who said something racist.**

These testimonies, a tiny microcosm of black rage, are three generations apart in the early twentieth century, and as the stories and the rage evolve, *we are bound to consider* what has gone into the intergenerational and developmental process of black people's lives that has perpetuated the process of black rage.

This question from a student is pertinent to working through the process of black rage:

How would a white counsellor deal with a client who has suffered racial abuse?

The question here is how much is the white counsellor prepared to learn about black rage and internalized racism, and to support these processes? This question might also be important for a black or Asian counsellor who is unaware of the impact of racism, as we cannot take it for granted that they will be the best qualified to work with black rage.

Dennis (in Carroll and Tholstrup, (2004) advocates that

> Supervisors need to be aware of how 'race' and cultural issues are taught and indeed how they themselves have learned about these areas: messages are transmitted and translated across generations of therapists and embodied within the family of the professional institutions with which they are aligned. Whether the family of the institution enables its offspring to separate in the way that can produce new ideas and changes to the institution or whether it simply maintains the status quo is a key question.

Dennis goes on to suggest that

> An integrative approach to 'race' as cultural issues is a framework containing four key features: language, power, identity, and institutional dynamics. These features aim to transcend theoretical underpinning of therapy and the training of counselling and supervision; however, this is not always the case. (p. 48)

It cannot be taken for granted that therapists will feel confident to address these specific contexts of racism and black rage. Ultimately, the same questions about using reflexivity and responsibility in the supervision process apply, and they must be associated with black rage and clients' experiences. When it comes down to it, I would say that giving up is not an option. Those therapists who fear black rage need to work through their defensive position, because giving up on a client where their material makes it seem too hard perpetuates rejection and abandonment, and these harsh experiences are already common features of racism. It is both the therapist's and the supervisor's responsibility to observe signs that racism may be having an impact on the therapeutic or supervisory relationship. Here are some indicators:

Indicators of the impact of black rage on the therapeutic triad

- White or black therapists, for different reasons, may omit to inform their supervisor about their black or Asian client's cultural and ethnic identity.
- Sometimes white therapists idealize their black clients and consequently avoid or underplay concerns about racism and black rage.
- Black therapists may identify with black rage and feel this is enough to support the client. This can lead to assumptions about the client's experiences and inhibit them from processing their unique story.

Below are some manifestations of internalized racism that I am sure many readers will be aware of. At an unconscious level, we may see denial of racism and expressions of internalized anger. A common presentation of internalized racism is overworking to be better or accepted. Another feature is assimilation and internalization of white ways that marginalize cultural origins. In its extreme, internalized racism manifests in skin lightening and adversity to kinky hair and African features, sometimes causing self-harm.

Manifestations of internalized racism

- Denial and internalized anger
- Dismissal of cultural origins
- Being unaware of the impact of racism
- Overworking to be better or accepted
- Name changing/containment of dialect
- Skin scrubbing, bleaching and hair straightening
- Depression, low self-esteem, self-harm, suicide.

As a community of black and white people and various shades in-between, we share common victim and perpetrator patterns of denial, silence, distraction, disassociation, collusion and, ultimately, rage – sometimes overt, and at other times internalized, yet projected in attitude and behaviour. We must acknowledge the lived experience of rage within the psychology of black peoples. This rage may be suppressed and somatized, causing common illnesses such as hypertension.

Sometimes, expressed and mentalized rage and fear draws attention from statutory services, causing over-representation of black people in the mental health system. Not attending to black rage in the therapeutic setting may predispose clients to the mental health system and cause destruction and collusion with underlying causes of black rage.

Whilst some psychological theories offer ways of conceptualizing this predicament, we need to consider creating frameworks to understand and process the impact of racism, past and present, in developmental processes, thus internalized alongside other oppressions. We also need to consider the function of fear intrinsic to internalized oppression and how fear can lead to mental ill health.

A student counsellor proposed this important question concerning black mental health:

> Why are blacks labelled badly most of the time?

This question evokes insight about black people being seen as bad rather than sad when they are distressed. The bad label is more likely to be applied when black people express their rage and the injustice of racism is not attended to but silenced due to fear. Badness is seen as a punishable offence, and if black individuals end up in psychiatric care, they are likely to feel punished rather than supported.

This was borne out in a review conducted by The Sainsbury Centre for Mental Health (2002). The review concluded that fear has the following impact:

- Service users delay seeking help and therefore present to mental health services in serious states of crisis.
- Families and carers are reluctant to become involved in services because they fear the outcome for the person they care for.
- Professionals do not have access to safe spaces to talk about issues of race and culture.

- Black people do not believe that mainstream mental health services can offer help, and services do not understand the pervasive effects of racism.
- Use of stereotypical or individualistic approaches can be unhelpful.
- There is a lack of accounting for the historical and sociocultural context of situations.

It is clear that these fears impact negatively on the interactions between black people and mental health services. There is no blueprint for working with the impact of racism and black rage. The courage to go there is what is needed. A starting point is exploring fears black people have about mental illness and mental health services and to acknowledge that these fears are rooted in the legacy of racism and disadvantage. Even if it is not an appropriate time to address these issues, therapists can take them to their supervision. I also encourage therapists to take to supervision a high degree of expectation that they will be supported to evaluate how their own experiences link with black rage. We need to recognize the lived experience of black people in relation to services for mental health and psychological trauma, and their past and everyday experiences of racism.

I see fear as a component of recognition trauma. There is real fear linked to racism, and we need to provide a space for these fears to be expressed. Paranoia of police and white people is a classic result of fear based on racism. You know you are black when you become aware of racism at work and within institutions, and there are numerous examples of individuals feeling afraid to speak out about their experiences of racism at work. Expression of fear can sometimes be mistaken for rage, and there is plenty of fear about black rage.

For this reason, therapists should recognize the importance of having some background information of the times in clients' lives when they became aware of experiencing or witnessing racism. This history can be taken at the time when concerns about the impact of racism are being raised. It can be useful to ask when the client first experienced racism or when they experienced feeling angry about other oppressions. These enquiring questions give clues as to how much rage the client may have internalized, or how far back the hurt of racism was instilled. Finding out about how clients have coped with racist experiences might also be useful. In so doing, these points about fear can be considered and black rage given a voice.

Clients often fear:

- The enormity of the impact of racism
- Isolation and rejection by peers due to recognition of racism
- Associating powerful feelings linked to racism
- That the damage racism caused cannot be repaired.

Considerations:

- What approaches to empowerment and recovery from racism and black rage are being used, and are they sufficient to unpick the intergenerational impact of slavery, colonization and recognition trauma?
- Can we honestly say that we take issues linked to the challenge of racism and black rage to our clinical supervision?
- Can we acknowledge that we understand where racism and internalized racism may be transferred into the therapeutic dyad? And if this is so, do we process these issues so that we can be fully attentive to the history and intergenerational processes of black rage?
- What do therapists see, hear and understand of intergenerational scars? If we could visually see the scars, would we pay more attention to them?
- Can we see through assimilation, and can we keep in mind that some attitudes and behaviours may be historically and culturally embedded in past experiences and heritage of black and Asian people?

Tayo's story (written by Onyeka (1999), in Ocheing and Hylton, 2010, p. 276) offers some insight into this intergenerational context:

As far back as Tayo could remember he had always looked back in anger. He did not have a blueprint of how to stay alive, but plan or not, he was definitely going to stay alive. Tayo felt that he had been thrown in at the deep end of a very large river. Without coaching or guiding, he logically should have drowned but it was not that easy to kill. He was part of a race that had been subject to every form of abuse and ridicule known in history and yet was still around to tell the tale. He had that same spirit inside of him, uncompromising, undaunted, and angry. As a baby if anyone ever touched his pram he would scream, he was cross then, but he was as mad as hell now. A fire burned inside him, which he could not fully control. Almost as if the rage of 100 slaves butchered in the middle passage had taken out his soul and replaced it with their own.

This passage exemplifies the build-up of rage, possibly linked to slavery and undoubtedly linked to everyday racism. I have mentioned a black empathic approach. There is nothing new about this approach, but use of this concept means considering the importance of naming racism and getting on with the work that specifically reaches out to, and supports and assists the development of, black peoples, as there is denial of black rage and much work to be done.

hooks (1995) reminds us, 'Slaves were denied their right to the gaze.' We need to ask the question, what does denial do to the back gaze? And can therapists place this in context when black rage is a feature of the therapeutic process?

A black gaze can:
- Reflect and reinforce cultural capital (the client's positive feelings about their background and ethnicity)
- Reflect and promote cultural connections and dialogue, offering opportunities to explore personal development in the context of racism
- Promote exploration of African and Asian identities and heritage
- Contradict racism and internalized racism
- Counteract the impact of Eurocentric dominance in psychological support.

A student posed the following question:

How can I be present with a black client who is constantly blaming the white people for his predicament?

What is blame but an expression of hurt and anger? The question here is not how, but are you willing to stay present? Are you willing to accept there is hurt underneath the blame? Are you willing to understand and accept that the black client knows and understands where the racism experience is coming from? It means they may be experiencing recognition trauma, and it means they may be ready to explore the hurt and rage that they may have internalized from racism. This is where compassion, congruence and a black empathic approach is needed.

Rage ignites despondency, revenge and hateful thoughts. Rage causes war in small communities and on a global scale. If we look at the facts and figures of deaths in custody and the mental health system, it is clear that black people expressing their rage have attracted both external and psychological threat to their well-being. Black people have plenty to rage about. On top of our history of slavery, we are impacted by immigration status and the disappointment of the 'promised land' that has left the debris of poverty, unemployment and black-on-black killings. Successful black people do not escape the impact of racism, as racism has no class. Frank Bruno's story is a prime example of this. Another student expresses specific concern about the position of black males:

> Why do black males struggle in society, in general fail to succeed, in comparison to white males?

Large numbers of black male children are referred by their schools for therapy or anger management. Exclusion of black boys from school is a known factor of families and the education system not dealing appropriately with black rage. In addition to their life situations, their predisposition to rage about racism may not be recognized. This is often the beginning of the route to the mental health system. In recognizing this, let us not forget that domestic violence and black-on-black violence may also be features of black rage.

There is a need for self-reflection on behalf of the therapist. In addition to considering the impact of slavery and colonization, we must view the anger of black males in a holistic light that includes the impact of ongoing racism and their personal development process. The black male is often viewed as more aggressive than the white male and less easy to control. Mental health and prison statistics suggest that he is prone to be pacified by these systems due to the irrational fears of the indigenous population. The report quoted below shows that the helper or therapist must become aware of how their fear of black male violence may be laced with racism. Male and female professionals may experience different levels of understanding about black male anger, due to their own experience and their racial projections. It could be said that racial projections underpin statistics on black people in the mental health system.

> Research indicates that more African Caribbean and other Black people with psychosis are being admitted to hospital for treatment because of the way they initially got in contact with the mental health services. Evidence suggests that they are more likely to have been in contact with the police or other forensic services prior to admission. They are also more likely to have been referred to treatment by a stranger rather than by a relative or a neighbor. It is important to note that this happens despite the fact that they are less likely

than white people to show evidence of self-harm and are no more likely to be aggressive to others before admission to a mental health hospital. (Ethnic Health Initiative 2010)

This research also suggests that although there is no evidence indicating that African Caribbean people are more likely to be aggressive than their white counterparts, staff in mental health hospitals are more likely to perceive them as potentially dangerous. The outcome also suggests that psychiatrists are more likely to consider this group as potentially dangerous to others. 'It is therefore possible that African Caribbean people are more likely to be diagnosed with psychosis because of bias among those who treat them. Research in the US shows similar results' (paras 17–18).

Although I am assuming that referring to 'other black people' in the report means Africans and Asians, I am also aware that the predicament in the mental health system may be different. The term psychosis as a generic term has been loosely used and sometimes inappropriately applied, without reference to the background experiences and cultural implications of individual distress.

This was borne out in a report on mental health problems in the South Asian community Harrow, North West London. Research was carried out in March and May 2010. The report written in November 2010 by the BME pilot campaign summarized the following:

Shame, or sharam, fear and secrecy surround mental illness

Mental illness is a taboo subject, meaning there is little open discussion about mental health problems.

People with mental health problems agreed that their diagnoses were something to be kept private and not openly discussed, even with immediate family –

One participant said they had kept their illness secret from their spouse for more than 20 years.

Part of the reason for this is the need to preserve the family's reputation and status at all costs – indeed, one group argued that all problems tended to be hidden, not just evidence of mental health problems.

Preventing community gossip, which can go on to negatively affect the whole family is paramount. Community gossip was mentioned by many participants as the most damaging behavior of all due to its high level of impact both on the person with the mental health problem and their close family.

'They have a fixed psychology, [it's] how they've been raised, how the community behaves. You do not discuss anything around mental illness because it's a no-go area.'

'They think there is no need to go to the doctor – the doctor won't do anything.'

Caring for people with mental health problems is the family's responsibility, largely because many in the community do not believe that a mental health problem is a medical condition that can be managed and treated professionally.

Fear of damaging the family reputation

Instead, there is often misunderstanding about the causes of mental health problems. These include:

- Black magic – which can also be a possible cure
- The will of God
- Genetic
- Bad parenting

Isolation due to fear of family stigma

One participant spoke of how his relative was treated:

'He doesn't go out so he doesn't have the chance to do something irrational or look out of place. If he doesn't go out, you're not going to see what his behavior's like. So his brother, mum and dad don't want him to go out because they don't want to be talked about.'

'It's like a taboo, not really wanting to get their hands dirty or exposed ... it's a really selfish attitude and selfish view, that if I'm associated with that person then my immediate family are going to be subjected to isolation... the stigma that's associated with the individual that's suffering with this illness will affect me.'

There is a deep-rooted misunderstanding of mental health problems passed through generations. People with mental health problems must battle to get the right professional support and treatment while also struggling with ingrained attitudes that promote stigma, discrimination, isolation and sharam.

The report suggests that many Asian individuals delayed therapeutic support because of reasons such as shame and fear of gossip. These delays often meant that by the time they sought help, clients would be more severely distressed and isolated. It is important that this situation not be interpreted as passivity and that underlying concerns be taken seriously.

In looking at the part that therapy and supervision can play in providing appropriate services, I interviewed Barua, an Indian therapist. She describes the cultural challenges that she experienced in supervision, and her experience and growing anger at the lack of awareness and support available when working with Asian clients and for her own cultural knowledge as an Asian therapist. Attention to how cultural marginalization and oppression features to perpetuate racism is important here.

Barua: It felt so important to me to work with a woman of colour and the reason for this was the questions I faced within myself; how will I be understood by a white supervisor? How will I bring culturally sensitive client issues to a white supervisor if she cannot understand me as an Indian woman? When I looked for an Asian or black psychodynamic supervisor I could not find one, so for the time being I started working with a person centred supervisor, an Indian female. Over a period of time I realized that I just wasn't getting what I needed, there was a relational depth missing, not enough engagement from the supervisor's part, and when I bought cultural issues to supervision my supervisor responded only with questions such as 'how did that make you feel?' I knew from my transcultural training that something felt 'wrong'. As a result of this, I felt stuck and frustrated when working with clients, as I didn't understand how I could engage in issues of colour with clients.

This meant that the therapeutic relationship was not at a level where my clients would open up, and I struggled to support them in waking their unconscious processes. An example of this was whilst working with a young Indian female who was clearly putting me on a pedestal, and when I asked her the question 'how is it working with a young Indian female therapist, being an Indian female yourself', the reply was, 'absolutely fine'. I knew there was more to it than that but I was unable to delve in. Maybe due to my lack of experience or my fear of asking the wrong questions. It was times like this that I realized that I needed to change supervisors. I had so many cultural-related questions that were causing turmoil inside me and I wasn't sure what to do with this turmoil.

I decided to switch supervisors and still questioned how I could work with a white supervisor, how could I talk about culture, colour, racism, oppression and such topics with a white supervisor. It was a big decision for me, but I realized that I didn't actually have to have an Indian supervisor to address issues of colour in my practice. I needed a supervisor who was empathetic, culturally aware and able to engage with me on this level. So I started working with a white middle-aged, female psychodynamic supervisor, which changed my practice dramatically, and I really enjoyed our work together. My supervisor helped me link client issues to a psychodynamic way of working, which changed my relationships with my clients too. However, I am also aware that there were still some limitations.

One example of this was when a client brought some issues around black magic to supervision. In Indian and Muslim culture this is practised a lot where people put bad spells on others to cause a lot of destruction in that person's life. I, myself, personally do believe in black magic, and when I talked about it in supervision my supervisor told me that she doesn't believe in it, and there was a very awkward moment between us, at which point I felt like I was a crazy person and then my supervisor steered us away from that conversation. I felt extremely stupid, stuck and shut down. For me this was massive because the effects of black magic can be severe and people seek healing from things like this.

Other issues that came up for me in practice were issues such as counter-transference and over-identifying. Interestingly enough, now that I look back on it, I chose to practise in an Asian location, an unconscious decision at the time but definitely worth reflecting on. I think I felt more comfortable working with Indian clients because in my mind they were more relaxed, not so professional, and that meant that if I made mistakes they wouldn't be so noticeable. This was me internalizing my fear and projecting it into my practice. In my culture, relevant boundaries that exist in a therapeutic setting are frowned upon or mocked, such as time-keeping and confidentiality. Deep down inside I knew, for this reason, I had some leeway as a new therapist and I have addressed this in supervision.

The majority of my clients were Indian females. I haven't been in practice long and was aware that whilst working with some clients in particular I was over-identifying with them. One of the archetypes that I identified with was having to be the perfect 'understanding Indian' therapist, just like a few of my clients felt the need to be the perfect Indian daughter or perfect Indian wife. I was able to take these issues to a transcultural group supervision with Isha, and also my second supervisor was able to work with these cultural issues, to some extent, because she related it back to projection, counter-transference and internalizing, especially when working with issues around self-esteem, the 'good and bad' Indian woman and family rejection from an attachment perspective. We looked at issues of colour and how to work with them. This helped in my practice by contributing to the one-to-one supervision I was having, and as a result I was able to connect culture with psychodynamic practice even more.

When I found a new supervisor, I did find that I was able to bring up such issues like arranged marriages, honour crimes, affairs, self-harm and depression. This was because my supervisor was culturally sensitive, empathized and explored all these issues with me. My clients began bringing more cultural issues such as the expectations that parents, partners and the community have on them, how they lack support, are terrified of who to talk to, have feelings of isolation, shame and guilt, as well as failure and fear of being outcast within the community. Other issues included having to be strong, and always being there for partners and family no matter how bad or down one was feeling. This reminded me of the black archetypes of being a strong woman, always having to cope with the world on your shoulders just because 'that's what we were supposed to do as women'.

Isha: What made it safe for you to do so?

Barua: I would want to check in with an Indian female client, whom I over-identified with during some of our sessions and was fearful of ending with her after we had finished working together, and what was coming up for me?

My supervisor was patient, empathetic, and culturally sensitive, though this did not always mean she had the capacity to work with every cultural issue, though her awareness of cultural topics was useful. She was comfortable talking openly about our skin colour, gender and age. She asked a lot of direct and challenging questions, helped me reflect, pointed things out that I just had not thought about, and sometimes she was able to support me using a psychodynamic approach when working with issues of colour.

Isha: What were the limitations, blocks, difficulties that got in the way?

Barua: I had a good experience with my second supervisor; however, somehow I did feel that oppression was a missed area in my supervision.

Isha: Was the issue of oppression still missed with your second supervisor?

Barua: I am really not sure what I mean by this, but I know it's a strong feeling coming from inside that gets lost, loses its voice, something I don't have words for, but something that became closed off in supervision – vital cultural aspects of client work that I just couldn't advocate in supervision, such as black magic. I feel a part of me held back in supervision, the human part, the spiritual part, the person-centred part, the part that was able to really relate to clients from a cultural aspect. Though I know some of it was over identifying. Something was also shut down.

Isha: There is strong feeling here and you have lost your voice. Can you try and articulate the feeling in relation to the challenge of racism? Have you been able to work through some of this process in your own therapy?

Barua: I feel I need more understanding of cultural issues and racism. I also feel that there's something about the history of what we as people of colour have been through which was completely missing from supervision. I wasn't able to take certain topics to any supervisor except in the transcultural groups, which were limited in time. I wanted to have more of a voice in my supervision about racism, about the rejection that some of my clients felt in their families, and what that meant for an Indian woman in a tight-knit community.

I think there needs to be more Asian and black psychodynamic supervisors, so I plan to become one myself in the future. I feel passion and commitment to getting to know the cultural core of what a client is missing. It's the essence and being of who we are, and I just cannot see how we can work without addressing issues of colour. It almost makes me feel angry that these issues are not spoken about enough and how little people engage with clients on this level. For me there feels like a voice inside which is directionless, not knowing where to go, and not knowing who will listen or understand. I wonder how many clients feel this way too. I also wonder how exactly can I, myself, work with my clients around this when I feel my own voice is shut down?

As we can see, black rage is not a homogeneous phenomenon. It occurs for black and Asian people in different ways, influenced by cultural experiences and the stereotypes that keep shame and fear in place. Therapists must be concerned with how individual rage has been dealt with intergenerationally and the different personal and cultural expressions of rage. We must curtail our judgements about the expression of black rage. We must know that it is healthy to express rage about oppression and make safe spaces for rage to be externalized. How many therapists can lay claim to a clinical space where their clients can scream and shout and bang things without feeling they will be hushed up, restricted by concerns about mental health or intruding into the quietness and privacy of other therapeutic territory?

It is clear that rage evoked by racism and injustice needs attention because this may not be a temporary condition. The psyche finds a variety of ways of coping with these intense feelings, and they may cause ongoing symptoms of trauma if not expressed. How individuals cope depends on their basic self-understanding, emotional security and awareness and how they have been conditioned to express or internalize powerful feelings about racism. Professor Angela Davis (1990), an African American liberationist in the 1960s, became aware of racism in her neighbourhood from an early age. As a young child, she observed where the hurt and fear about racism was being re-enacted in the playground:

> The children fought over nothing over being bumped, over having toes stepped on, over being called a name, over being the target of real or imagined gossip. They fought over everything split shoes, and cement yards, thin coats and mealless days. They fought the meanness of Birmingham while they sliced the air with knives and punched black faces because they could not reach white ones. (p. 94)

Angela Davis, a US equal rights activist, was imprisoned and accused of murder, kidnapping and conspiracy and eventually acquitted on all counts (Davis, 1990). She writes about her controlled rage whilst campaigning for the release of her peers the Soledad brothers, accused of the same after incarceration for rioting. They were all victims of institutional racism,

> But we did not feel afraid, we did not feel impotent. And we vigorously applauded the heroes of our struggle as they strode proudly, courageously, powerfully into the courtroom. The chains draping their bodies did not threaten us; they were there to be broken, destroyed, smashed. The sight of those shackles designed to alarm us, to make the prisoners appear 'dangerous' 'mad', only made us itch to tear the metal from their wrists and ankles. I knew that my own anger was shared by all. The bile rose in my throat. But more powerful than the taste of outrage was the dominating presence of

the brothers, for the brothers were beautiful. Chained and shackled, they were standing tall and they were beautiful. (Davis, 1990, p. 263)

The above quote shows acceptance of black rage and the courage to witness injustice. We need to be aware of the specific nature of racism that concerns us in the present time. Knowledge about the effect of racism can be useful. Racism does not only happen to footballers and people in the public eye. It is not just about name-calling and exclusion from jobs. Racism can be very personal and difficult to evidence. This is why we sometimes doubt whether our feelings about racist experiences are valid. I will try to address this by exploring another poignant question from a student:

> How would a white counsellor deal with a client who has suffered racial abuse?

First and foremost, white counsellors need to accept that some black clients may have internalized their feelings about racism, thus creating ongoing trauma that can influence their well-being. Second, white counsellors need to acknowledge to themselves and their clients that they are aware of being in the perpetrator group and the dynamics that this role may create in the therapeutic relationship. This does not mean expressing guilt about racism (which should be taken to the therapist's own therapeutic space). This acknowledgement may open a space for clients to share their experiences. Third, all therapists must be able to accept the experience of racism as told by the client, and make attempts to empathize specifically towards the hurt of racism and related feelings of rage. This approach should be supported in supervision. From this place of openness about racism, trust can be built. All therapists should consider the historical impact of racism on a black person's psyche. This means that the client can be encouraged to share both past and present experiences of racism and its impact on their personal development.

Racism at its most challenging can be unconscious and deep within interrelational dynamics. Individuals who find it difficult to identify racist dynamics and challenge overt racism tend to internalize the hurt it can cause. Sometimes they might dismiss the racism and try to deny their feelings. Whilst this can be a temporary safety measure, racism can cause harmful, deeply painful symptoms of emotional hurt. These symptoms have been addressed as internalized racism and can manifest as feeling silenced when experiencing racism or other negative and harmful outcomes. Racism plays a part in how rage is processed. Rage is fundamental to racism and it can be a driving force for creativity. Rage can be as equally challenging as racism in the therapeutic process, and we must be aware of what we do with the rage of our clients and the rage within us.

It is common to hear someone say, 'don't be angry', as though the expression of anger is not a valid emotion. So where does the rage go if it is not expressed? Messages about internalizing rage are fraught with anxieties about disclosure and shame. Shame is also an important factor for those who are impacted by racism – shame about skin colour installed by the racism itself, shame about powerful unexpressed responses to racism, shame as an ongoing stigma, linked to the taboo of externalizing and challenging racism rather than storing the feelings in our bodies.

Confronting the taboo of black rage means understanding and exploring the multidimensional effect of mistrust, fear, guilt, confusion, ambiguity, shame, self-blame, internalized anger and internalized racism, and the silencing nature of oppressions as they impact on the self expression and self-esteem of family members.

Mothers of abused children identified feelings of mistrust, fear and paranoia, and that they wanted to withdraw from others, leading to isolation and addictions in order to cope with the powerful feelings. Rage in the black community is stigmatized. Black men are labelled as violent, and black women labelled as aggressive. When people are too traumatized to talk about the painful feelings related to sexual abuse and violence, they may internalize their anger.

A black mother whose husband abused her 10-year-old daughter was interviewed by Barnard (2001): 'I felt as if I was swallowing my anger. You begin to feel paranoid. As if everyone is thinking you should have noticed something. I feel afraid to trust anyone' (p. 43).

A father whose six-year-old daughter was abused by her stepfather, reports, 'I am either feeling very angry or withdrawn. I don't know whom to trust anymore. I was even afraid to acknowledge the abuse myself so it feels easier to shut myself off from everyone. I'm more fearful and I feel as if I have become a different person' (Barnard, 2001, p. 43).

Therapists and care workers need to question whether they are working on themselves in this area. Whether support workers are black or white, these aspects of psychological demeanour will need to be understood and taken into account so that trauma and powerful feelings can be unpacked. Rage needs to be accepted as it is. The history behind the rage should be processed in supervision. The client's rage should not be interpreted as madness. Black rage cannot be measured, and the experiences and feelings that lie beneath must be valued.

Rage is what it is, and it can teach us about individual healing needs and the struggle to overcome injustice, instilled by racism – in other words, rage coloured by racism needs attention, yet more often than not a raging black individual faces more racism and rejection rather than a space to vent anger and share the hurt of their experience.

There is no doubt that responses to rage affect the psyche and influence coping mechanisms. If the response to rage is less than positive, an individual is likely to develop hiding patterns rather than sharing patterns, and rage can then become submerged. At the age of four years old, witnessing the response to a bombing of a house of a black family on a segregated street, Davis (1990) describes the hidden fear underneath her black rage.

> Crowds of angry black people came up the hill and stood on 'our' side staring at the bombed-out ruins of the Deyabert's house. Far into the night they spoke of death, of white hatred, death, white people, and more death. But of their own fear they said nothing. Apparently it did not exist, for black families continued to move in. (p. 79)

So, here we see that fear can be a hidden element of rage. It is not always clear that rage can camouflage other feelings such as sadness and fear. It is important, therefore, for therapists and supervisors to bear in mind other emotional features underlying black rage.

Summary

Racism plays a part in how anger is processed. Unexpressed black rage can create stuckness and splits in the psyche, causing inability to be open and fully connected to feelings. Unexpressed rage can create depression, yet there are dangers of expressing rage openly, due to misinterpretation and fear of racist responses, including mental health labelling. Cultural influences and intergenerational experiences play a role in the levels at which black rage may be expressed. The roll of shame can inhibit expression of black rage and create isolation and further shame about mental health concerns.

Black rage is a challenge to racism. This behavioural response to racism may at times feel overwhelming; even so, it has a powerful influence on defending vulnerable emotions hurt by racism. Sadly, this intergenerational feature has created stereotyping and lack of support due to its unsociable nature in the white world. Misconceptions about black rage can isolate black individuals and cause therapists to disassociate with clients who express strong feelings about racism. Alternatively, silence due to fear of repercussions when challenging racism can create the same response. Unheld emotions can sometimes be influenced by racism or the internalized racism of the therapist and supervisor. It is not true that black rage equals violence, and it is not true that Asian people do not experience rage. As spoken by Maya Angelou on OWN, on 19 January 2014, 'I am a human being. Nothing human can be alien to me.'

Pointers:

- Therapists must be aware that stereotypes about the way black and Asian people express rage can prevent appropriate connection with client material.
- Therapists and supervisors must remain aware that black rage is likely to be linked to past experiences of racism and will be intensified by other oppressions and vice versa. It is the therapist's and supervisor's responsibility to assist individuals to untangle the different threads of rage and bear witness to how black rage may have been instilled early in life. Cultural directions of rage must be considered.
- Trust in the process and stick with the challenges. Therapists need to make close connections with their supervisors, not subservient connections, so that they feel they have secure backup in facing these challenges.
- Develop a working awareness of black rage and the challenge of racism.
- Develop new concepts for understanding that include a black empathic approach.
- Use interpretations that reflect a positive black gaze.
- Consider recognition trauma in the light of individual developmental processes and the impact of contemporary and intergenerational racism and black rage.
- Develop ways of being present in the client's experience and process of cultural identity development, oppressions and black rage.
- Engage with clients in anti-oppressive, empowering ways that facilitate black rage and intergenerational racism.
- A space to express black rage without judgement whilst connecting empathically must be provided.

Part II

Identity, Shadism and Internalized Oppression

The challenge of racism and developmental processes has to be sensitively negotiated when working therapeutically in the context of cultural diversity, assimilation, family fragmentation and mental health. When the psychological challenges of living with diversity are not taken into account, a client's whole experience can become denied or split off from their experience of being black, or having a Caribbean, African, Asian or an immigrant background and belonging to a group whose origins differ from the host population. In this section of the book, problems of personal and institutional disassociation, and the process and healing of internalized negative cultural messages and racism arising from within the family and from the social environment will be addressed. Here, the concept of 'ancestral baggage' will be explored. The cultural origins of black and Asian families are integral to personal identity and personal-development processes. Therapists are generally trained to think in Eurocentric mono-cultural ways that do not fully consider the impact of 'Britishness' and assimilation processes that can emerge when distresses become apparent. Part II will also reflect on the melting pot experience of diversity and sameness, and the implications of shadism in intra-cultural and intra-racial dynamics. Gender as a contributor to assimilation will be addressed as a vital component linking to intersecting identities and the challenge of racism.

We must consider how identity repression can ultimately perpetuate taboo and lead to mental ill health. One very stark black Western archetype that black people grapple with is the concept of beauty and the way that skin tone and hair texture have become a measure of this in the white world. This is a particularly pertinent area for black women and evokes a huge dollop of internalized racism to contend with.

Hernton (1973) suggests that black and Asian people have become objects of desire and objects of envy and hatred based on their skin tone and hair texture.

The stereotyping of light-skinned black women with less kinky or straightened hair portrayed in the media has created a discourse of confusion about desire and black sexuality, creating divisions between us. This is borne out in the prolific sales of skin-lightening and hair-straightening products and, more recently, ways to plump up the lips and buttocks of women. The manufacturing of skin-lightening and hair-straightening products sold to black women emanate from archetypes about blackness as bad, dirty and unacceptable and about nappy hair as abnormal. These archetypes instil negative identity into the personal development of people with African heritage. This also creates a split between African and Asian people, due to the similarity between Asian hair and European hair. This will be addressed more fully in Chapter 5.

The Melting Pot

The UK is a melting pot of ethnic and cultural mixtures, but often the assimilation process associated with this is marginalized, misunderstood or misinterpreted. This chapter will address the challenge of racism and assimilation as a feature of the client's personal development and identity process. The function of internalized racism will be explored in relation to assimilation and black or Asian identity development. Some attention will be given to how racism impacts on ways that immigrant families can be confined by attempts to be British.

Assimilation

Assimilation can imply bringing together old and new to make new forms that create social discourses. Humans begin assimilating and internalizing culture at birth. This is evident in the ways that young children discuss their appearances in terms of beautiful and ugly. Good and bad. What we do with these early messages as aware adults is our choice. The influence of family, educational and cultural heritage and levels of assimilation within the intergenerational context are what make us who we are. Conflicts such as Britishness versus authenticity may arise for clients struggling with this process. It is, therefore, important that therapists remain aware of assimilation processes and the ways that normalizing can impact individual psychology and responses to the experience of racism.

Assimilation is an internalizing process whereby an individual absorbs the cultures, habits, attitudes and behaviours of their surrounding environment. For someone whose background does not originate in the UK, taking on new sociocultural experiences can mean a loss of cultural identity and community. Ways of being become challenged in a new environment. Due to war, colonization and migration, there are many examples of cultural assimilation across the world: the British assimilation into North America and the colonies; Arab and Israeli assimilation into Europe and America; post-slavery assimilation into Nova Scotia; the Irish, African Caribbean, Asian and Eastern European assimilation into the US and the UK. Mass-migration asylum and indentured labour have often meant loss of culture and community, taking on the identity of the host population and putting away what has previously been familiar. For black and Asian people, this experience can be compounded by racism.

Standardization of language, legislation and social policies that reinforce citizenship create a life in part context of individual ontology. In addition, this can mean disassociation with former customs and attempts to reidentify the self in the context of a new environment. Social policies can also influence members of minority groups in their host population. Patriotic and anti-gay attitudes and legislation reinforce assimilation of women, men and LGBTQ individuals. The campaign against pathologizing people who are gay, and psychotherapists who try to normalize individuals by changing the mindset of homosexuals are prime examples of this.

Assimilation of traditional approaches to psychotherapy can sway ideas about identity and working with oppressions. Reassigning a new context for living has a relational and intergenerational impact, and individuals are bound to unlearn aspects of past cultural associations and feel compelled to replace them with present and future reference points. Loss of cultural capital can have devastating effects. Ways of being and doing become eroded, and a split in cultural associations may occur.

A young woman, age 27, was having difficulties assimilating into British culture after arriving from the Seychelles with her grandmother. Being third-generation and feeling abandoned by her mother, who had moved to Bermuda with a new husband, she was feeling lost and unsure that she wanted to stay in Britain. Her father had resided in Britain for 10 years before she arrived. Her encounter with the children of her father's new family contributed to feelings of abandonment and insecurity, since she had not been informed of her siblings' existence prior to her arrival. Her father was a disciplinarian and he was also dependent on alcohol to survive long working hours and unsociable shifts. In addition to arriving into an alien culture, she was experiencing difficulty getting a college place because she had not completed her education in her homeland. Her description of negative attitudes towards her sounded like a familiar story of institutional racism. Although she had not seen her father for 10 years prior to her arrival, she was drinking heavily to try and overcome her difficulties around settling in the UK.

These are the consequences of ancestral baggage, which can mean that coping skills and behaviour patterns linked to immigration and racism in the UK may be passed on to future generations. A familiar feature of this phenomenon is a confused mindset when individuals are trying to understand past from present, or when younger people searching for their real identities rebel against rigid boundaries of family and cultural origins.

On the other hand, if individuals have a childhood experience of integrating knowledge about their family origins, and black and Asian pride, this can serve as cultural capital and buffer oppressions that they encounter in their daily lives. The following paragraph exemplifies how cultural capital can be utilized in the client's experience of racism and loss of heritage:

Black therapist: My client had the same name as me, but we originate from different places. My background is Jamaican and her parents are from Malawi. Her parents have returned home and they only have email and phone contact. My client complains that her parents approach British culture as a model for personal progress and they do not seem emotionally strong enough to listen to her feelings about life in the UK. Work as a theatre hand is going well, but the client does not trust colleagues or friends enough to share her concerns. The client feels abandoned by her parents and has been feeling depressed. On arriving in the UK at age 11, her parents emphasized the importance of living and behaving as the British do, so they could fit in. The client's experience of being the only black African child in school was traumatic and left her feeling that she does not fit in, the opposite to her parents' expectations.

This sounds all too familiar to me – a clear case of ancestral baggage and internalized racism. The dilemma for this Jamaican therapist from an immigrant family was multidimensional. Whilst they both were women of African descent, therapist's and client's diverse experiences of being African Caribbean and being a direct descendant from Malawi, both regions formerly influenced by British colonialism, set them apart. The therapist's immediate response to the client having the same forename initiated projections about the significance and Britishness of their names. A brief conversation about their names had taken place at their first meeting. Although the therapist also had experiences of being the only black child in school, in later sessions, the gap between their cultural heritage became apparent.

Both dissociation and association are likely to be features of their dynamic relationship. This predisposition can cause the therapist some conflicting thoughts about creating a safe alliance. The therapist in this case offered a black empathic response influenced by her awareness of institutional racism, but this did not seem enough to support the client's internalized feelings about abandonment by her family and rejection caused by racism.

In supervision, we came to an agreement that the diversity in the client–therapist relationship needed to be acknowledged to enable a shift in the client's depressive thoughts about abandonment. A risk of the client feeling further abandoned needed to be faced in order to offer a space to explore the client's loss of origins and cultural heritage. This could be viewed as a means of supporting cultural collateral, esteem building and repairing dissociation due to the client's assimilation process. The term cultural collateral signifies that if a black individual has enough positive input about their black heritage, they are more equipped to manage the impact of racist dynamics on their well-being, education and developmental process.

Thinking strategically about dissociation, assimilation and parental heritage and ancestral baggage on behalf of the client was found to be supportive in this situation. The therapist's association and assimilation processes were also considered when addressing stuckness with this challenge in the supervisory process. Although this challenge may not necessarily include experiences of racism, racism is implicitly a part of the assimilation process.

Multiculturalism and assimilation

It is often assumed that minorities are expected to assimilate. This is where racism and other oppressions can play a role in excluding or marginalizing individuals who do not conform to stereotypical roles and the customs of a majority white culture in the UK. These premises arise from the British idea of civilizing the natives of their colonized territories.

Whatever forms the blending of migrants into societies takes, a level of dissociation is likely to occur. Jews who uprooted themselves and fled the pogroms to Western Europe altered their names so as to fit into society. Many Nigerians have also relinquished their traditional names to alleviate problems of assimilating and outward association with their African background, due to lack of acceptance caused by racism.

There are differences between having your home invaded like the Native Americans and Indigenous peoples of Australia and the plundering, trafficking and enslavement of Africans and those who flee from ethnic cleansing and become a minority through migrating to another culture. Each situation has its problems that influence the assimilation processes of future generations. These processes can exacerbate taboos and secrecy and influence concerns about how majority citizens will understand or perceive particular characteristics and traditions of minorities.

Normalizing as an aspect of assimilation has many dimensions, depending on individual cultural experience. For example, a child raised in the Hindu faith may be aware of the collective nature of their family and community; therefore, normality is the shared context of extended family and community customs and attitudes. Thoughts and attitudes about familiar ways of life and behaviours outside of these norms might cause guilt and anxiety about breaking boundaries. In therapy, communication issues such as the client, therapist or supervisor putting a part of themselves away or revealing hidden cultural territory may arise. Support to work with disassociation of this nature must be considered in the supervisory process. Care about not homogenizing different cultural minority groups must also be taken.

If we look at diversity within the Asian population, it is very clear that features that indicate an Asian heritage do not indicate that all Asian people originate in India or China. Koreans and Japanese are different to Asians born in and raised in Africa, who have a different experience to Asians born and raised in the Caribbean, or raised in the UK, or the US. East Africans may have a different experience to West Africans, North and South Africans. Caste systems, spirituality religions and levels of contact with the white world and colonization will influence how different groups present themselves. An understanding of family practices and traditional influences on groups that migrate to the UK from Asia, Africa and the Caribbean is an important feature when considering homogeneity and racist stereotypes.

Professionals and supervisors must be willing to explore the impact of assimilation and normalizing and not take this for granted. It is difficult to talk about assimilation without reflecting on internalized oppression as a critical source of this process. We cannot easily see internalized racism, but the manifestations of it are all around us.

Comments about skin tone, hair texture or breadth of nose, dished out over a young child can metaphorically be absorbed through the skin. I have heard that some parents have gone to great lengths to alter the features of their children. A range of behaviour such as pinching or pegging the nose to raise it and stop flatness and plastic surgery to make lips thinner have been reported. Comments about hair texture add fuel to this fire. Such comments about identity can cause deep trauma that often gets carried throughout life.

I met an African American man in his 40s who explained how at the age of 14 his mother became concerned about his adolescent behaviour. After several visits to the doctor, they decided his problem was the size of his lips and sent him for surgery to thin them down. He showed me the scars on his mouth and explained that they were nothing compared to how ugly he had felt as a young boy. The truth is that he was made to feel ugly by internalized standards of what a black person should look like – that being a closer version of the white man. This is a classic story of the physical and emotional scars instilled intergenerationally because of internalized racism.

I, too, had my fair share of internalized oppression. In my training, for example, I was informed that people who were raised in care did not have a 'secure base', and therefore they were likely to remain in the borderline psychotic category of mental health and it is unlikely that they would gain from psychotherapy and counselling. This perspective of early childhood influences came from perceived ideas about Bowlby's attachment theory and the influence of insecure bonding on relationships. For me this meant that because of my background I was relegated to the no-hope group. The same applied to people over the age of 45 who were deemed less likely to be open to emotional and behavioural insights and change. From these pearls of wisdom, I internalized feelings of unworthiness and began to assert my need to be valued as a black trainee.

At no time throughout my training did I feel confident to acknowledge my past experience of being in care; so that became a taboo subject. I have always had a strong determination to fight back, but disclosure was risky once I became aware of the marginalization of black people's experiences and institutional racism. In being silent I was assimilating, putting a part of me away so that I would feel normal and fit in as much as my skin colour allowed me in a predominantly white, mainly middle-class, group. On reflection, I can see that some of my behaviour was intergenerational, as prior to this training I had never felt confident in educational situations. I felt that if I could just go through the motions and pass to prevent the humiliation of failure, that would be OK. I could manage my life sufficiently and there was no need to excel at anything so long as I fitted in somewhere. Fitting in is an assimilation process that created confusion in my own training process. Therefore, looking back, I can see that I must have spent most of my training period in a dissociative state.

My own therapy and supervision

I have had three experiences of long-term therapy and clinical supervision with white women. In all three of these situations, it took me at least a year to begin talking about my experiences of being black, my heritage, experiences in care and racism. I was never encouraged to explore my parental history, my interracial heritage or early experiences of racism, so I stayed in the present with my everyday life whilst building a dossier of the lack of attention to anything I said about being a black person. I became enraged by the attitude of these white professionals who were engaged to support my journey. On reflection, it is now clear that they had neither experience nor appropriate training to assist me with these matters.

When eventually I expressed my accumulating rage, my therapist and primary supervisor acknowledged their naivety, and these were points at which the therapy and supervision were drawn to an end. My therapist said she did not have a white experience, and I felt that her attitude became that of anger towards me for provoking this insight. My supervisor seemed to give up when her lack of experience and training in this area was disclosed. So we did not have the opportunity to work through this phase of the fear and guilt evoked by their recognition trauma, and any possibility of exploring my internalized racism was remote.

Internalized racism

It is clear that institutional and internalized racism work together in persuading individuals to submerge parts of their identities in order to normalize and fit in. We only need to look at how hair straightening and skin lightening fit the model of shadism that pushes dark-skinned people and nappy-haired black people to the bottom of the 'beauty' pile.

Shadism is a term used for describing prejudice that divides black people based on different shades of their skin from light brown to black. This divisive attitude was set up during slavery and maintained intergenerationally and through colonialism, via apartheid, classism and assimilation.

Similar attitudes underpinned the caste system in India and the old apartheid regime in South Africa. Assimilation on a huge scale has perpetuated media portrayal of the tanned, silky-haired woman as more desirable than the dark-skinned, nappy-haired woman. These elitist models of acceptability perpetuate assimilation and can influence self-esteem, work performance and job seeking.

The black student quoted below grapples with her internalized racism and work performance, whilst reflecting on her experience with a white client:

> A recent client wanted to know about me, and I did not want to get into that with her. I told her I was married and a few things and I said she is open to fantasize about whatever. One of the things she said to me was, 'as a Nigerian, (I must have mentioned to her I was Nigerian), you have gone through a lot and you have reached maturity.' I did not add or dismiss what she said; I just thought she could keep whatever fantasies were hers. But sometimes I am left thinking did that mean she may have thought I was not good enough to be her counsellor?

The conundrum of racism and internalized racism with a black counsellor and white client is demonstrated right here at the centre of this therapist's well-being and the well-being of the client. The client is curious, yet offering some understanding that the therapist must have experienced racism. Something of what the client was conveying in her attempt to empathize with the counsellor triggered the counsellor's internalized racism. In consideration of the client's naivety, it appears that for a moment the counsellor was being responded to as though she were the client. On reflection, this raises two questions. Thinking psychodynamically about projections, could the white client have been infantilizing the black counsellor or making attempts to gain control of the session? Thinking with a person-centred cap on, what did the client want from the counsellor, and what was she trying to convey about herself? The counsellor did not answer, and yet a powerful response was triggered. A rupture may have occurred and the counsellor seemed to be experiencing recognition trauma, unawarely prioritizing this over the client's curiosity. The question of 'am I good enough?' was raised for the black female counsellor, and this question interrupted an empathic response.

Bearing in mind that being black/Nigerian and female brings a conglomeration of experiences and multidimensional oppressions, I am wondering about this counsellor's assimilative processes. She became disconnected from the client's process and temporarily disempowered, gagged, silenced by her internalized racism in a moment of recognition that the client may have meant something racist. At this point she also became assimilated into the role that racism often assigns to black people. Unable to fully engage as a professional, she was stumped at the voice of the other, incongruent and unable to account for that moment of connection and misconnection in the room. Out of this experience come three questions. What happened next within the therapeutic alliance? Was this stored away for further reflection? Did the therapist feel able to take this experience to supervision? The counsellor may have been trying to ignore the racialized context of the interaction, due to her assimilation processes. Supervision in this context would require attention to the overt expression of black–white diversity, awareness of the multidimensional context and working with the unspoken racial content. An analysis of the following question from another student portrays a multidimensional concern coupled with internalized racism, possible racism and a question of machoism:

Why can't my white male client bring his white pain to a black woman?

Different strands of oppression are being observed here, and the diversity of black–white and male–female is an essential feature of this relational process. Not only may this man have coping mechanisms built on his disposition as a male, at the risk of homogenizing, I speculate that he might be unable to see his pain; he may unconsciously fear overcompensation from a woman, as we are usually designated the role of primary caregiver. In addition to this, the power dynamics of racism where white men are on top of the list in terms of white supremacy and patriarchy have been reversed. The challenge for this black counsellor is to utilize her observations and become active in addressing the diversity between herself and the client, and what this may mean for the process of a white male sharing his pain with a black woman. I have experienced black female supervisees who become aware of the racialized dynamics in their therapeutic work and forget the gender contexts. Allowing vulnerability in supervision may be the key to deepening exploration of this multidimensional context.

Supervision

Just as denial and rage, assimilation issues also get transferred into the supervisory relationship. Both therapist and supervisor carry their personal identities into the professional arena where accountability for their work is scrutinized. So, for example, if a straight white Jewish man and a black lesbian woman are working together, their cultural, linguistic, religious and sexual orientation will be present in the ways that they communicate and process the client work and their supervisory relationship. However, challenges about racism present in life experiences and this work will also be part of the supervisory dynamic. Personal experiences of assimilation will affect whether the challenges of racism are disclosed and whether racialized identities remain hidden or presented in supervision. An excerpt from a 2014 discussion with two white therapists (Ian trained at the Institute of Group Psychoanalysis; Jenny trained as a play therapist at Roehampton University) shows the challenges of this situation:

Ian: The cultural context is important. Things here may be difficult for you. If you have been living in Syria, the cultural context makes a difference to how psychopathy is managed. I would not look at a person's psychopathy on its own. If you are black and experiencing racism, this is a context. You can't make the assumption that if you are poor, you can't expect to be dealing with your problems if you can't pay your rent. My training taught me to solely look at the psychopathology and that was it, as if you would take it out of how you live. Of course, psychoanalysis is changing now. I had a black male client who was keen to talk about racism. He was affected by his relationship with his father and what was going on in his job. He wanted to sort himself out. Of course, cultural context influenced how his own father was affected by racism. I know from my black male friends that this context can be powerful. Somehow, the older black man can become crippled by racism and take it out on his own children.

Jenny: I had a client who was not directly bringing an issue of racism. She was having a really difficult time and she felt it was racism, but it was not named. It was difficult to pin it down and I helped her as much as I could.

Ian: Well, it can be really difficult to suggest, because people will come and discuss the intimate details of their problems, but they won't talk about the issues here about I am black and you are white. They won't talk about racism because I am white. What am I going to be like if they talk about this? It's the thing that comes in that they are scared because it might mess up the relationship.

Jenny: I can't recall this occurring with my clients. I will often try to get a black therapist, as children may need a positive role model instead of another white therapist. All you can do is try and work against it. If I am the only therapist they can get, I have a range of toys that are reflective of black children and Asian children, but it does not take away the wanting to be white.

Ian: I am comfortable around black people, having gone through a lot. It feels natural now and I can risk it. Before, I would have held back. It feels alright to talk about it, as I have enough experience and back-up. It's not such a big issue. When I was younger, no. That's why we need to have this in training.

Jenny: I have had only two black supervisees. With the first black woman, I had a lot of difficulty, where my racism was tying me up in knots. There was something about her that I found difficult. She wasn't very good, I don't think, but there was something else. I kept getting mixed up between racism and her. It was down to the relationship. Not naming her fear of working with a white woman could have been in the mix.

In this discussion both therapists are white and being supervised by white professionals. Both had become aware of the impact of racism and both are willing to address their difference to the black client. There are differences in their attitudes to racism. Ian acknowledges using his empathic awareness to acknowledge the importance of cultural awareness, class issues and racism. In his group therapy sessions, he supports the dynamics of a mixed black and white group. He has had two black supervisors and he trusts that his white supervisor is willing to discuss the challenges of racism and cultural diversity in his practice. He acknowledges the need for more CPD (continuing professional development) in this area.

Jenny has experienced some confusion about whether racism is in the room and found some difficulties being clear about addressing it directly. On the other hand, she refers clients on to black therapists so they can experience the black role model, but she does not seem clear about the possibility that she might offer a positive black gaze in her responses to clients. She acknowledges that she is not reading about black issues and she seems complacent about increasing her knowledge and further CPD.

Working with clients with a visible difference such as skin colour will require some consideration of racism and willingness to continue developing in this area. Identifying with similar cultural experiences and oppressions can bring about a renewed awareness of how multi-dimensional oppressions permeate everyday lives. Along with this awareness comes some ambiguity influenced by forms of denial about the therapist's role in oppressing other groups. Denial may also be present in the supervisor's responses. Both therapist and supervisor must remain aware of these influences. This is where the process of assimilation kicks in.

Bits of our personalities that appear as shadow elements or taboo subjects often get put aside so that our priorities with clients get explored within one-dimensional Eurocentric frameworks. We sometimes deny who we really are, our cultural needs and how we view our client work via an assimilated looking glass. Like Alice in Wonderland drinking the assimilation potion, we become smaller and shrink our visibility so as not to draw attention to our identities, or we grow larger and swollen with a false layer of protection against institutional humiliation and responses to being real.

I worked occasionally with a black woman who came specifically for supervision with me because she wanted to unravel her responses to a client's experience of racism. The supervision was supplementary to regular fortnightly clinical supervision with her white male supervisor. I am usually quite clear with supervisees that our work does not include discussions about their personal therapists and other supervisors. On this occasion, I became concerned because the supervisee informed me that she felt that she could not take her work with black clients to her supervisor. My concern was about her missing out on learning from facing the challenges of working through racism with her white supervisor. Therefore, she was not benefiting from the parallel process of her client's experience of racism. Through this dialogue another dynamic became apparent, that her supervisor also being male further made him a member of the dominant power discourse. I encouraged the supervisee to take a look at what was getting in the way of expecting a professional response to the challenge of racism that she was experiencing from her supervisor.

Sometimes we expect that responses to the challenges of racism must be perfect, precisely anti-racist and empathically connecting. So what if they are not? We then have an additional learning, that of mistakes as a result of this challenge, and further opportunities to work through a process of change. This approach gives us opportunities to learn about discouragement, disappointment and growing from our failures. Racism is no different from other oppressions in the ways that it can disempower us and make us feel afraid of failing or falling short of our professional standing. Some individuals died from symptoms caused by their relentless struggles against racism. Others were assassinated because of their boldness, and some remained terrorized into silence and numbness. The choices are many, but most of all, in the professional role of therapist, we must create circumstances that enable us to think clearly for the benefit of the client. This may mean that risks will need to be taken so that we can open our hearts compassionately to members of the oppressor group, remembering that they may project their own hurt and terror onto us, thus causing confusion and doubt about our ability to hold the client through the challenges of racism. This applies to supervisor, therapist and client, who can at times all be in the oppressor role. So, there becomes a point of opportunity to interrupt this process rather than continue in the same patterned way.

Summary

I have addressed the profound influence of assimilation on individuals. This effect, which is rarely considered as a contributor to racism, can be seen as a feature in the personal development of individuals and, in particular, clients of African Caribbean and Asian heritage. Families from these heritages became influenced by the melting pot and British colonialism, and generations that came after will have been impacted by assimilation into white Eurocentric British culture. We must consider whether time is given to the challenge of racism and assimilation processes in the client's personal development. There may be parallels in how these needs are met in client work and supervision, causing a ripple effect through training and accreditation processes.

Confusion about working through the challenge of racism in supervision may occur. Time constrictions and prioritizing essential elements of the client's process may be seen as more important. Working through the confusion may be hindered by assimilation and assumptions of homogeneity. For example, all clients, no matter what their ethnic designation, can be understood in blanket terms by interpreting their behaviour using a traditional Kleinian approach. Klein developed a psychoanalytical approach based on child observations and interpreting unconscious responses to anxiety. She encouraged the exploration of defences such as splitting and the projection of unbearable feelings onto others.

Therapists and supervisors addressing the challenge of racism can work through such assumptions by broadening their outlook and reflecting on traditional concepts with a third eye. Splitting and projections of the client can be explored in terms of their cultural influences and assimilation processes. Adult dilemmas in relation to early parenting experiences can be considered in the light of the client's cultural background. Ethnic origins can be taken into account, giving clients an opportunity to unravel their assimilation processes. Defences can be understood in relation to experiences of racism and multidimensional oppressions. Remember, there is no blueprint for working with racism, but we can develop our approach using awareness and a degree of risk-taking in the practice and supervisory process.

Generally, supervisors are supportive and attentive to the client's and therapist's well-being, but sometimes their personal assimilation processes can cause unwillingness to break the silences that uphold denial and racism. This can limit willingness to explore the challenge of racism in the supervisory relationship and the client–therapist dynamic.

Fear and shame in this process can cause shutdown-ness, and these restrictive elements underlie assimilation. These distresses can remain hidden in a variety of ways.

A sound framework for therapeutic process depends on how much individuals' lives have been influenced by assimilation and the intergenerational influences of racism and other oppressions. This also depends on whether individuals experience freedom of choice to liberate themselves from the cultural restrictions associated with assimilation.

Working with a black or white client when you do not come from that group and not addressing the differences, either with the client or in supervision, must become a thing of the past. Therapists and supervisors must consider what they put away because of their assimilation processes and how this can restrict emotional development. Censoring thoughts about cultural influences in clinical work, due to fear or guilt, is a feature of assimilation and a condition that with awareness can be utilized for the therapist's and supervisor's personal development. In addition to the challenges, there is learning and self-discovery in being aware of assimilation. Therapists and supervisors can use their insights to support clients through their own assimilative processes.

Pointers:

- Be willing to consider that assimilation will have influenced the developing identities of clients.
- Do not take it for granted that assimilation of black or Asian individuals means that they have not experienced racism.
- Consider that internalized racism may need to be explored.
- Therapists must expect to explore the impact of their own assimilation process and how their identity may contribute to attending to the client's presentation.
- Black professionals must avoid assumptions of similarity that cause glossing over individual identity and internalized racism (i.e. judging by levels of blackness, language and ways of expressing self).
- Develop confidence to voice the often challenging and unspeakable impact of multidimensional oppressions.
- Explore individual resilience and help seeking patterns.
- Use an anti-oppressive approach and, where possible, process specific oppressions such as sexism and racism and their link with assimilation and identity.
- Reflect on the process of homogenizing clients.

5

African Heritage, Asian/Indian Heritage, Mixed Heritage

This chapter will address concerns about homogeneity and perspectives that include diversity within African/Caribbean and Asian families and mixed-heritage experiences. I shall take a look at the problems of tarring everyone with the same brush, so to speak, and how the therapist can use diversity and sameness to get to know the client's acculturation processes. The challenge of sociocultural stigmas and assumptions about being black enough, white enough or mixed culturally and racially will be explored. The client's ability to retain their integrity and their right to be who they are and define themselves in the sense of their heritage is of primary importance. Therapists and supervisors will be encouraged to explore the question, who am I in the therapeutic space and in the context of my role as a therapist, and with clients' identities? Using empirical material from a supervisor, therapist and a client, the role of a racialized identity in self-esteem and psychological development and support will be addressed.

A homogeneous approach assumes that black people are all one Caribbean bunch or one African bunch or that Asian people all originate from India or South Asia, marginalizing Eastern Asian experiences of Chinese, Japanese and indigenous peoples. It is important to be aware of languages, religions and cultural and spiritual denominations that form the make-up and origin of diverse groups; however, unless one has extensively studied world peoples, it is unlikely that we would have a full knowledge base of traditions and migrations that make up the background of our clients' historical journeys.

Due to colonization and the emergence of the Commonwealth, the British have marked a powerful global influence that lingers internationally. This is the background status of white privilege. A key area of transcultural therapeutic work, therefore, is to understand some of the particular heritages that influence extended family origins and the intergenerational impact of 'Britishness' for clients in the UK.

Britishness in itself assumes a notion of homogeneous peoples. Racism is one aspect of homogeneity, yet it also diversifies groups and individuals. The most common manifestation of this notion is the English language as an international source of communication throughout Europe and the world.

Racism operates on both sides of the fence, and taboos about mixed relationships are embedded in both black and white people, in Africans, Caribbean people and Asians. These taboos also affect same-sex couples. Painful dynamics create taboo surrounding black-on-black sexual relationships, mixed-race relationships and mixed-cultural relationships such as African and Asian and their offspring.

External racism

Clients of African heritage who are challenged by racism harbour hurts they have experienced from an early age. A range of different hurts about skin complexion, body features, language and cultural heritage may have impacted them. Black children become aware how society categorizes them at an early age in terms of beauty, skin colour and hair texture. I call this a negative or misrepresented gaze.

Eye colour, hair texture and skin tone are viewed as markers of beauty and success in the white world (see Jane Elliott's exercise, Elliott, 1968). These features impact sociocultural responses on the privilege spectrum and how young people measure their worthiness. White children attract certain responses based on their lightness, their hair colour, texture and eye colouring. For example, favouring blond over brunette hair and brunette hair over black hair, with ginger frizzy hair at the bottom of the pile. These similar light-over-dark preferences condition Caucasian identity development, but they appear less overtly. The subjugation of these elements of whiteness gets projected unconsciously via racism, where lighter-skinned black people gain more privilege and inadvertently serve as agents to the oppressor. As previously mentioned, shadism of this nature has permeated African and Asian countries, creating class and cultural divisions. The impact of this is intergenerational and intercultural.

African/Caribbean children have great pride in their looks and family origins unless otherwise persuaded by parents, carers and peers. It is a contradiction that many use hair-straightening products and skin-lightening cream. Whilst many African/Caribbean and Asian individuals achieve high academic success, others get caught in a cycle of low achievement and low economic status. This positioning, impacted by racism, can lead to low motivation and low self-esteem linked to skin colour. Also, for some individuals who achieve success in their jobs, striving against racism in their employment and daily lives becomes a burden.

Internalized racism

Like other oppressions, racism is internalized from an early age. Once a child is influenced by negative remarks about their skin colour, facial features and hair texture, their esteem is imprinted by feelings of not being good enough. These feelings can impact a secure base from which their life skills develop.

Things said such as 'you are too black' or giving preference to the lighter-skinned child can have far-reaching effects. These responses to black beauty constitute a negative gaze and can prevent the child from experiencing themselves as black and beautiful.

The story of 'Ugly' written by Briscoe (2006) portrays the inner thoughts of a young Caribbean girl raised in the UK. Her mother said her nose was too wide and that she had plunger lips. In addition to this, she writes of a childhood influenced by her parents' emotional neglect and, in particular, bullying from her mother. One of eleven children, she was singled out and beaten by her mother for bed-wetting. Her mother displayed inordinate violence to her father and withheld food from the children. Ugly (the name her mother addressed her by) survives the abuse of her mother and stepfather, and as a young adult in her second book, *Beyond Ugly* (Briscoe, 2008), she makes a decision to put herself under the knife to enhance her appearance and this makes her feel better about her looks.

Sadly, she feels that this is the best way to not feel the pain of her 'ugliness' and to feel better about herself. Ugly survives her vicious childhood, and, eventually, through her determination she pursues a legal career and elevates to a highly respected profession as lawyer. Unfortunately, the abusive behaviour was passed intergenerationally to her sister, whose child was removed from the home due to similar behaviour. The story of Ugly portrays abuse associated with black identity.

Alongside the blight of comments about physical appearance is the internal impact of hurt and emotions instilled by being put down as a black child. These inner feelings can often be buried as a means of self-preservation. A frequent message conveyed by African/Caribbean individuals is that black parents told them that they 'would have to work harder than white people to achieve respect and success'. Otherwise, they would never amount to anything. Messages from family members who may have internalized these thoughts about themselves are the content of ancestral baggage. These early messages have repercussions and have created adult distress patterns about not being good enough that have come to light in therapy. Young black identities can be influenced by cyclical blurts that interfere with them achieving their full potential. Feelings of failure can compound the competitiveness associated with these messages, as doubt and powerful negative messages about who they are set in, coupled with racism and striving to compete with others rather than for themselves. These messages have manifested in distress patterns that signify compulsive independence, workaholism and inability to recognize or challenge workplace racism and other oppressions. Such behaviours are consequences of a negative gaze.

Whilst achievement and motivation are important for young minds they can be unconsciously distracted by skin colour and competitiveness with white people. No matter how infrequent experiences of racism occur, messages about failure due to skin colour and refusal to accommodate parents' wishes can be an additional blight on self-esteem.

In Asian families, accommodating family wishes and fulfilling traditional roles within the family may be paramount to acceptance. Secrecy and shame function to bind families and guide young people to their future paths. Senior family members often take for granted that these roles remain unquestioned. This causes some clients to experience intergenerational conflict. In this context, racism can manifest as judgemental attitudes towards closed cultural values upheld within Asian communities and family settings. Therapists may need to check they are not being judgemental about these ethnic customs, even if they disagree with them. This may manifest in pro-assimilation thoughts and homogenizing. The focus must be placed on the client's experiences of shame and trauma caused by the oppressions they may be experiencing.

These contexts may be brought into the therapeutic space and need to be explored. Racism may not be raised directly by clients because due to stigmatizing and taboos about challenging racism that they may have carried with them throughout life, assimilation has caused them to need permission to talk about it. This is also true of some therapists. This means that therapists must be prepared for discussion about the challenges of racism. The therapist's denial or silence about racism will reinforce taboo and stigma about the issue, and non-action will be unsupportive to the clients in a quandary about identity. What may appear to be low self-esteem due to feeling overwhelmed by work can turn out to be the result of undisclosed previous or current bullying and racism.

Langston Hughes (1955) in his novel *Not Without Laughter* portrays an incident where the early hurt of racism became internalized:

> Her first surprisingly and unpleasantly lasting impression of the pale world had come when, at the age of five, she had gone alone one day to play in a friendly white *families* yard. Some mischievous small boys there, for the fun of it, had taken hold of her short kinky braids and pulled them, dancing round and round her and yelling: 'Blackie! Blackie! Blackie!' While she screamed and tried to run away. But they held her and pulled her head terribly, and her friends laughed because she was black and she did look funny. So from that time on, Harriett had been uncomfortable in the presence of whiteness, and that early hurt had grown with each new incident into a rancor that she could not hide and a dislike that had become pain. (p. 88)

Hughes portrays an early experience of racism, not dissimilar to experiences shared by many of my black clients. In addition to this, black clients have shared experiences of racial hurt from their parents, siblings, carers, educators and in public and the workplace.

Where does an individual take their long-term pain about racism? Clients suffering from the impact of racism often question their identity and blame themselves for not recognizing the racism they were experiencing. The challenges of cultural misunderstanding and societal racism weigh heavily on the psyche when held internally for long periods. This is the nature of internalized racism.

The following student's question portrays curiosity about difficulty in addressing these concerns:

> I wonder why I have experienced difficulties asking my black, Asian clients about their experience of being black, Asian and how it might relate to the issues they are bringing?

First of all, therapists may need to reflect on the nature of this difficulty. Could it be associated with their own internalized oppression? Could it be that they are gagged by fears of being seen as racist or unable to empathize? Does the therapist have appropriate support to reflect on the concern and move forward with the client?

It is not necessary for a black client to mention racism for the therapist and supervisor to be aware that racism may be a key feature of their past or current situation. This is where the therapist's response to the whole of the client's experience must be considered with care and sensitivity. Some black clients may not want to acknowledge that they are impacted by racism. This does not mean they are not affected by it. If a client is naive about racism they may still be affected by it. Here, the therapist's skill in connecting in a black empathic way is important.

I have explained the term internalized racism to clients and they have appreciated the use of this term in helping to understand their responses to the oppressions they are experiencing. Providing terminology for these experiences can be liberating and a reflective education for clients. Using intuition and racial sensitivity, the therapist and supervisor can approach the subject of racism, that is, they are holding the experience of racism for the client and working through ways of supporting the client through their experience and, ultimately, the process of recognition trauma. The work between therapist and supervisor needs to include exploration of the degree to which the client may be aware of racism and the degree to which they may have internalized racism and negative messages about their black identity.

Unpicking internalized racism

There are several distress factors that must be considered when working through the process of internalized racism. Racism does not stand alone in its infringement on the human psyche. Racism impacts both from an intergenerational and personal position and can be one form of much oppression that affects early development and ongoing existence. It is important to remember that racism evokes powerful emotions such as guilt, shame, sadness, rage and humiliation. These human emotions that are learned from an early age, even if they were not attached to experiences of racism, can be exposed by present-time racism and growing awareness of internalized racism. Internalized racism can only be supported when the therapist is offering a black empathic approach and a positive black gaze.

Therapists and supervisors may need to be reminded of the intrinsic link between the experience of racism and the coping mechanisms that individuals enlist to protect themselves from the impact of hurtful experiences. In due course, therapists must become aware of the components of racism, because human elements of self-protection become activated when the challenge of racism is present.

Having worked with several clients who have been impacted by racism at various stages in their lives, I have become aware of the different levels of defence that may occur. A victim of racism may experience an immediate and ongoing impact of a racist experience. Dormant feelings about racism may be evoked. There may be disbelief, fear, rage and feelings of humiliation. If the individual is loaded with guilt from their past, they may feel deep shame at their awareness that they have knowingly or unknowingly received a wound related to their skin complexion. They may have retorted angrily, or swallowed the pain associated with racism, causing a delayed response. Shame at the realization of being in a space where they received racism may be experienced. Guilt at their response or feelings or inability to challenge or remove themselves from the situation may be experienced. The many ways that individuals feel responsible, caretake or dismiss the behaviour of others may be evoked at the point of experiencing the racism. These feelings and behaviours are all features of recognition trauma.

White clients discussing their experiences of being in the perpetrator group may need to explore the relevant guilt and shame that may have arisen ancestrally due to their intergenerational influences. Racism arises from hatred installed early in life, which grows into toxic behaviour within the carriers of this negativity. The early lives of white people are a feature of their responses to the challenge of racism. Those who have been educated about the crimes of slavery and colonialism may have been influenced in less negative ways. On the other hand, cultural beliefs, intergenerational wounds and irrational beliefs about black people may not have been adequately processed.

Guilt and fear about reparation and being singled out as a racist can prevent empathic responses to clients impacted by racism. Responses from white therapists or supervisors such as 'racism is in the past', 'are you sure it was racism', 'but I don't see you as black' or 'I am not racist because I have black friends or family' are not helpful. These types of comments fuel denial and dismiss the client experience of racism. If racism is being acknowledged, it should be taken seriously because the implications of not being seen or heard serve to perpetuate racism. It is crucial that therapists and supervisors do not lean on post-racism perspectives. They must remain aware that past hurts within black and Asian families and between African and Asian communities exist and may impact on individual responses to day-to-day racism.

Asians

The Jati caste system in India served numerous closed communities, each one having their own rules and regulations and agreements about their internal systems of living. This created diversity within geographical regions and class groups, and separation of land and society in India and Pakistan. The Punjab and Bengal created divisions between Hindus, Sikhs and Muslims, resulting in refugee communities and stigma. These divisions carried intrinsic prejudices, for example high caste preferences, white over low caste Indians and Africans. Community, faith, language and culture became stereotyped through these procedures. This backdrop has also influenced second and third generations in European countries. The historic impact was brought to the UK, and Indians faced the additional oppression of white racism. Many tried to maintain support within their own communities in places like Southall, Bradford, Birmingham and Green Street. They faced corner-shop racism and Paki bashing. It sometimes appeared as though they would take any abuse, because they were reluctant to complain. The strength and support of their communities sustained them, but this does not mean they did not feel the pain of racism.

The vast lands of Africa also comprise a variety of villages, tribes, languages and customs. Some parts of Africa and the Caribbean also have mixed African and Asian communities, with chequered histories impacted by slavery, colonization and indentured labour that reinforced servitude and class systems. Diversity within African and Asian communities is deeply rooted in the past and intergenerational discourses that are likely to influence black and Asian identities. Attitudes to diversity may not always mean taking seriously diversity within black and Asian communities. Therefore, to avoid homogeneity, therapists may need to consider unlearning their bias and addressing what may appear to be blind spots.

People of mixed heritage

People of mixed heritage and people in mixed black-and-white relationships face the challenge of racism and shadism whether they are black, white or people of colour from Asian, mixed African and/or Asian heritages. Their challenges often tend to be marginalized or invisible.

Attitudes to different mixtures, rooted in the sociocultural and historical impact of slavery, colonialism, partition or ethnic cleansing, are important factors and must be valued. The following voices portray these experiences.

Pearl, age 56: I identify as African/Indian/Caribbean heritage. In Jamaica there was a huge taboo about Africans and Indians marrying; that is why my parents married in England. In my early life, I identified with my African side; now I know I am an Indian woman. On the monitoring sheets, I classify myself as 'mixed other'. Both my parents are Jamaican. My mother was from an Indian family and my father from an African family. There has always been incongruence between what I feel and how I look, and this has been influenced by the way we were treated. I mostly came into contact with Jamaicans. I grew up with lots of aunties around me who are married to the Indians, and they did not accept my African heritage. I also had to cope with anti-Indian prejudice from African Jamaicans. It was very hurtful on both sides.

Then there is the whole Caribbean experience; as a child, when my friends visited and were offered food, they would refuse. I discovered that not all Jamaicans ate the same food and dhal and roti were deeply Indian cuisine. We were five siblings with different complexions and this created a dynamic. One brother and myself were the darkest. We look like our father. The others were lighter like Mum. My brother and I experienced a lot of abuse from the Indian family members. We were from two completely different cultures. The Indians were used by the British to undermine the Africans, and this was strong within my family. Black men see me as exotic. Will I ever be seen as who I am? Living in a racist society compounded all this. The Enoch Powell era (a white politician who spouted racist ideology and fuelled rejection of black people in the UK) was a backdrop for this.

Social stigma and internalized racism contribute to the ways that these taboos are displayed in attitudes and actions. One example is teenager Emmett Till, who was killed in 1955 in the southern US for whistling at a white woman (Anderson, 2015).

Hernton (1973) presents another example suggesting that the taboo of the white woman creates a hidden ambivalence towards all women. A black male, age seven: 'I received a beating for associating with a white female. My grandmother put a fear in me that I have never forgotten. Her body trembled as she installed the terror in me that she had felt. I was awakened to a vital part of me that I would have to kill and it was only then that I began to cry' (p. 56).

Hernton continues:

> His ego is inflicted with fear of the other and his sexual identity is tarnished by internalized racism. The child was instilled with a fear of relationships with forbidden white fruit and fear of the wrath of the black matriarch. At the same time he believes that no person will ever understand what this dilemma is like. There remains in the black man an undefined sense of self-mutilation. He is castrated. From these incidents, the black female remains an enigma. The black male learned to despise the black female due to her subservience to white folks and the comparison with white goddesses. He views her as tarnished and untouchable. The black woman in turn becomes resentful to the black man for his resistance to her mannerisms, social graces and womanhood.

Here, the effect of beatings as discipline to a young child, combined with the effects of racism and internalized racism, clearly demonstrate how early the experience of multidimensional oppressions get laid in. Education about the taboo of white womanhood has been instilled by a black parent at a time when childhood development is likely to be highly influenced. In Hernton's words:

> the effect of racism is 'psychopathic'. Deep in the psyche of black men is their rejection of a black mother and the desire to have a white mother. Consequently, if the black man offends the black woman she is full of resentment towards him. She denies his masculinity and his skin color and humanity. He is no longer a man he is a black bastard. (p. 57)

These harsh words fit a harsh reality, and they are worthy of consideration, for, where do the archetypes and hurtful responses to mixed black white relationship come from? A variety of socially constructed terms and attitudes have evolved from negative responses to individuals of black/Indian and black/white mixed heritage. Examples of these are mullato, quadroon, dugla, coolie, half-caste, Anglo-Indian. Other terms for specific mixtures have evolved. In the US, the term biracial is common. Although terminologies to describe identity mixtures have evolved, I believe that people of mixed heritage have a right to define themselves and should not be defined by others in terms of their parentage.

Even though there may be some naivety or denial of origins or personal background, these individuals can be supported to discover their identities. Therapists and supervisors therefore must be aware of how their own experiences and prejudices might interfere with this process. Some of these concerns have been identified in a discussion with Nicky, a white cognitive behavioural and mindfulness therapist. Nicky also shares how she works with the following student question about client racism:

> How do you deal with clients who assume it is OK to be racist and who have no reservations about disclosing this in a session because they are convinced that as a white woman I share the same thoughts?

Nicky: Obviously I am a white therapist and I would say that I have had to talk about racism a lot more with my supervisees who are from different parts of the world than me as a therapist talking about my own issues about racism. I have worked with kids of all different nationalities and backgrounds, and racism was a small part of that work, but a lot of it was dealing with mothers who were going to court about losing their children. So, a lot more of the work was around child protection issues and 'you don't understand me', and risk and safety.

One of the women that I spoke with, her children were being taken away from her, and risk was a really big part, because she was a white woman who had had relationships with older black men and her children were mixed race. Her children were being taken away from her, and it was about the identity of those children moving from London to a foster or adoptive parents in Gloucester. She felt quite strongly about the idea that they were not going to be brought up as black people even though the mother was black.

Isha: The fostering mother was black?

Nicky: Yes, and I was helping her to come to terms with not having any control over the future of what was happening with the children. So, I never have problems with talking about racism with clients; it's a subject that I am comfortable with naming when it comes up in the room. Sometimes it can be quite uncomfortable because if somebody makes a racist remark I have a principle that I always say, 'I need you to know that when I hear that I have an emotional response to that. I need you to be aware that when you talk in this way it has an impact on me.'

Isha: *How does that work with clients when you challenge them in that way?*

Nicky: It does close them down a little bit, and I am aware that it can close them down, because I have a very strong moral sense of this, but they have to be aware of it, that I have a response to what they are saying. I do talk about non-judgement, but they need to be aware of the impact on me. And are they aware of that when they are with other people? I try and explore where it comes from.

Isha: *Is this someone that is making a racist remark?*

Nicky: Yes, someone living in Downham. For example, one client would say, 'all those black people'. I would say, 'What do you mean by that? Is it the colour or the behaviour? What do you mean by that? What is it?' It's generally stereotyping or a cultural thing with people that they mix with, where it's OK to just say things like that.

Isha: *So the client is actually challenging you because of your openness about it, and you find a way to challenge them.*

Nicky: Yes, and sometimes it can get in the way, because you are dealing with anxiety and you are dealing with maybe agoraphobia; sometimes it can be a story that they have told themselves, 'my environment is not safe', and it becomes a conflict, I find. So you want to reduce the anxiety and you are often doing some exposure work. This thought that you are having, is it based on anything? When you are out on the road and people are watching you? Does it matter what colour they are? Is it worse if you see a black man or a black woman and they look at you than if a white woman or white man is looking?

Isha: *So in terms of their relationship with you and that interruption, I would call it, that has happened, are you able to reconnect with the client and does it work in the therapeutic process?*

Nicky: Yes, it's an interruption, that is what I would call it. I think sometimes they might view me differently in the sense that 'I know Nicky doesn't like that point'. I can connect back to them and they might say, 'I'm not going to say that because I know it will offend you.'

Isha: *So there has been some learning in that connection, because they are internalizing that that kind of language and racism is not OK in front of everyone and that it has an impact.*

Nicky: Yes, there is a consequence. Sometimes I will name about how that can distract me from everything else that is going on, how it comes higher up my agenda, and when they say things like that, it does distance me, and how can I come back to helping you, in supporting you, in caring about you and respecting you?

Isha: I respect your openness about that and that you can go through with the client about how this also affects the relational process. For me, that really gets to grips with how racism ruptures relationships.

Nicky: There have been one or two people in 8 to 9 years who have taken great offence to me challenging them.

Isha: And then what happened?

Nicky: It's taken time, and I think if I were only doing six sessions with this person I would not be able to deal with that the way I do. I would probably have to let it go.

Isha: So I guess it is similar to when you hear something in the street and you hear something racist that is happening, and you have to be discriminatory about how you respond, even though it has impacted on you.

Nicky: Yes.

Isha: That's what I call everyday, ongoing racism.

Nicky: I would be thinking about who is around me – would it be safe for me to challenge, have I got my children with me, you know, doing a sort of 360 check. Although, neighbours in my personal life, they say things like 'it's them darkies over there', and I say to them, 'I cannot have you making comments like that to me' – I challenge that. That was quite difficult for a few months.

Isha: Did you see the information about the white policeman in the US who went into a cafe where there were a group of campaigners after the Ferguson police killing of a young black man? The young campaigners, after a discussion with the policeman, asked him to hold up a placard and take a photo of him. The placard read, 'I resolve to end racism @work and to end white silence'. Soon after, his phone started ringing and the photo was all over the Internet. Many negative comments were made about his attempt at anti-racism and what he had said. He was accused of calling the authorities racist. Lots of resistance came back to the statement that virtually brought tears to my eyes in the light of what is going on now in the streets of the US and the UK. I think people are realizing how institutional racism has permeated our societies and causes death.

Nicky: We live and work in Lewisham, and I do think that therapy should be a reflection of real life. The domestic violence project that I work on is much more multicultural. I have had some Turkish people, black African, black Caribbean, South African, white British, French, much more multicultural clientele.

Isha: So you also get an insight into the prejudices that these groups face.

Nicky: In a mixed relationship with black and white, when I am observing I found there was a lot of derogatory comments by black women to white women who have children with black men. That they were not taking care of their hair or their skin in the way that these black women felt was acceptable.

Isha: So the black women were making derogatory comments towards the white parents?

Nicky: And the children.

Isha: No respect really for the fact that they are children. When I look at how some Caribbean people behave in their own environment and sometimes in the UK, they will look at you and say what comes out of their mouth – there is no respect for feelings and that it might hurt. But it is not everybody.

Nicky: No, it's not everybody. It's judgement.

Isha: So, when you have these challenges do you feel able to take them to your supervision?

Nicky: Generally, yes.

Isha: And do you have discussions about it?

Nicky: Not always, because I do manage it in a way; we talk about it, if it's something that I feel uncomfortable with.

Isha: When you do talk about it, what makes it safe you to do so?

Nicky: I have a very trusting relationship with my supervisor, so I can talk about any discomfort, any awkwardness, you know, if I feel I have behaved in a way which I'm ashamed of or maybe I came down too hard, or I was afraid of saying something. I can own up to it.

Isha: That relationship between you and your supervisor, when the challenge of racism is present, does that feel safe enough for you to actually explore that a bit deeper?

Nicky: Probably. I haven't had to, and I don't know if that is because it is an aspect of a relationship between two white women.

Isha: So you manage it and you feel confident because you manage it in your daily life as well. Is there anything that you feel may be a limitation or a block when you are managing the challenge of racism in your therapeutic practice?

Nicky: No, with my current supervisor I have never had a block; with my previous supervisor I found her quite hard sometimes, as an individual she was not consistent, so sometimes she would feel safe and open, and there were times when I felt there was something wrong with me.

Isha: Was this happening specifically when you wanted to discuss the challenge of racism or was it any way?

Nicky: Any way.

Isha: So I guess that would create a kind of a block if it were a period when you felt there was something wrong with you, as that safety needs to be there in order to open a deep subject and a subject that is very volatile. With your own therapy do you bring issues of racism?

Nicky: I am not in therapy; we don't have to be in therapy. It's not part of the requirement in CBT training. I have never been in therapy.

Isha: Do you feel that you might need some therapeutic support as a result of things that might get raised for use as a therapist?

Nicky: It is something that I have considered because people have said you should know what it's like to experience therapy, but I have not done it because I have never felt that I needed it.

Isha: So obviously your life is fairly stable and you are fairly supported in your life.

Nicky: Yes, I can't say that it is always on an even keel – there are things always kicking off – but I deal with it. I have support from other women in my life. My experience with certain key people helps enormously to ground me.

Isha: Is there anything you want to say about supervising therapists who may bring some of these issues?

Nicky: I have a few students who have had difficulties with clients, and I have always been the one who has named, is it racism? I recently had a young black woman seeing a white client. The client kept saying repeatedly, 'I do not want CBT', and I wonder, is she saying 'I do not want to work with a black woman'?

Isha: How do you approach these issues? Do you question openly with this supervisee?

Nicky: We have gone away and had a think about what is going on with the decision to talk about it.

Isha: I think it's good that you are open to checking it out with your supervisee, given what I have heard about some white clients who have difficulty working with a black therapist. The black therapist is sometimes unsure if they can take this anywhere. Did she seem open to that?

Nicky: I think she was quite surprised.

Isha: What do you think works well in your approach?

Nicky: It's much more difficult to look at these issues with students because they are having to adhere to a model which is much less holistic and much less therapeutic than my model, so there is always this tension between what I would want to say and how I would want them to work and actually what their training needs are. The model does not really address these issues. In CBT there is no real space for the relationship between the therapist and client; I am helping students to develop a style and also bearing in mind their training needs. This is a major conflict, so having respect for the client, especially when there is stereotyping about race and feminism and teaching them how to deal with that, has always been about 'don't avoid it, but do not spend too much time on it'. Probably far less then a psychodynamic approach would. So in CBT you would develop a closer relationship with what comes up in the mind, getting people to understand, what do you believe, where does it come from? So, it is appropriate to say I am observing, that there is some tension here around race or the fact that I am a woman and you are a man.

Isha: Has it always been like this for you? Because you would have had the same training as them.

Nicky: I did not have any of it; even though I had a black supervisor during my training, we never discussed it. I went on a course where I was the only white person and the course was about helping people in the BME community. Participants asked, 'why are you here?'

Isha: So how did that feel?

Nicky: Well, I think they were grateful to have me there because the group was so small.

Isha: What are the challenges for you?

Nicky: People make judgements about me – that I have had a privileged life, and what do I know? Would I really be able to understand them?

Isha: What sort of people ask these questions?

Nicky: Anybody, really, but I think it sometimes becomes more polarized with BME clients.

Isha: Did you find that a bit of a challenge, when they had those projections?

Nicky: Yes. I once worked with a black woman who was very anti other black people. It was like she did not really want to be a black woman. Trying to undertake that was very difficult.

Isha: Did you have any progress in terms of her thinking about her identity?

Nicky: No, she was absolutely rejecting of anything I discussed and she rejected me in the end.

Isha: That must have been a massive challenge with this client. Is there something in your reflective process about that experience which might be useful to convey to other therapists who find themselves in that situation?

Nicky: I don't really know; it may have been more helpful for me to be more challenging earlier. She was so fragile that actually containing her and nurturing her and allowing her to develop was difficult because she came from a very difficult childhood of abuse and disappointment about her parenting. I tried to work on that area of the therapeutic relationship and I failed her and I never knew how.

Isha: It felt like you failed her because she was failing everybody who tried to help.

Nicky: Yeah.

Isha: It sounds like you stayed in there, but it was very challenging because it would not move anywhere.

Nicky: I think I felt enormous badness and I could not shift that badness. This was a woman with so much potential, but she would not allow herself to go there.

Isha: *It is a common feature with some black people that they deny their blackness, so they are angry with those other black people out there. Does that make sense from your perspective?*

Nicky: **I am very aware that I don't have enough experience of this; that was just one situation. I have a black colleague who shared a similar situation where a client was denying his black identity. It is an area that I am very interested in, but it is not something that I necessarily get to face that often. Those clients that I pick up are suffering from anxiety or depression, and my work is very focused on that.**

Isha: *Are you familiar with the term 'internalized racism'?*

Nicky: **Yes.**

Isha: *So you don't get much opportunity to work on that deeper level of internalizing because you work with those main themes.*

Nicky: **Yes, it is not a big part of my work because I am a CBT therapist.**

Isha: *How did you feel when reflecting on these questions?*

Nicky: **It is something that I don't get much opportunity to reflect on. In supervision, your focus is all about risk to the client, status of the client, the efficacy of what you are doing. Sometimes you don't go and look at these issues, and that is probably a product of my training.**

Isha: *So did it raise that experience while we were talking?*

Nicky: **Yes, I kind of found myself observing myself, how things have been, how I have felt.**

Isha: *Do you have opportunities to do that kind of reflection in your supervision?*

Nicky: **Not a lot. I probably do it more in my own mindfulness practice. I do get that opportunity to sit quietly and listen to what is going on in my thoughts and what is coming up for me.**

Children produced from different ethnic and cultural mixtures inherit the impact of both mixtures and divisions. In addition to this, they may be impacted by intergenerational gaps in cultural experience. Often, black people raised in a white setting where they may not have acquired much black cultural capital feel a loss of their black identity, yet they may have been subject to racism. Outside of Europe this experience may be reversed, where white individuals may be raised within a white family, but in a predominantly black environment.

Having this background experience does not exempt them from racist attitudes.

Black and Asian people are born with a variety of skin complexions and can be subject to a three-dimensional oppression of racism, shadism and internalized racism. This triangular oppression will also apply to someone of mixed heritage.

The brown paper bag test in the US was one way of defining whether a person is black enough. If their complexion matched or was darker than the tone of the bag, they were then accepted as a black person. If they did not match this criterion, they may have suffered discrimination and attracted responses from black people that demeaned them because of their lighter skin and association with whiteness. On the other hand, they were likely to receive racism from white people because of their brown skins or their association with black people. Parents of black mixed-heritage people have also been victims of racism because of their union as a black-and-white mix and the racism towards black individuals.

Whether a relationship is black-on-black or white-on-black, the children may suffer from the intergenerational and intercultural influences linked to racism. The root causes of racism and shadism emanate from history and mythology, and assigning blame does not help with healing this blight.

Ina-Egbe (2010) suggests that children and adults of mixed racial parentage need to work through internal conflicts and guilt about having to develop an identity that might not incorporate all aspects of their heritage and need to resist internalizing society's negative attitudes. Ultimately, successful identity formation, or a satisfying feeling of wholeness, requires that people of mixed racial and cultural heritage appreciate and integrate all components of their heritage into their lives.

The colour conundrum and internal racism

Damage can be done by receiving negative messages about skin colour, hair texture and body features. What gets listened to, what gets dismissed and what gets internalized are key areas for emotional-repair work with black people and mixed-heritage people.

India.Arie's (2006) song states, 'I am not my hair, I am not my skin, I am the soul within', and this strongly emphasizes a personal plea to be accepted for the person she is rather than the way she looks. Responses to racism clearly show that this is not generally the case. Hurt experienced by individuals goes far deeper than the eye can see. The heart is broken at an early age when comments are heard referring to how black or not black enough a person appears to be, or how nappy or loose their hair texture is. This experience, referred to as shadism or colourism, informs the fertile mind with early messages that influence cultural attachment and rejection.

The colour conundrum results in internal racism that can lay dormant until other life traumas occur. When my client Paulette's marriage was breaking down, she began to realize that her employers were also exploiting her. The hurt that she experienced from the relationship was similar to the pain of being constantly excluded from opportunities for promotion in her job. During our weekly counselling, she was supported to unravel some early hurts about being excluded within the family. She felt that her father did not love her because he favoured her younger sister who had 'fairer' skin. Her sister was given priority in family decisions, whilst Paulette was relegated to a sort of Cinderella role within the family. She received less affection and appreciation, and was given more practical tasks within the home. Her heart was broken early.

The final blow came at age 9, when she was sent to stay with an aunt whilst her parents took her sister and brother on a weekend break. Her aunt fussed over her and made her feel special. This experience gave her clues that something was not quite right with the relationships in the family home. Paulette was determined to prove her worth and she went to college and trained as a nurse, a role that gave her many challenges and also lots of appreciation. As a professional, she was highly sought after and relied on by the domiciliary team. Sometimes she had a feeling of being burdened with too much responsibility that could have been shared. When her marriage began to crumble due to similar experiences of being dumped on and not appreciated by her husband, it became clear that her broken heart needed repair.

Therapists need to be prepared to unravel cultural and racialized messages that may have contributed to personal trauma and self-esteem early in the client's life and during periods of identity-building. This aspect of what I call ancestral baggage, due to the roles assigned to the house slave and the field slave, perpetuated via African, Caribbean and Asian family structures, is a cultural element of shadism and all that goes with the physical aspects of prejudice within black and Asian families, communities and in society. The media generally reinforces this.

According to Ina-Egbe (2010), 'In a society that emphasizes race but often denigrates the black race, a strong racial identity enables a black child's self-esteem to cushion the messages of inferiority they receive from others. A strong sense of black cultural identity therefore may be more likely to result from having black parents than white.'

Summary

The subject of African, Asian and mixed-heritage therapeutic work is huge. Obviously these areas merit their own space in the field of therapeutic literature. I have touched on some important, sensitive areas that need expanding and warrant far more discussion and reflection. The challenge of racism is present for Africans, Caribbean people, Asians and people of all mixed heritages. Social stigma and ancestral baggage about skin colour and shade underpin the prejudices that get passed on intergenerationally. Societies that house predominantly black or Asian communities are just as responsible for how racism imposes diversity and stigma as white society is. The problem of sociocultural racism, shadism and internalized racism is massive. There is a huge job to be done on building self-esteem where it has been eroded by stereotypes based on racism and prejudice within communities. I want therapists and supervisors to pay attention to the hurts within African, Caribbean and Asian communities, between those groups and for individuals of mixed heritage. Early hurts from families and care systems about skin colour, skin shade, physical features and hair texture matter. Curiosity about the impact of these features of racism that individuals harbour is paramount to therapeutic work with African, Caribbean, Asian and mixed-heritage clients.

Pointers:

- Therapists must be prepared to explore the different dimensions of shadism and cultural diversity that clients encounter in their personal development process.
- Value African and Asian heritage equally, within their own merit. Remember that both continents have been influenced by slavery, colonization and cultural fragmentation.
- Encourage clients of mixed heritage to find their own identity.
- Clients of mixed heritage, whatever the mix, can be encouraged to embrace their whole self and parts that make up their whole self.

- Therapists must be aware of their own judgemental processes and stereotypes about black-and-white relationships.
- Therapists need to be aware of the three-pronged oppression of racism, shadism and having a mixed heritage.
- Be prepared to work with the challenge of sociocultural stigmas and assumptions about being black enough and white enough.
- Work with the messages of external and internalized racism and the hurt they can cause.
- Expect the supervision process to support and develop an understanding of ancestral baggage and historical links to a misrepresented gaze for Africans, Asians and mixed-heritage peoples.

6

Gender Influences and Racism

Stereotypes of black men and women persist in permeating the lives of people of African/Caribbean and Asian heritage. In this chapter, some exploration of the impact of these particular engendered and racialized stereotypes on black psychological processes will be offered. Often, the context of gender and racialized material becomes marginalized in the support process between supervisor and therapist, and a blind spot can occur. The position of initiating discussion and the context of inter-gender and intra-gender communication and challenge, as an important area, will be supported. For example, some women find it difficult to address the context of their relationships with men, and some men say they prefer to share their feelings with women. Individuals in both gender groups may find it difficult to challenge within their groups.

In Chapter 5 we considered racism in the context of heritage and identity, and the various ways that racist discourses can impact. In this chapter, the role and designation of black and Asian men and women will be considered in terms of therapeutic approaches and the therapist's and supervisor's roles in responding to the emotional challenges of these particular multidimensional contexts. Using personal experiences, this chapter will support therapists and supervisors to counteract the harmful process of stereotypes and their influence on the therapeutic triad. Racism and gender often feature in a one-dimensional way, and it is rare that the spotlight gets focused on how individuals cope with intersecting oppressions; so, this chapter will take a look at the challenges of working therapeutically within a multidimensional context influenced by gender oppression and racism. The challenge of parallels between interracial dynamics and gender discourses will be addressed.

The black woman may excuse her black man's behaviour in the home by her understanding of racism in his everyday experiences. She may also exhibit compulsive independence and 'don't discharge' patterns, being unable to display her grief at the pain she experiences. Black people were conditioned to repress a range of emotions as a survival strategy during slavery; therefore, the stereotype of them being able to withstand overwork and pain often inhibits appropriate understanding and support for relational concerns. This type of response to the black woman creates a distorted mirroring of her femininity. Of course, these stereotypical images may not apply to all black women, but most modern families would have been touched by the discourses of colonialism and slavery and these elements of racism in some way. It is the therapist's and supervisor's task to be fully aware that not showing pain does not mean there is no pain.

The strong black woman as a black Western archetype is seen as infallible, and she is often less supported then her contemporaries. From slavery, the mammy archetype has infiltrated her psyche; she can be driven by her distress as she tirelessly serves the extended family and the unreasonable demands of her employers. When she expresses her rage about the injustices that she is experiencing, her hurt is often not seen, because she is viewed as aggressive rather than vulnerable. Her cries are internal, and even when she is visibly crying, the responses are less empathic, less connecting, less supportive because it is rare that she shows her vulnerability and she is usually the one to support others and push her own needs aside.

hooks (1993) talks of decolonizing the mind by countering dominant stereotypes, and of the black woman who refuses to occupy the position of 'step and fetch it', or Aunt Jemima, or to submit to the phallocentric gaze (p. 122). Her empowerment threatens the status quo and has generated anti-black-female backlash. She is seen as aggressive rather than progressive, a combination of fierce racism and anti-feminism, suggesting that this turnaround threatens black life. These contradictions have made it difficult for some black women to practise the art of loving. She may have learned to put her emotional needs aside and instead look as though she is in control, to cope with the multidimensional impact of racism and sexism she faces.

Caring may need to be distinguished from love. Internalized racism and self-hate often stand in the way of love, and due to capitalism, love has become a commodity. Capitalism gives rewards for material goods, and dressed-up objects attract profit, so deals are made based on our ability to gain access to material goods that emphasize a white outlook and love becomes secondary to appearances (hooks, 1993, p. 136).

Emasculation and power

As a woman, I must admit that I know very little about men, and, rightfully, I have turned to them for guidance. Lee Butler (Butler and Homer, 2010) identifies several features of growing into African American manhood. He suggests that in the absence of discussion, black men will continue to define themselves by stereotypes and mythology. Key to this is the role of black men in the family and community. I do not think the plight of the African American male is different, as many African and Caribbean males have inherited similar intergenerational traits from the legacy of slavery.

During slavery, the role model for the black man raised on plantations was the slave master who treated the African man and his black brothers and sisters as goods and chattel. The black man was therefore deemed to be a failure, as he could not emulate the white slave owner. The phenomenon of siring brought distortions of the fatherhood role and a perception that the number of children a man created made him more manly. Consequently, many black women today remain in a lone matriarchal position within the family, and a woman cannot give a boy what he needs to become a man.

How do you love completely when your ancestors were forced to disconnect and forget about loving? There was love between couples and within families, but there are strong judgements about ways of loving in black communities. The gaze of white supremacy and Eurocentric standards of love dictate what is 'normal' in the white world.

In therapeutic relationships we must consider the position of the black woman and be concerned about what kind of rites of passage the black man has experienced during his transition from boyhood to manhood. Could he have been raised with enough cultural capital and black male leadership to assist a positive, confident identity development, or was he initiated by fire, using sex, drugs and the gun? Poet Dr Lemn Sissay, poet Dr Benjamin Zephaniah and actor Ashly Walters are examples of young black men who have gone though the fire and discovered ways of turning their oppressive experiences into something positive, as role models for the future.

I will begin by taking a risk and speculating that there is a tendency to process one oppression, as opposed to viewing the multidimensional context of oppression. The psyche tends to create a hierarchy of oppressions depending on social and emotional priorities. My days of dungarees and feminist badges are an example of the discourses that influence this hierarchy. Going into women-only groups, I was once questioned about whether I was black or a woman first. The shock of being confronted with what appeared like a demand to choose between the two identities was overwhelming. As I recall this incident, feelings of confusion and rejection surface. The questioning of two precious aspects of my identity was a challenge that made me feel that I was attending an exclusive group of women who had their own political reference points about who qualified as woman.

At the same time, my early feelings of rejection began to surface. I left the group, taking my humiliation with me. This was a point at which I realized that stereotypes of women and black identities are fragile emotional contents that dwell in our inner being and can be easily split by discourses and internalized distresses that individuals harbour. This situation shows that within minority groups there are prejudices and splits.

Going further back, I recall as a young child being called names such as 'darkie', 'blackie', 'black monkey' and 'nigger', and schoolteachers referring to all the black children as Jamaican, in an aggressive manner. At a girls' secondary school, I became a spectacle for the black Caribbean girls. They would circle me and demand to know whether I was half-caste. I felt that, somehow, in their eyes I needed to justify who I was to be accepted by them, yet the white girls accepted me as a 'nice one' due to my light brown skin and clear English-speaking language. They were under the impression that this gave them licence to make racist remarks about my black friends in front of me. I hung out with both black and white peers, but I felt more accepted by my black friends. During this period of my life, I fell in love with Caribbean music and food and braved the iron comb to straighten my hair, not being aware that I was toning down some of my blackness and trying to turn up my femininity. My personal experience of my cultural and ethnic identity was therefore vague and confused, until the age of 30 when I sought after my heritage and identity as a black woman. I had very little black cultural collateral until this time.

These hurtful aspects of my early development were not shared with adults, not even in my therapy. As I matured into adulthood, I began to read books written by black women. I realized that given the right setting, bits that were missing could be reclaimed. Through this life process, I am more aware of how oppression operates to play down our significant identities. I am more accepted as black than Jewish, because I wear my African heritage on my skin. So, I favoured a female and black identity over my Jewish identity. Clearly, my ancestral baggage has played an integral role in these aspects of identity development.

During my training as a therapist I frequently referred to myself as black, and the response from my white female therapist was confusing. Emerging through this process of identity-building can be likened to rites of passage. Therapists can play a significant role in supporting this process, as this student's question implies:

> How can I, as a white middle-class woman, relate to a black woman, or vice versa, how can they relate to me – is it possible?

This pertinent question has become familiar in my training experiences. It is an important question for all therapists and supervisors to consider. Class, race and gender conspire to divide women and men of all nationalities and ethnicities. There is no blueprint for this process of identity development and interracial context. The answers are within our experiences and awareness of how these oppressions impact on our lives. Working-class black women suffer the same racism as middle-class black women because racism has no class barrier. It's just that middle- and owning-class black people may have greater means to protect themselves and recover from their experiences. Middle- class white women curious to understand this question may need to educate themselves about black issues and expose themselves to the necessary risks involved in understanding and processing the challenges of racism.

First of all, it is important to accept that racism exists and is a felt experience for many black individuals. One problem that often occurs is that of disbelief; where the victim of racism is expected to describe in detail their experience of racism in order to evidence the experience. Racism is also a volatile theme, and sometimes individuals slip into denial and fear of the reality that it continues to exist. Having to educate the white person adds insult to injury where the white person, having not immediately witnessed the racism, cannot fully accept that this experience consciously exists. One of the reasons for this is that racism is not always experienced in covert ways, such as name-calling and physical attack. This is similar to the discourse of sexism, where society seems more accepting that women get sexually harassed or treated less than men, even though this is not always directly apparent. This whole challenge is about white women taking on board that as women, in spite of their role in an oppressed group, they also inhabit the perpetrator group. These concerns need to be addressed in supervision settings. Therapists and supervisors must be aware of defensive responses about their role in perpetuating these oppressions and work through them.

The way individuals survive and emerge from oppressions is tantamount to their lives as adults; therefore, these aspects of life experience need to be seen as key to the developmental process and identity-building. We can therefore assume that the impact of racism early in black women's lives adds to the imbalance that sexism and gender issues create. I am sure at this point readers may be thinking that this must be true of other oppressions. Turning assumption on its head, we could suppose that black women suffering gender oppression at an early age would be more susceptible to an imbalance caused by racism. Whilst this may be true, on the basis of this proposition, due to the nature of white racism we cannot assume that white women or men will be in the same predicament.

I have never had a white client or student who has linked their adult oppressions with the oppression of racism at an early age. I have shared the experience of Irish individuals who experienced similar persecution between communities in Ireland and with their families arriving in the UK. These families shared the humiliation of the 'keep Britain white' attempts from landlords and jobs that displayed signs saying, 'NO BLACKS NO IRISH NO DOGS'. They were not welcomed by certain factions of British community, and their families were blighted by British prejudice and racism. Many Irish people therefore have a disposition that affords them a level of deep empathy with black people experiencing racism and the impact of colonialism; however, they can never claim to be walking in the shoes of black people. In the same way, other white individuals may not have a deep empathy with the Irish or black individuals, and vice versa.

I once had a black male client who wanted me to suggest to him what to do in a situation where he was struggling with the behaviour of his white partner. I considered the enduring racism that may be present within his relationships, but I was in no position to point this out in the initial meeting. He did not continue to see me, because he came for suggestions that I felt unable to give him. Had he continued to attend, I would have considered the dynamics of racism, sexism and black male oppression in my clinical supervision.

A gay Asian man wanted to figure out his dilemma of leading a double life and not coming out to his Hindu family. My background as a female raised in Christianity did not permit me to fully empathize with the nature of his Hindu upbringing, but I felt able to connect with the dynamics of secrecy and taboo that shrouded his situation.

A young Punjabi female was concerned about her family wanting her to get married as she was approaching the age of 30. She was habitually surfing the net for an Asian partner so that she could make her own choice of a husband. She felt this would please her parents and get them off her back about arranging a marriage. In this situation there was a wider context to consider, the intergenerational and intercultural context of second-generation Punjabi experience – a young woman feeling oppressed as a woman in the face of cultural heterosexism and her Asian/British background. This was a tentative situation, as there is no training blueprint for working with multidimensional intra-cultural concerns. I was being asked to hold the multidimensional aspect of her dilemma, without judgement or bias, yet my principles as a fairly liberated women needed to be curtailed in order to allow her to explore her own cultural needs and decisions.

A black woman of Jamaican heritage was experiencing oppression from her Jamaican live-in partner. Again, this situation stretched my empathic capabilities, because whilst I am aware of how the dynamics of racism and sexism may impact both individuals, I cannot assume anything about their early experiences of racism or oppression. I was aware that this woman had come to me as a black therapist offering a black empathic approach, but I was also aware that I couldn't on this basis assume that we are alike.

In all of the above situations, ancestral baggage played a key role in how the individuals felt about themselves. All situations included inter-gender dynamics, and considering the role of family members, they would have also experienced intra-gender dynamics. It would be counterproductive to assume that black or Asian people all suffer from dilemmas related to early childhood racism, sexism, heterosexism or gender oppression. I can only assume that at some point in their lives they may have been impacted by racism or sexism or other oppressions. The challenge here is to keep in mind that racism is usually the least attended-to experience that may contribute to how clients process their presenting concerns. This is an area that as a therapist I can take to my own clinical supervision.

Approaching this theme that is personally relevant to me evokes challenges. It is almost like an inner synchronicity – the challenge of how difficult this is, how painful it can sometimes be and being a woman, being a successful black woman. I feel it's about me because I challenge these issues rather than support the oppressor's viewpoint, and I take the risk to present my challenge to the oppressor in support of clients who may be victims of the oppressions, so that they know that I am on their side. It is not always easy to be compassionate when I am hurting from oppressions, but I do my best to remember that hurt equals hurt, and this means that the oppressor may also be hurting.

This perspective is based on my experience through years of working with clients who have felt silenced by racism and sexism. Although I do not represent all women, or all black people, the experience of millions of other women and black people supports my challenge to racism and sexism. As a result of my powerfulness, I sometimes suffer situations of disrespect, dismissal and marginalization. This I take to my therapy.

I once challenged the term 'My Bitches', voiced by a black man in a movie. I thought out loud, 'I don't like this, it is horrible.' The response from a close male friend who was laughing at the film was, 'It is only a film.' I was hurt by his response. I assumed the fact that I was feeling hurt was enough to convey my situation and I trusted that I was loved enough to gain some empathy. This was not so. I forget that men have also been hurt and many are somewhat naive about how their sexism impacts on us, just as white people often deny the existence of racism.

On sharing my feelings, I was criticized for having feelings about the oppression and was called an activist. I was no longer a woman; I was now an activist. I was viewed as oversensitive in my expectations of support rather than collusion. My challenge inflamed the situation, and we as friends became disconnected. My equilibrium became unbalanced and I was sick from this incident and all past attacks on me as a woman. Both the perpetrator and I suffered recognition trauma. Yes, it was only a film, and I am aware that social media reinforces negative stereotypes of women that get colluded with in the name of comedy. His rationale was that the expression of 'bitches' was not directly aimed at me.

I am every woman, and I experienced double wounding because someone I trusted dismissed my experience of oppression. 'Acceptance is a form of complicity' (hooks, 1996, p. 11). When women shut up, we shut the oppression inside ourselves and suffer from the impact in silence, causing us to mistrust men. We internalize the shame of being a woman, the shame of fighting for our self-respect. Some of us turn to other women for support, and it is possible to feel empowered if they are not colluding with sexism. If we transfer this situation of mistrust into a therapeutic context, it is not difficult to imagine how therapists who have not worked on their gender hurts might rupture the therapeutic alliance by lack of empathy with clients who express their hurt about sexism. The challenge of racism is similar to this, and these oppressions coupled with intra-gender collusion can evoke hurts that are twofold, combining the pain of sexism and racism.

Men in the throes of sexism dislike gutsy women, and their distresses make them want to overpower us and make us feel small. Misogynistic cultures reinforce the notion that we should be and act powerless. In the past, I have dissociated with my power and suffered emotional and physical violence and abuse from men. Disassociation causes us not to notice ourselves, and it can stop us climbing out of our suffering. White individuals who are unaware or defensive about racism can evoke similar feelings of disempowerment and attitudes towards black men. Many women confuse female support with male-bashing because they have not processed their own hurt from men. If we women have sons, brothers, fathers, grandsons and nephews, we must heal from the hurts of men in order to support women and men in an unbiased way. The same applies to men.

I had felt abandoned and rejected in response to my friend's insults. I was furious and I hurled some unsavoury insults at him as a man, which humiliated him and vexed him to no end. He then punished me with silence. Or, should I say, I felt punished by his silence. After the initial withdrawal, I realized that I was thrust into a reflective space.

During the silence I visited a female friend. I did not share anything about the incident to my friend. Coincidentally she offered me a document called 'Making women visible'. For me, this is proof of ancestral guidance. I displayed the document on my dining table for a few days where my male friend could see it, without referring to it in any shape or form and I allowed it to do its work. During a later conversation about our differentiation, my friend expressed some awareness of his deep-seated sexism. From this sharing of naivety and defensiveness, our wounds began to heal. Fortunately, our reflective silence healed the rupture evoked by the wounds of racism and sexism between us.

Our words for challenging oppression can be as harsh as the oppression itself, and we cannot always be aware of the multidimensional nature of immediate oppression. This is an important feature of the therapeutic healing process, and therapists and supervisors can support the connections that make up the jigsaw of oppressive circumstances and responses. A girlfriend that I explained the story to was empathic and validated my upset and my power as a black, Jewish woman. From this I figured out that my early abandonment and feelings of betrayal by an African Caribbean father who passed away and was unable to raise me were all connected and mixed-up in my distress. I learned humility from this important trial. I learned about my diversity and how when oppressed I internalize the hurt, and in my unconscious attempts to get attention on the hurt, I can hurt others. These psychological patterns that develop from oppressive experiences need to be taken into account when working with multidimensional oppressions.

As I edit this piece, the news has come in that two young black males who attempted to kill my son have been jailed. At this moment in time, I have compassion only for my son, the victim of their male violence, and I am confused about the intra-gender context of black-on-black male violence.

We must be aware of how inter-gender and intra-gender hurt and internalized oppression can be transferred into the therapeutic process. It is a brave but important step to attempt to assist clients to make a holistic connection between being black or Asian and female or male. Therapists and supervisors can process the risky aspect of intervention, so that rather than disassociating, clients are enabled to unify the oppressed parts of their psyche. Learning to love all parts of identity is essential to working through multidimensional oppressions, and therapists must account for their responses to all oppression. The question proposed below relates to ways that therapists can dismiss diversity and blame the client for their significant oppressions:

> Is a good counsellor good regardless of race, gender, disability, age, sexuality, etc. – is this a transference on the part of the client?

A 'good' counsellor is one who is open and aware of multidimensional oppressions – one who takes into account their identities and oppressions and works through them in preparation for the client's diversity. The 'good' counsellor acknowledges their naivety and mistakes, and works through their own pre-transference, transference and counter-transferences. They can then engage with the client's transference and identity development and the challenge of racism and gender oppression. If I were not to answer this question as though it were significant to the challenge of racism, I would be diluting the importance of attending to racial equality and other oppressions. I am suggesting that recognition of therapist, supervisor and client responses are a vital key to the ability of the therapist's process, whatever their ethnicity and gender. In situations where transference may be apparent, the exposure to racism and awareness of racism is what matters. The important context is that too much focus on the client's transference can dampen empathy and distance the therapist from engaging with the challenge of racism and other significant oppressions.

Sociocultural elements of the transference are maintained within ancestral baggage and the traumatic impact of racism. Via black Western archetypes, they reinforce mythology such as 'all black men are rapists' or that they are eager to use sexual domination to express their rage about racism, or that black sexism is more heinous than white sexism. The myth of 'sacred white womanhood' is one such archetype that perpetrates racism. In an intra-gender context, the black woman's inferiority to white females is compounded by the use of skin-lightening creams and hair straighteners. In Freud's typology, the African man and woman have both been castrated; therefore, although they may achieve sisterhood and brotherhood via empathic connection and via experiences of racism and marginalization, a key area for consideration is their struggle to form lasting bonds.

Berger (1993) suggests a male intra-gender, interracial phenomenon:

> The white men's competition with black men for social authority is also played out on sexual terrain. white men articulate a fear of racial difference through concern of black men's power over the bodies of white women. ... Sexual practices are the locus for the expression and exercise of power (both oppressive and resistive) between men and vice versa: consideration of the colonized other. White men succeed in colonizing black men to the extent that they are not subject to black men's dictates regarding their (black men's) women (i.e. black women). (pp. 9, 10)

It just so happens that the transcultural supervision groups that I have been facilitating have mainly attracted black women. A white woman who started in one of the groups dropped out when she fully realized the impact of being a minority in the group and that those experiences of racism that impacted the black members' lives and professional situations would be discussed. She acknowledged to the group that she had become aware of the depth of the work she needed to do on herself, as a member of the perpetrator group, so that she would feel more able to engage with the themes.

Understanding these processes and the immediate impact of opening a dialogue about the challenges of racism can create diverse support needs for black, Asian and white professionals. Supervisors need to be aware of these diverse needs so that they respond appropriately and with a view to the impact of multidimensional oppressions.

An Asian supervisee attended the group to reflect on how her Hindu background affected her practice. Some therapists join the transcultural supervision groups because they want to understand what internalized oppression is doing to them and how it affects their therapeutic work. Internalized oppression is a key area in therapeutic work.

The oppressive experiences of black and Asian women and men cannot be taken for granted, because they are understood via association with the therapist's or supervisor's same gender or same cultural background experiences. White women do not know what it is like to be a black woman. Black men do not know the full colonial impact on white men. Asian men can empathize with some other Asian men based on similarities in their spiritual or cultural influences, but they do not have identical life experiences. For example, a Punjabi Sikh may not be able to fully connect with a Muslim or a Hindu. Diversity in these areas is a meaningful locus point for transcultural work and the challenges of racism in therapy.

In our everyday lives there are examples to remind us that the psyche absorbs racism and gender oppression. These barriers uphold social constructs and permeate the education of therapists. It is therefore important not to underestimate this process. Therapists and supervisors must make the link between everyday oppressions and the client's traumatic experiences and relational processes. In the cycle of these deep hurts, there are usually competing oppressions and it is helpful for therapists and supervisors to discuss them in the process of supporting their work with clients.

Black therapists must be aware of their anger and fear when these situations occur. You will have to hold on to what you know and find a way of not shaming yourself in the process of challenge. During this process you may become aware that you may harbour your anger and carry it into your client work. You can choose to work on this during your own therapy or personal development. You may be aware of situations with your clients that command your attention to gender oppression and racism. These situations may challenge your success with building a safe alliance, and I am sure they will hit on experiences of racism, sexism or male oppression in your life.

You may have done a great job with a white client, and suddenly it could look as if it's not a great job because the client is looking powerless, like they looked when they first came to your consulting room. You may begin to feel despairing of your work with the client and wonder why these feelings of despair have hit you so very hard. You may have forgotten, or not be aware, that you are actually doing the job as a black or Asian person. This may be where the experience of everyday racism can press down on you, as it is set up to make you feel as if nothing you achieve is good. If you have not been processing your therapeutic work in the context of gender oppression and racism, or your diversity with the client, the oppressions may kick in at this time as an unfamiliar imposition.

You may need to find a way to overcome the oppressions that you have held inside, so that you can see yourself as the experienced professional that you are and someone who has been really useful to your client, in spite of their oppression. This approach can bring black and Asian people through difficult situations.

White therapists may face blocks in their attempts to assist clients to explore multidimensional oppressions. When these blocks occur you need to be aware of the ways that internalized oppressions such as racism and sexism can create havoc with our psyche and victimize our self-esteem.

I would like to say to you that these situations will not arise again, but I know that they may rise again in other forms. Our lives are made like that. We think we've done the work on ourselves, in certain areas of our lives, and we think that we dealt with it. Then suddenly another situation occurs and reminds us that there is still a big dollop of internalized racism or internalized sexism, or, in the case of men, internalized emasculation inside us, making us feel we are a failure because we are black or male or female. This can happen even if we are not fully aware that racism may be affecting us. A discussion with Eugene, a black male integrative arts psychotherapist, clearly shows how he experiences internalized racism as a black man:

Isha: So what can you tell me about being a black man in your role within the organization? Because your identity is important.

Eugene: I am the one who does the race and culture sessions that we have. I am in this funny place at the moment; I was talking about this the other day. The organization wants someone to move into the position of director and there is an internal battle with me about that, about being the figurehead.

Isha: As a black man?

Eugene: As a black man, or the main person. I am pulling back. There is a big work issue there and being a black man in that position, not wanting to be there first. There are loads of issues about that, and being a black man is a central issue as well. It is hard to explain that I may feel really awkward in that position. Being a black man, I do lots of training and consultations and I'm often meeting new people. I remember when I first started, there was a working-class family and they had adopted three children. And the mother did not want me to be part of the team. She was claiming that an Asian man had beaten up her son and she did not want me there.

Isha: A white child?

Eugene: Yeah. There was a lot of discussion about how to handle this. That was my very first case there. That was how I started. At the time, the organization was saying, 'Well, this is a team. If you want the team, fine; if you don't, then you will have to go somewhere else', so she went with it and it worked out. There is the feeling of, will I be accepted? I come in to work in such a way that it is not going to be an issue, and I get in there as a professional. People seem to accept that I have this role as an expert in this field. There are some cases where the feeling does not go away and there is wariness.

There was one incident where this white couple adopted a not overtly black looking girl of mixed heritage. They did not see the value of keeping that part of the culture alive. I struggled with this particular person and in the end it all fell apart. This was a very young child, so there was a rationale for not doing any therapy and waiting to see how things develop and come back to it later, although I felt it should have happened at the time. That was another point where there was a lot of tension between this couple and me. You know, can this child pass as 'white', in quotes. That is not really the whole story and it was difficult trying to get that across. Down the road, I can see that this will be an issue for that child, when she starts to think about her identity. So, yeah, I am aware of being a black man and sometimes that fades away.

Isha: I guess you would take some of those issues to your own supervision.

Eugene: Being a black person in the organization does not really come up. It is not something that I bring up.

Isha: Why not?

Eugene: I kept feeling that they would not quite know what to do with it, but I have not really tested that out.

Isha: How long have you been in the organization?

Eugene: About 8 years.

Isha: That is a long time having to hold your experience as a black man and not really feel you can get support with it.

Eugene: Yeah, with the clients and me that's been OK, but me as an individual in that place has not really been explored.

Isha: So you can take the clients, whether black or white, and you work with them and you are kind of seen as a black expert, but when it's about the impact on you and the interrelational process with you as a black man in that situation, you don't feel safe enough to take it. Is that right?

Eugene: Yeah, that's probably right; I think there is a safety issue. I think there is some embarrassment from white people becoming conscious about the racial dynamics. There is a sense that it will make people uncomfortable and there is a part of me that does not want that as well. A sort of 'looking after' process that I am aware of in myself around these issues.

Isha: So they might get uncomfortable because you are raising the issues, and then you might feel you have got to take care of them and you don't want to do that?

Eugene: Yeah, I don't want to take care of them and I don't want them to feel uncomfortable either.

Isha: As you were talking, I was thinking you expressed a kind of reticence about getting into this role of being a director, and I'm wondering about the link between you already being seen as a black expert, having all those years where it appears as though there was nowhere to take it within the organization. Then there is this big responsibility that you would be taking on, and I get a great sense of isolation.

Eugene: Yeah, as you were speaking I got this image of myself. Which is slightly different from saying, 'if I did not grow up in London...'. Some of my African colleagues and people I know have grown up in Africa and came here. They feel like they can go anywhere in the country. London, Scotland, Yorkshire, and they kind of feel OK. My experience going out of London was with a black friend. My friend was asking me how I was feeling. I was feeling wary about what was going on in a white area. He grew up in Kenya and he did not have the same feelings that I had. It feels connected with me being head of this organization. Like coming out of London, I just want to get back into London. I know it is about my experience of growing up in the UK that is different from the experience of my friend from Africa. I'm trying to put some metaphors in there to help me understand it because I have not really spoken about it in this way.

Isha: That is what I call cultural collateral. You know, if someone has enough black juice behind them they feel more confident when they are in groups of white people. It seems as though you are saying that you do not have an

opportunity to take what goes on for you as a therapist to the organization. Do
you have a chance to take it outside anywhere?

Eugene: Yeah, I would mainly take it to the black men's group.

Here we see how the process of accepting racism and emasculation can
be healed by intra-gender and intra-cultural support. Black people who
do not accept racism do not remain untouched by it. Not accepting
racism can often cause the individual to be shamed and feel shame.
Upsetting the norms of subservience harshness and lack of love attracts
isolation and marginalization by both black and white people.

The effect of civil rights protests and the black renaissance gave black
folks hope of greater self-love without reliance on white folks for vali-
dation. However, the great white hope betrayed many people who left
their lands to a better world; this betrayal helped reinforce the work
ethic of black people trying to get homes and work. We must remember
that within the struggle for equal rights, women were also struggling
for equal recognition. Forgetfulness about this context of oppressions
within oppressed groups may be an inherited reason why quite often
gender is prioritized over racism.

Black Western archetypes create negative models evolving from
slavery and colonialism. The image of the sacrificial mama and matriarchal love permeates African and Caribbean families. Love means
caring for others over and above self-care. Often, this approach is
backed by religious connotations that to care for self first is selfish
and sinful. So, many black and Asian females are raised to care for the
whole family – children, men, cleaning and cooking, and less time for
love. To reject this model for love can mean being seen as betraying
self and family.

hooks (2001) discusses the cause of self-love for black women and
clearly states:

> Black female self-love could be fully recognized only when individu-
> als no longer internalize negative stereotypes. ... Following the path
> of Sojourna truth and otherwise black women elders, black females
> must constantly assert our full humanity to counter the impact of
> dehumanizing forces. Expressing our full range of emotions is heal-
> ing to the spirit and engages us in the practice of self-acceptance,
> which is so essential to self-love. Underneath the stern expression I
> saw my mother and many of her friends. There was an ongoing fear
> that if they let their guards down, even for a minute, they would be

disrespected, hurt or violated in some way. To laugh we have to let fear go and live faith-based lives. Living in faith means that we recognize, as our wise black female ancestors did, that we do have the power to decolonize our minds, invent ourselves, and dwell in the spirit of love that is our true destiny. (pp. 100, 112)

Individuals raised by men who are emotionally shut down may be present, but emotionally unavailable. They may have experienced a model of distant parenting or lack of a primary male model. African and Caribbean men have been known to mask their vulnerability. They want to be loved but they are often confused about giving love. Giving love is seen as women's forte. Hence, there are many fatherless children.

Black folks love and care about their families, and harsh discipline has come from the intergenerational process of parents fearing for the safety of their children. It does not make it all right for children to be beaten, but this aspect of black life needs to be understood in the context of intergenerational trauma. As black people, we have a great heritage, and these are some of the blights imposed by slavery, war rivalry and family fragmentation. Hence, this student's question is important:

> As a white woman, should I see the colour of my client before the person?

In attending to this question I talk to an experienced Ghanaian male therapist who highlights the importance of paying attention to what we may not know or understand about black and Asian communities and how gender and racial dynamics can go unnoticed:

S: **Transformation depends on who goes to the training. My therapy and supervision is with white females. I have never taken racism to my therapist or supervisor because they would never understand. They see a black man who is white-educated. I am a lot more and they would not understand this. I was able to point these issues out with Clarkson when she was my trainer. I did not come across anyone else who could understand. Your questions have pointed out things that I should have been aware of.**

Isha: *We are looking at internalized racism in the therapist. What informs your practice?*

S: **My practice is integrative and it takes a different perspective. I have not come across any book that deals with a perspective of a black** therapist – I would turn more to the US. There is more. I look at it from a historical perspective. You make your own project, as there is no model. You make your own structure from a historical perspective. I haven't yet named the form. I agree that an integrative approach includes working with oppressions. A person is painfully familiar with their situation and they do not engage with therapy because the approaches do not suit them.

Isha: The issue of going back into the client's historical and social past is not addressed.

S: It disempowers the white therapist because of guilt, and the black client feels voiceless. Part of the oppression happens in the room. There is also a master/slave mentality going on that is almost never addressed.

It depends on the experience of the therapist, to be able to be aware of these dynamics. The client may not be aware of this and have difficulty with it, but may not know what it is. It's expressing it in the language of the client. What happened a lot is that the therapist is expressing it in the language they have been taught, not in the language of the client. The client becomes alienated. My experience of a black male client: the black male will not admit his weaknesses to another black man. The language is multi-layered. So we are dealing with many issues – the inability to express on a multi-layered level.

Isha: What do think about the idea that the impact of racism goes on alongside the impact of machoism?

S: When a few areas of oppression are operating, these issues are smoothed over – a kind of a seesaw effect that we are not given the tools to address.

Isha: What is your experience of bringing this to supervision?

S: I have a lot of experience of how racism impacts the supervisory relationship – if a therapist is not equipped for this and does not bring this into supervision. They give it other names, like transference. This goes further than just being labelled transference. The therapist is impacting the client, and the history of this is not addressed on a racial level. I have yet to have a therapist who brings the racial aspect to supervision. It disappears and is not mentioned on my part as well. I should be educating the therapist on these matters, and I don't. It gets missed because I supervise white females who are counselling white females. The element of race should be addressed, and it's not, because they have not encountered it. The transference is an overall label and they reduce it to therapist and client stuff. I don't think they would hide the racism issues, and they are not aware of the dynamics between them and the white client and between them and me. They see that I am their supervisor with a Eurocentric view. They have got to take into account my background and my multilingual ability. I have not supervised a black therapist. I see that not addressing the racial issues is a new challenge.

All my knowledge is from a Eurocentric model. It does not work to try and take an integrative model and try to address it into an African context; it will not work. So, there needs to be an education where you cannot hold these approaches as the only approaches. My supervisor is white because there are very few black supervisors. It doesn't work, and this is why I need to reach outside and read other works. My CPD is plateauing because I am not getting sufficient input on these issues' concerns.

The transparency of my discussion with S exposed for him his predicament of not disclosing his need to include his identity as a black African man in his therapeutic and supervisory dialogue. Although he is aware of his African ontology and the racism that black people experience, the consequences of his silence are clear. His white clients, supervisees and supervisor do not fully see him, as he denies his black male self in the role of supervisor, client and supervisee. A parallel process is operating. Whilst he is clear about how Eurocentric perspectives have influenced his training, he appears helpless to engage with the missing bits in a constructive way. He is gagged. Receiving therapy and supervision from white women and attending to white clients constructs a false framework for the therapeutic process. He is trapped whilst behaving in accordance with a white Eurocentric framework and a training that has denied him the liberty to be fully himself.

Summary

I have outlined the context of gender influences and how the imposition of racism can be put on a back burner if there are defensive responses or denial. In doing so, I have shared some of my own experiences to support the empathic elements to these concerns and to help open discussion on areas that are sometimes difficult to address. This is my main reason for presenting the voice of S, who in his own words portrays his naivety about the impact of using only white female professionals to support his therapeutic work. In summarizing, I can only say that it is vital that therapists and supervisors be more engaged with the duality of gender and racism and their intrinsic links with ancestral baggage and intergenerational influences. We are left with two key questions. Can therapists be aware of the consequences of inter-gender and interracial dynamics in their own supervision and support forums, and in their client work? Do racial concerns get prioritized or pushed aside when gender dynamics are present?

Pointers:

- Therapists must make it their responsibility to address the context of gender and the impact of racism in the supervision setting.
- Supervisors must equip themselves to support therapists in these areas.
- Gender influences and racism must be held as a dual phenomenon, both with clients and in supervision.
- The consequences of splitting off gender from racism must be considered.
- Being aware that prioritizing gender over racism or racism over gender can diminish the nature of specific oppressions, as with any other dualities.
- Therapists and supervisors must be aware of interpretations such as transference over and above gender oppression, or the impact of racism.
- It is important to be aware of what gets shared and what might be dismissed or unacknowledged, both in the therapeutic setting and in supervision.

Part III

The Traumatic Effects of Slavery and Colonialism

Racism continues to cause and compound trauma and depression. It is often forgotten that slavery was damaging for both the perpetrators and the enslaved and that both parties play a significant role in moving on from this atrocity. Silences about the impact of slavery and colonialism within the psychotherapy profession often mean that black clients may not have appropriate support for the intergenerational impact of this trauma. This section will offer some insights about ways that therapists and supervisors can process the post-slavery traumatic impact and the intergenerational duality of contemporary coping mechanisms. It will give meaning to the concepts of black Western archetype and ancestral baggage.

The Intergenerational Context of Internalized Racism

I am a melting pot,
bubble bubble, toil and trouble,
outcast,
half-cast,
Mixed-race,
histories' disgrace,
the joining and tearing apart,
the unexpected cause of Immigration, emigration, a new part of a nation,
pollution? or a part of a dream?
The next chapter, the unforeseen,
She dead but she na lie down.
She live inside me deep deep down.
She smile but she still have a frown.
Her ethnicity is black and white
but she brown.
Like dirt,
like mud
it stick,
from it, she get sick

Dom Powell, 6 February 2014

The above poem aptly portrays the theme of this chapter: the intergenerational context of how racism and dominant Eurocentric culture has impacted black people. You will find that sometimes I use the term 'black peoples' to acknowledge the diversity between us and within our origins, in the diaspora and in the UK. Together we will face the challenge of unpacking how internalized racism influences unconscious processes. Attention will be given to the way that the hurt of racism gets taken into the psyche and re-enacted in the daily lives of black peoples, for example creating a 'false self', and assimilation processes such as hair straightening, skin whitening and negative mirroring of identity and appearance. This exploration will inform and support the challenge of engaging with the impact of intergenerational and social racism on the developmental processes of black peoples and in the responses of white people.

The theme of intergenerational influences and internalized racism is a tough one, because we need to consider both collective and individual aspects of consciousness and unconscious processes. Behaviour assimilation and self-esteem are key areas of consideration when exploring these themes. Intergenerational influences of cultural and familial behaviours and attitudes that may be passed on by those who care for us and our educators and in social situations are key areas in this framework. Internalized racism is usually seen as an unconscious process by which individuals assimilate and take in harmful behaviours and attitudes aimed towards skin colour, hair texture and features. This divisive undercurrent usually gets instilled at an early age and can erode self-esteem.

As I consider this theme that goes deep into the hidden impact of racism, I feel a fear of making mistakes. My own process of internalized racism gets stimulated because I am conscious that if I make mistakes I may get fired at from all sides. Eurocentric theory and attitudes are challenged when we work with family origins, cultural context and the intergenerational trauma of the African Caribbean population. These challenges can cause their own trauma. On the other hand, I do not profess to be an expert on African, Caribbean and Asian peoples, and my words may not fit the experiences of everyone.

Fletchman Smith (2000) begins from the position that slavery was damaging for everyone concerned with it:

> As in all situations in which there are perpetuators and victims, it is what the victims do in their own minds with the horrors they experience that to a large extent determines the future state of mind of that individual. (p. 7)

As previously noted, the maintenance of an approach based on a post-racism mythology is likely to hinder the intergenerational process of surviving the past. Once individuals become aware of how racism has affected their lives, both survivors and perpetrators can decide whether to liberate themselves from racism or remain in a post-racism silence.

First of all, I want to affirm the goodness of intergenerational characteristics that get passed to individuals via the immediate and extended family and those who care for us. Our beauty, tenacity, creativity, music and capacity to love are all extensions of ancestral and intergenerational, cultural processes; yet for those of African heritage, they have been marred by the impact of slavery and colonization. Many white people, whom collectively I have referred to as members of the perpetrator group, have also recognized the damaging effects of slavery on their ancestors and current attitudes towards black people.

I recently went to a supermarket with my 25-year-old son. I noticed that he packed the shopping cart in the same way that I do, carefully separating the non-food items and the cold items from the rest of the shopping. When we left the supermarket I asked him, 'Did you learn that from me?' And he answered yes. Naturally, as a proud mother I immediately noticed where he was imitating one of my good habits. On the other hand, there are plenty of strange and challenging behaviours that my children have exhibited, and some of these I must take ownership for, but without blame, for I was pretty naive in my practice as a parent, and some of those behaviours were handed on via my assimilation processes and my historical and intergenerational influences. I have called these negative features ancestral baggage.

A black client's emotional situation may be affected by his or her upbringing and also by his or her ancestors' modes of response to oppression. This is a proposition about intergenerational patterns of relating that can be impacted by past family attitudes and behaviours, whether conscious or unaware. Learning situations that raise awareness of ancestral baggage provide us with opportunities to rewrite the negative aspects of these scripts and transform our lives. Psychotherapy and counselling is just one way of supporting the inspiration and insights that can contribute to this process.

Awareness of the transpersonal elements and sociological lag of those gone before can help develop appropriate mirroring. I mean transpersonal in the sense of shared empathy and shared Eurocentric experience. In addition, the consequences of Eurocentric socializing and different generational experiences will influence this outcome. By sociological lag I mean those elements of our origins that got lost or transformed due to immigration and moving through different cultures. My parents, for example, were both from immigrant families. They settled in the UK as citizens and spoke the English language. They assimilated aspects of their past histories, and cultural frameworks were left behind in their countries of origin. In my father's situation, part of this transition was leaving a colonized island to reside in a country inhabited predominantly by generations linked to white colonizers. A question proposed by a student about this predicament is presented below:

> Why don't we leave the past alone if it appears to be irrelevant to the present?

If this question was turned on its head, we might consider viewing it like this: why don't we leave the present alone if it appears to be relevant to the past? It may then be possible to consider the function of fear and denial that is so often associated with the challenge of facing the impact of racism in colonial history. The dynamic of the 'don't go there' signal is ever present in therapeutic relationships, and it is often linked to past experiences of oppression that render individuals speechless when processing minority issues. This gagging is tantamount to the ways that slaves were robbed of their right to love and communicate painful feelings. It is important, therefore, to be aware of how the therapist's own denial in the present time may prevent them from acknowledging the historical and cultural context of denial within individuals and the black family. The past will only be irrelevant if we refuse to contextualize the present. Leaving the past alone in this context would be a form of gagging.

Some hurtful traits of everyday racism can be traced back to the influence of slavery. One example mentioned in Chapter 5 is the pecking order based on shadism. Another example is the fear that many black people have about challenging white racism. White people, due to their membership in the perpetrator group, have also inherited a number of coincidental traits, for example white guilt and fear of being singled out as racist. Besides the inability to fully accept the traumatic impact of racism and related feelings, their self-esteem has also been eroded by racism. This becomes apparent when they are challenged about their responses to racism.

In my doctorate study (Mckenzie-Mavinga, 2005), the issue of denial, mistrust and internalized racism became paramount when trainees attempted to discuss the challenges of racism. White trainees expressed concerns about identifying their racism. Black trainees became concerned about hurting their white colleagues if they shared their experiences of racism. The mistrust perpetuated fear within these discussions. The discussions then became conditioned by the source of their fears – racism. As a result, the fears of white trainees inhibited their ability to listen to black trainees, and black trainees' fears focused on their white colleagues. This situation diminished the level of support and personal development that black trainees received. Here we find a dilemma for the black client in a cross-racial client–therapist situation. Likewise, the black client may inadvertently be placed in the role of taking care of the white counsellor instead of being free to fully express their experiences. If the white therapist is unaware of this transference, they may collude with clients and maintain a status quo of post-slavery subservience (that perpetuates the black Western archetype of 'step and fetch it') with black clients.

Looking at it from another angle brings into focus the needs of black therapists and clients working together. How then do therapists place aside their ancestral baggage about racism and become fully present for their clients, without racism conditioning the agenda? I once had a client who brought a huge dollop of internalized racism into her first session. Noticing that my skin was a lot lighter than hers, she conveyed her concerns as a darker-skinned woman, because she had once experienced hurt from a lighter-skinned manager at work. By nature of my light skin and mixed black-and-white heritage, it is important for me to remain aware that due to shadism, I may unconsciously oppress others due to my life experience of having part of my heritage within an oppressive group. The context of these experiences and difficulties can usually be traced to family dynamics (ancestral baggage) and training institutions that have not sufficiently recognized and supported the historical backdrop, impact and dynamics of racism. A graduate drama therapist, author of the above poem, describes his personal development process and awareness using the term ancestral baggage:

I can identify the scars that are the wounds of my Ancestral Baggage taking the form of my Internal Oppressor. Often this manifests as my inner voice that negatively comments on the way that I present myself to the external world and that holds me back from being my authentic self for fear of being stereotyped and judged negatively.

I have found that creative writing has enabled me to process on this experience affectively. It has shifted; that rock that I have been under, it has been removed, allowing me to be free and seen for what I am, but am I embraced because of my race or because I am me? My relief is short lived, as I can see the rock slowly falling onto my peer. I feel embarrassed, humiliated and ashamed. Why confine a group of people? Why not be open? Why put someone else through this? As a minority group what are you promoting? Two wrongs don't make a right; is this Ancestral Baggage? Your way of protecting the image of your cultural identity by keeping it closed? I can't breathe. I am torn. As I look into my peers' eyes filled with painful tears; she looks to me for the answers. I give answers that I believe are required in order to sooth the wound, but as I look and answer, I don't believe that we are together in our suffering. We have not met each other at the bridge where her wound starts and mine ends. I feel this mirror is only reflecting one way; I am still disappearing, being swept up and sucked in by her whirlpool. I am worried how I will be perceived. As she implores me for the good enough answers, my trauma is triggered thinking of my Austrian grandmother who must have had experiences of this in her life, being white and married to a black man. My identity is contaminated, pulled and pushed; I am universal, able to feel experiences from both sides of the table. (Powell, 2013, pp. 25, 20)

This excerpt offered by Powell demonstrates his struggle to connect empathically and make sense of responses from the other, bound up in Eurocentric dominance, internalized racism and intergenerational gagging.

Whether the therapist is black or white, the sole use of a Eurocentric approach may underestimate experiences of the black family and the impact of racism on individuals. Deep wounds connected to family experiences of racism and colonization can contribute to low self-esteem, and if not addressed, this can lead to depression. It is vital that therapists become aware of the potential for black clients to harbour these symptoms, whether they are made explicit or not. This preparedness contributes to the development of good practice that addresses black issues and racism for therapists, supervisors and their clients.

Having said this, although the term black is generally used to affirm the rich African and Asian heritage of colonized peoples, it is important to be clear that not all Africans, Caribbean peoples and Asians identify as 'black'. Indeed, a Caribbean artist friend alluding to black as a transitional phase through authentic identity development, insists that 'you are black until you are African', thus suggesting rites of passage that may include building cultural collateral by learning about African heritage in the context of individual and collective identity. No matter how individuals define their identity, unless the construction of racism is addressed, racism remains a precursor to their self-esteem.

Attention to the racial or cultural predisposition of the black or minority client in the therapeutic process is three-dimensional. The first aspect of this is the personal and psychological impact that derives from experiences of individual overt or covert racism that become embedded in our interactions as though they are real. Scheurich and Young (1997) define this civilizational racism:

> The civilizational level is the level of broad civilizational assumptions that, though they construct the nature of our world and our experience of it, are not typically conscious to most members of a civilization (Foucault, 1979, 1988) ... 'Not all people [i.e., civilizations, in this case] "know" in the same way' (Stanfield, 1985, p. 396). In addition, large, complex civilizations often include a dominant culture and one or more subordinate cultures. In this context, subordinate cultures, races, and other groups often have different civilizational assumptions. (p. 5)

The example by Hughes offered earlier (in Chapter 5) showed how a five-year-old experienced overt racist attack based on skin colour. The child became disempowered and internalized the trauma of the experience. According to Scheurich and Young (1997), this forms a basis for 'epistemological racism'. They go on to say:

> By epistemological racism, then, we do not mean that the researchers using, say, positivism or postmodernism are overtly or covertly racist as individuals. Nor do we mean that epistemological racism is a conscious institutional or societal conspiracy in favor of whites (B. M. Gordon, 1993, p. 267). Epistemological racism means that our current range of research epistemologies – positivism to postmodernisms/post structuralisms – arise out of the social history and culture of the dominant race, that these epistemologies logically reflect and reinforce that social history and that racial group (while excluding the epistemologies of other races/cultures), and that this has negative results for people of color in general and scholars of color in particular. (p. 8)

This means that even if the individual does not accept they are being racist, epistemological racism therefore occurs out of discourses emerging from institutional racism and Eurocentricism.

Scheurich and Young (1997) explain the second aspect of racism as 'social and educational', evidenced by intergenerational oppression and trauma that can be seen in everyday attitudes. A 15-year-old teenager stands in the centre of a cultural carnival in London and states, 'There are Chinkies all around me.' A small child points and laughs out loud at a 'little' person in a shopping centre; a 17-year-old states that he would kill himself if he were gay. An African Caribbean child hates her hair because it is not silky and straight. These snapshots of early oppressive attitudes, expressed publicly, are influenced by social, cultural and educational reference points and get passed on intergenerationally. They are usually evident when unconscious psychological processes are exposed. Therapeutic work creates a dynamic emotional situation that can uncover these 'civilizational' and intergenerational modes of response to diversity and culture. Eurocentricism impacts on responses to these social and educational dilemmas and can determine how, for example, the oppression of racism will be responded to. For both individuals who are victims of racism and those within the perpetrator group, emotional distresses attached to responses to racism need support.

The traumatic effects of slavery and colonialism have created misunderstanding and lack of attention to the cultural aspects of anxiety. Several indications of these anxieties have become apparent. First, negative or sole identification with the same group and rejection of members of the perpetrator group is one aspect of isolation that can occur. When support has not been forthcoming, isolation and depression can occur on an individual level.

There is strong evidence that 'don't discharge' signals emanating from the trauma of slavery prevent some individuals from crying or raging about the oppression of racism. During slavery, white people were led to believe that African people did not grieve or feel pain, and this message became internalized and passed on intergenerationally. This was how the enslavers managed to carry out such atrocities on our people. Their ancestors created this belief and they, themselves, acted as if they felt nothing. This is the background to modern Eurocentric denial about the pain of racism. They were also taught not to feel anything about black people's pain, as many of them gloated over the beatings and lynchings and rarely interrupted this vicious cycle of violence. This numbing of the reality of slavery destroyed their empathic connections with black people.

A second context of this trauma-related anxiety is the better than or less than ideals that through caste systems and shadism have widely permeated identity development. The concept of black Western archetypes may assist with understanding the historical context of this phenomenon and how these archetypes get interpreted into damaging stereotypes that get internalized. Situations where an inappropriate collective gaze, portraying dark skins as negative, have resulted in individuals self-harming, by scrubbing or scraping their skin to try and escape their blackness and fit the stereotype of light skin and soft, long hair.

The third aspect of trauma and the cultural aspects of anxiety can be seen when denial of the experience of racism or denial of being a member of the perpetrator group become apparent. Fear of the enormity of the impact of racism forms a major part of this type of response. For white people this can mean fear of isolation and rejection by peers due to recognizing the powerful position of being in the perpetrator group, or naming the oppression.

In addition to these fears, individuals often experience fear that the associated powerful feelings caused by racism cannot be repaired. This is where the concept of recognition trauma comes in. I have stated that I believe there is a process of recovery that can happen once recognition trauma (an understanding of the powerful feelings associated with racism) is acknowledged and worked through in a therapeutic setting. These positions of servitude permeate black psychology in the white world. They restrict identity development of black peoples. When this process remains outside of individual awareness, this can become a restrictive normality, reinforced by white privilege and ignorance of black people's cognitive dissonance.

DeGruy (2005) talks about post-traumatic slave syndrome (PTSS), which reinforces cognitive dissonance. From this mindset, white nations, due to their privileged position, see black people as bad, and black people internalize this concept and feel bad about themselves. This may happen on an unconscious level. One example is the inherited negative gaze that causes us to feel bad about our natural hair. The shame inherited from these assumptions passed intergenerationally from slavery causes generations to be raised on shame. DeGruy goes on to say that PTSS is a threat to mental and physical safety because there has been no exchange of power, no structural changes and no statistics to evidence a post-racism period. It is our job, therefore, to help people who have never had a chance to heal in this area. In assisting the healing of PTSS it is important to remember that cognitive dissonance, in this respect, is a feature imposed by white privilege. This may impact those who display shame about their heritage and having an African identity. Racism is a system of advantage built on cognitive dissonance, so this is the basis from which we need to support healing.

I have spent some time reflecting on intergenerational trauma, and the best that I can offer you is some excerpts from my own everyday experience and the experience of others. I used the black Western archetype concept to describe how racist psychological patterns inherited and perpetuated in the collective unconscious within social structures can be repeated and manifest throughout history and perpetuate cognitive dissonance. An interview with Dr Aileen Alleyne regarding the challenge of racism in therapeutic practice describes how cognitive dissonance can feature both in the work with clients and the supervisory relationship. Alleyne identifies the 'internal oppressor' as specific to the impact of racism:

> From my long-standing observations, now confirmed by the findings within the study, I have concluded that the particular experience endured by black workers in the workplace is workplace oppression. I use the term in a deliberate sense to address complex organizational dynamics and silent forces that give rise to difficulties involving issues of power and powerlessness and of the dominant and dominated. To see these experiences of black workers as simply stress, scapegoating, bullying, harassment, or personality difficulties is to do a huge disservice to an unexamined phenomenon and all its complex tenets within organizations, which represent a microcosm of society at large. It is a well-known fact that black and other minority ethnic groups easily become containers for projected, unwanted and negative feelings from the other (Obholzer and Roberts, 2000; Shur, 1994). (Alleyne, 2005, p. 4)

Aileen: The example I wish to share for the discussion on how we work with race and racism in the consulting room is concerned with a white female psychotherapist bringing to supervision her work with a black male client. Her client wanted to talk about his personal experiences of racism in his workplace. I noticed in her presentation that she herself did not ever mention the word black. Her tendency also was to wait until the client had brought up the word, and she would make the standard intervention of, 'how do you feel about that', and, 'how did that make you feel'. I actually think there is nothing wrong with such interventions; they are helpful, client-centred, Rogerian-type therapeutic questions, but, when it came to exploring the client's powerful feelings and workplace dynamics at a much deeper level, she didn't actually know or feel confident to go further.

So, what I recall raising with her was about what was happening to her level of curiosity. She was naturally curious about everything else that happened in the client's life – his early childhood, his relationship with his partner, his estrangement from his father – and it was noticeable

that her curiosity was free and open. She was just very 'normal' in her facilitation and wanting to know about these areas, but it was striking that when her client started talking about his experiences of racism in the workplace, her curiosity noticeably had dried up. It seemed to be shut down.

Curiosity for me is a major issue when we are dealing with racism in clinical practice, and it's a puzzle that very efficient, intelligent, competent therapists seem frozen when they encounter issues of race and racism in the consulting room. It seems very remarkable. So I feel that the supervisor questioning the absence of the therapist's curiosity where race and racism are concerned is perhaps a helpful way to keep these themes at the front of the stage. Curiosity is a very small, almost benign word, which when explored in supervision can make the challenge to the therapist less combative, if you see what I mean. If the supervisor were to use a more pointed approach, for example if you said, 'I noticed that your client has been bringing issues of racism into his sessions, and you have not picked them up', in my experience, I feel that practitioners would think they have done something wrong. And when they feel they have done something wrong, particularly with a black supervisor, they could end up feeling shamed or having failed. So I think we have to be mindful of not re-shaming the shamed, and as a supervisor, I have to be mindful of an enabling way to help the practitioner whose curiosity has been shut down.

This particular practitioner was honest in admitting that her curiosity did not go further than checking out the client's feelings. And she also admitted that this was an area that she was not familiar with or competent in, so she felt that by just asking the client about his feelings she was at least giving attention to something important to him. You see my point. It's OK checking in with a client's feelings, that's the first port of call and something one should do, but I think there is more to the exploration of racism in the consulting room, which requires the practitioner to facilitate other kinds of questioning. What I was actually thinking was how do we categorize helpful interventions that practitioners could make to fully facilitate work in this area. I would say that there are the obvious and basic client-centred empathic questions and acknowledgements that enable the client's expression of feelings, for example, 'How does that feel?' (question), and 'I sense your disappointment with your colleagues' (acknowledgement). But there are other kinds of interventions, which are more to do with the therapist showing a genuine interest and curiosity to stay with the subject of race and racism, and delve deeper into the murky waters of this difficult area.

Showing curiosity to stay and delve deeper and wider demands more than your obvious and basic person-centred, Rogerian approach. Other kinds of explorations are needed, such as, 'How do colleagues relate to you when you seem to be the only one challenging racism in the workplace'? (question), 'Tell me, what position does that put you into?' (question), 'That sounds like you are left torn between two loyalties' (empathic response), 'What are your choices when feeling trapped in such situations at work'? (question). These are mainly situational questions and empathic acknowledgements that demonstrate the therapist's curiosity, interest and understanding of the black client's struggles.

The sequence in the line of facilitation demonstrates that the therapist is prepared to travel and meet the client in their difficulties. There is a standing away from the 'mess', rather than a meeting with the client. The deeper questions are more situational and try to get a sense of the black client's position in his workplace. Working with race and racism is a bit like working with the family. You have to understand the system, so your questions are pitched to address things systemically, such as who are the other players, what are these relationships like, who is the scapegoat, who is holding what for which members, and so on. The therapist needs to show curiosity to venture to these murky and complex places and get dirty, not just remain lily-white and unblemished at a distance! Such an approach is bound to leave your black client abandoned and not very held in their distress.

Isha: So, after you challenged the practitioner about losing her curiosity, did she find a way to work with that situation?

Aileen: Based on my support and offering her a sense of what it might feel like for somebody experiencing racism in the workplace, I asked what questions she felt she could facilitate to help the client to feel he's been heard and that she was having a sense of what he was going through.

Isha: Did you specifically talk to the supervisee about addressing the racism?

Aileen: Yes, one of the questions I asked was if he was the first black male she ever worked with. The other question I asked was how she felt about the fact that he was a black male.

Isha: So you were working with her about the interracial dynamics between them to show her that clearly you felt it was important.

Aileen: Yes, the third question I asked was how she felt when this black male client was talking about his experience of racism at the hands of his white work colleagues in the workplace, bearing in mind she was a white therapist. How did she feel? She was actually quite honest and said it was difficult to hear what he was going through, and she felt much more conscious as a white woman and being his therapist. She also felt ashamed that people still experience this kind of thing in this day and age.

What I received at that point was her gushing about her own white guilt and about what her people were still doing to black people. I just accepted that she was telling the truth, and it wouldn't help to re-shame the shamed.

Isha: That's a very useful example of how traditional theories such as person-centred, whether used in a strict way or not, are not always sufficient in helping the therapists to fill in all the missing bits.

Aileen: Yes, it can lull therapists into a false sense of security in tackling race issues. I think when a client is talking about and experiencing racism, it is usually in the midst of other people. They are not in a vacuum, hence the systemic approach. We have to know the whole structure and the whole position, so that the questions about who are the other players in the group, and what are those relationships like, as one would do if one were working in family therapy, are very important. Where is the client positioned in the group and what do they do, and do they have a voice, are all key dynamics that must be explored. So there are some key points to hold in mind when working with race and racism. One is for the therapist to maintain curiosity; the other is to explore what happens to black people's voices and positions in groups in the experience of racism; and, finally, to remember that the client does not talk about racism in a vacuum, there is usually the 'other', in other words, racism involves other people who should be brought into the frame in therapy. The practitioner has to facilitate situational questions for that to come out more fully.

Isha: So do you feel you are playing an educational role with your supervisees?

Aileen: Yes, of course. I see supervision as having three focuses – the supportive, the managerial and the educative or tutorial roles. When I use these focus points with supervisees, it is quite normal to rely on the educated/tutorial element to explain, illustrate, educate and direct the supervisee towards further reading material. I might even share my own experience of racism or an approach I may have used in my own clinical work with a white client. I remember that I once shared a personal example of a white male client who said something like, 'I mostly go out with black women because they know how to treat men.' He also went on to say that he liked the patina of black women's skin. I asked my supervisee what she thought was going on between the client and me. She said she thought he was flirting with me. I said yes, I think that's the case, but I also added that I thought he was using race in a favourable way to prove to me that he was OK as a white client, that he wasn't prejudiced against black people/black women/this black woman who was his therapist. I went on to demonstrate to my supervisee how I used my curiosity to stay with the dynamic. I told her that I wondered aloud with my white client why he needed to tell me that, why he felt he had to stipulate that he liked black women's skin. I stayed with the line of questioning by wondering aloud what he felt he was trying to achieve by sharing such intimate details about black women to his black female therapist. I also told her that I thought there was an erotic transference presenting itself for me to work with, not to ignore. All of this kind of sharing with the supervisee contributes to good educative/tutorial supervision work with issues of race and sex.

Isha: In terms of the fact that your doctorate is specifically oriented towards the internal oppressor, I wonder if any of your clients or supervisees work with this or identify it.

Aileen: Yes, I would say that for the majority of my black clients, when I raise this issue of their own internal adversary, that is, the internal enemy, and I name it as such, they understand that we are addressing the function of the internal oppressor. When I work with it, they get it. I suppose they feel relieved that it could be named, because they could get hold of it and work with it in a more focused way. So, for example when a black client of Jamaican heritage said in her session, 'I ain't want me son bring home no African woman', I was actually quite shocked to hear that. She did not want her son to be going out with 'African women'. Then when she was talking in another later session about some problems at work she said, 'The bloody coolie man think because he is head of finance he can control my CPD budget.' And you know the term coolie man is quite a pejorative term. The other thing that black clients do when they are working with a black therapist is to say something like 'you know what I mean' following the derogatory comment.

Isha: So what do you do with that when it happens?

Aileen: Well, I usually respond with a smiling face because I don't want them to think I'm taking up some smug position, and I say something like, 'I can see you are wrestling with your feelings about Africans, because on the one hand you've made an apology for not wanting to be racist, but on the other, you've given your son a clear mandate not to bring no African ouman in yow ouse'. Lapsing into Creole tends to soften the challenge, but the thrust of the challenge is still there. And, let's say the client insists, 'Yeah I mean it, I don't want no African inna mi house'. I might then say, 'Well, do you feel this is one of the struggles for us as black people and the diaspora, that we still carry prejudices or dislikes for our own people?' I would say, 'Fancy that?' I think you've got to play with the issue, and even if they are a doubting Thomas, you bet they will go home and think about the challenge.

Isha: Yes, and you kind of go onto their side while you are responding in that playful kind of way.

Aileen: Exactly. I'm very mindful of not wanting to be smug, or wanting to outsmart the client. You don't want to come across as so right on that it makes the client shut up. I'm really conscious and mindful of that.

Isha: Some British people tend to see that kind of response as being politically correct, which is not therapeutic, really.

Aileen: Exactly, and I think with black-on-black dynamics, if you don't do that playful thing and be careful, the client may feel they can't be free with you. As the black therapist working with a black client, you don't want to set yourself so apart, as you may shut them and the process down.

To sum up – the key points for challenging racism is for the therapists to maintain curiosity at all times. We appear not to have any problems being curious about and facilitating questions about such signifiers as the client's age, their marital status, whether they are gay or straight, old or young, etc. But, when it comes to race, the interest and daring to be curious is absent. Things get slid over or not mentioned at all. Curiosity dries up, and I find this very remarkable!

Alleyne (2005) suggests that 'recovery from this ongoing trauma and its present day forms of racism is to start from within. The nature of the work of inter-generational trauma is such that each group must first see to their own healing, because no group can do another's work'.

In the conclusion of her study, Alleyne (2005, p. 293) suggests that

> although limited, there is indication that negative experiences of black people's historical past are still bound up with those of their present. This is not entirely new thinking and by no means a new concept. We have only to look to such writers as Lifton (1969), who examines the impact and effects. Invisible injuries and silent witnesses of Hiroshima on its peoples, and Dale (1988), Karpf (1996) and Schaverien (1998) whose works deal powerfully with the effects of the holocaust and aspects of Jewish identity. These writers show in their different ways how collective memory with its painful imprints can continue to transmit trauma and grief through generations of an oppressed group or race of people. Schaverien's work in particular provides us with a searing analytic account of the legacy of the holocaust and Jewish identity. However, although each of these human tragedies are uniquely different, there are areas of commonality that can help us to deal more effectively with collective trauma when it has specific regard to identity, understanding of the self and the process of healing. Here I am highlighting the strong possibility that powerful memory imprints from a legacy of a painful historical past might heighten oppressive workplace experiences for black people. This inescapable past, although a distant 400 years ago, seems still to be present enough to be creating a persistent post-traumatic syndrome. Therefore, the work of throwing off the shackles of the past and emerging from the entanglement of historical briars is still an important modern day (therapeutic) task for members of the black diaspora (and other oppressed groups). It would be true to say that a reflexive identity will only begin at the point where unconscious identification and fixation with aspects of one's history cease.

History has a way of being played out in present time discourses. Having labelled slaves who tried to escape as mentally ill, a cure of whipping and removing their big toes was prescribed. Although whipping and toe removal is now illegal, a present-day symptom of this labelling is borne out in the over-representation of black people in our penal and mental health systems and the causes, diagnosis and treatment of schizophrenia applied to black mental health patients. Cognitive dissonance and rebellion against Eurocentric imposition and assimilation are too often viewed as madness.

It is not easy to face the dark, violent, turbulent history of European behaviour and still assimilate with British culture, but we must face it in order to assist healing from the damage this has caused to African peoples. If we consider how this past confusion may have influenced the psychology of black peoples today, we can see there is a lot of work to be done. Therapists need to understand the intergenerational impact of slavery and transatlantic trauma in order to create appropriate empathic responses to current-day concerns that show up in the therapeutic process. It follows that those daily experiences of racism, sexism and homophobia, to name but a few, cause re-traumatization of individuals who may already be intergenerationally impacted by racism.

Therapists working with these psychological traumas sometimes ask the following question:

> What if clients are silent about racism?

Clients' hesitation to discuss experiences of racism or abuse experienced within the black family can appear problematic during training, due to Eurocentric domination of theory, education, upbringing and training. Breaking through silences and remembering that our shadow tricksters can make us forget, go numb and disassociate us when racism is apparent is a key consideration for therapists and supervisors. This is all part of working through recognition trauma. As with Klein's depressive phase (Rycroft, 1968), the therapist's recognition trauma must be worked through to develop their confidence to congruently and empathically respond to ancestral baggage in ourselves and in our clients' presentations. A balance of challenge and support must be managed in clinical supervision, otherwise re-traumatization from racist experiences can turn individuals into permanent victims of the oppression rather than activists in the development of their own psychology. This is the nature of internalized racism.

In order to examine the impact of internalized racism, we need to transcend shame, self-blame and internalized blame. Although these powerful expressions of self-worth do matter, it is necessary to be aware that fixating on racism can also give a sense of power to the perpetrator rather than rebuild self-esteem. Therapists and supervisors must find a balance when working with clients in this area.

hooks (2003) emphasizes the importance of a healthy self-esteem for black folks, suggesting that fixating on racism exacerbates self-doubt and dehumanizing. Therefore, 'the practice of self-love is difficult for everyone in a society that is more concerned with profit than well-being, but it is the negative perceptions of blackness we are encouraged to embrace by the dominant culture. ... The issue of self-esteem is integral to self-love' (p. 19).

hooks (2003) is concerned that being a victim of racism does not mean we cannot resist it in ways that build our self-esteem. In spite of living in a predominantly white society, many individuals do build a healthy self-esteem. She uses the term 'racial terrorism' (p. 19) as a way of describing the trauma that racism instils. Contemporary racism gets piled on top of PTSS, and sometimes these layers are not recognized in a therapeutic context.

Our intergenerational make-up includes shaming as a way to intimidate and break the spirit. This hugely powerful emotion was exacerbated by slavery and colonialism. Severe beatings administered by adults to very young children are an indicator of this. Shame is a deeply disturbing human emotion that becomes triggered anew throughout the life cycle, from birth to death. Shame is by no means confined to just one time of life. During each successive, unfolding phase of development, from childhood and adolescence into adulthood and old age, there are distinctive sources of shame. It is ever present in our lives, however masked it may be. This perplexing emotion is also passed from each generation to the next; the transfer is mediated directly by critical scenes of shame which become internalized through imagery but which then are reactive and re-enacted with others (hooks, 2003, p. 37). Shame constitutes a large proportion of ancestral baggage.

Due to Eurocentric assimilation processes, many black people have learned that if they imitate white people, even their own people might treat them better. We must remember that to therapeutically challenge racism and attend to the traumas that racism instils is to raise the self-esteem of black people. Self-esteem can only be raised if we increase self-love and love who we really are. This process helps to decolonize the mind of both black and white people and heal collective dissonance. In other words heal collusion with a status quo that instils and perpetuates low self-esteem and internalized racism. Living consciously does not mean madness. Frequent monitoring and extreme caution about not internalizing white domination can sometimes create mental ill health and low self-esteem. Many black people fear they are going mad when they attempt to live consciously and identify and challenge racism, yet there is no real middle ground, because racism permeates almost every aspect of our daily lives. The guilt of letting go of our ancestral baggage may cause confusion, and we survive this.

Fakhry Davids (2011) presents an example of how the police stop him as he is trying to drive to work to see his patients. He is delayed for his work. He thinks they are stopping him because of racism. He is trying to explain that he is a professional and perhaps they will understand that he has patients waiting for him; it is only about a broken side-light on the car. The questions raised by this scenario are pertinent to responses when facing the challenge of racism. In a training group this question was raised:

> Should we as therapists challenge this man for his fantasy that the police would not stop professionals, especially for the fact that he is a professional Asian man, as opposed to an ordinary young black man?

Divisions between Asians, Africans, and African Caribbean people can become merged with trauma when racist incidents are apparent. These divisions can influence therapists' responses in a variety of ways, depending on their ethnic background and their alliances. I would believe any person who feels they are experiencing racism, whether it seems to arise from internalized racism or external racism, because often we are not believed. Racism operates towards us and then we internalize it, and this can bring out the pain we carry about past experiences of racism and other rejections. The black–Asian divide has been opened up within this question, so there is a lot to be discussed. If you home in and challenge someone about their beliefs, whether black or Asian, in terms of experiencing racism, is that empathic? We must be sensitive when listening to these experiences of racism and the client's feelings. Such experiences come first, before our philosophical ideas about racism.

Internalized racism therefore is a form of psychological distress that must be given attention in therapy. The hurt created by racism often gets left unattended because of internalized messages about complaining and because of fear on the part of the therapist. Irrespective of how confident an individual may feel, they are likely to have internalized racism at some point in their lives and this will add to periods of low self-esteem. Black children raised or educated in predominantly white settings will have most certainly internalized racism. Black children raised in black families are also likely to have internalized racism from intergenerational effects via the family, care system and educational systems (ancestral baggage). These histories are key psychological factors in therapeutic settings.

Methods of repression have been handed down intergenerationally. Strict disciplinary methods to coerce children to behave well in the face of white society are an example of this. With regards to their self-esteem, this approach to discipline can serve to pass on negative, punishing attitudes to the next generation. Lessons about appearing to be emotionally untouched and harsh in relationships with each other and white people have been passed on and can add to levels of self-worth.

It is important not to confuse low self-esteem with the impact of racism, however; therapists should always be ready to link the two. On the other hand, we must be aware that the more racism an individual harbours, this will add to lowering self-esteem. We must be aware that to engage solely with the impact of racism can create denial of the whole self and this can inhibit a healthy self-esteem.

hooks (2003) highlights Brandon's six pillars of self-esteem: (1) being true to our own principles of behaviour, keeping our word and being faithful to our promises; (2) live consciously, cultivate awareness and ask questions that make you a critical thinker; (3) self-acceptance requires that we like ourselves just the way we are, and in that liking, we decide stuff we want to change; (4) self-responsibility means we are willing to correct and be accountable for our actions, for what we say and do; (5) self-assertiveness lets us practise honouring our needs, wants, values, and judgements and find the right time to give them expression; (6) to live purposefully, we look for the places of meaning in our lives – this could be family bonds, working for a cause, or practising kindness and compassion in everyday life. hooks adds to this content the need to heal the soul that has been stolen or exploited due to capitalism (p. 212).

Given the huge challenge that racism presents to the psyche, it is not surprising that the above principles may be difficult to maintain. As a result of this, many black people turn to spirituality to heal their soul from the impact of colonization. Slavery invaded the mind. The trauma left behind is of such magnitude that thinking about it is still defended against in order to maintain psychic integration. A brutally harsh regime of fear and humiliation was installed. House discipline, stolen names and emotional castration dislocated African populations and invaded the mind. Fletchman Smith (2011) suggests that certain 'middle passage' behaviours emanated from this tragedy. I believe that we must consider a transformation from middle passage to rights of passage, rather than initiation by fear.

According to Fletchman Smith (2011),

In accepting slavery the individual comes to thinking that he is regulated solely by something external with a sadistic power. It is the opposite of feeling oneself free to become self-regulating.

It is a mental condition that is still very prevalent. If an individual is really stuck with a belief in the sadistic power of the external world over him, and in his total helplessness to change that situation, then his life is likely to be a life of mental slavery and severely limited. (pp. 15, 16)

This writer confirms that understanding and exploring the intergenerational context of internalized racism means exploring a missing history and filling in the gaps left out by Eurocentric theory. It seems that when people are given information about this aspect of the history, even very carefully, it is hard for them to receive it, hold on to it, make sense of it and experience it fully at a feeling level. Therefore, a gap is left where history should be. This is the nature of the trauma (Fletchman Smith, 2011, p. 22).

Summary

It is not generally recognized that the intergenerational impact of racism, colonialism and slavery has created forms of post-traumatic stress syndrome. Therefore, therapists have not fully developed ways to approach the multidimensional influences of PTSS in black individuals. This aspect of PTSS creates self-hatred, hatred of skin colour and hair texture, and sometimes hatred of other black people.

A healthy self-esteem will incorporate positive aspects of ethnic heritage and equality. Racial integration has its benefits and pitfalls. It can be beneficial in challenging society to confront its prejudices and tainted history, as racial equality is often not practised and often ignored. Behavioural signs of racism often silence the victim, and on many occasions support is limited. As Alleyne (2005, p. 12) points out, this aspect of industrial and corporate life can sometimes devastate self-esteem.

Trying to overcome past trauma and the enforced dissociation linked to slavery and racism may be played out in a collective or individual need that can no longer be met. It may be difficult to see this clearly. Internalized racism can be influenced by intergenerational attitudes and behaviours and also by contemporary behaviour such as workplace racism. Early hurts from racism add to post-traumatic slave syndrome and intergenerational influences. This is an ongoing process that must be addressed. Low self-esteem and cognitive dissonance are features of internalized racism, and therapists and supervisors must be aware of the importance of reflecting on both these aspects of black psychology.

Pointers:

- Be aware of and support reflection on negative messages about identity. What gets listened to? What gets dismissed? What becomes taboo?
- Facilitate the process of working with negative stereotypical black Western archetypes and ancestral baggage.
- Give particular attention to individual unique experiences relevant to being black/white/Asian/mixed heritage.
- Confront and process the 'don't go there' signals.
- Become ungagged and assist clients to find their voice about racist experiences.
- Explicitly acknowledge experiences of racism, internalized racism and intergenerational trauma.
- Create and engage in a healthy supervision process that engages with the consequences of slavery and colonization, assimilation and internalized racism.
- Processing PTSS is about the therapist and supervisor developing their awareness of the impact of slavery on individuals. It is not about educating the client; it is about holding the space compassionately, with this in mind.
- Challenge the one-dimensional approach of Eurocentric theory.

8

Working with Recognition Trauma

Recognition trauma
Memoir, imagination
Intangible figment
Faded occurrence

A thorn in the side
Momentary choice
To cling on,
Or to not cling
Release or deny

A vision or mirage
Over whelming
Under influence

History inscribed
Internally tattooed
Hot irons tremble
Fleecing minds
Contemporary signs

Unmade identities
Forgiving God
As God forgives

Happening then
Happening now
Shame lingers
As cobweb
On branded hearts

Shame his story,
Shame her story
Shame is the story

An imprinted ankle
A shackled throat
Transgenerational
Poltergeist
Forgotten past

Present in process
Healing hatred
Will it cease
Can it erase

Songs of praise
Halting voices
Numbing the terror
Not yet rested

Isha Mckenzie-Mavinga, 2014

I previously introduced the concept of recognition trauma, based on identified responses to black issues. As expressed in the poem above feelings of fear, guilt and shame have been identified in relation to acknowledging that the experience of racism is a valid and recognizable situation embedded in the mutual history of black, Asian and white citizens. These feelings about racism can also block the individual from self-expression, causing self-doubt, depression and low self-esteem. In therapeutic settings where the emphasis is on sharing emotions, inappropriate responses to recognition trauma can block communication and cause rupture in the therapeutic alliance.

In this chapter, I will unpack the concept of recognition trauma and explore the use of this concept in the client therapist and supervisor experience. Ways of supporting an open dialogue about related feelings in supervision must be found so that clients can be supported through their own experiences of racism and recognition trauma that may often lay dormant in their psyche. In some situations, a therapist may need their supervisor to take a risk to go with them into this territory and support them to emerge from their own recognition trauma and the recognition trauma of their client. Most importantly, let us reflect on the experience of a receiver of therapeutic support. In this chapter, the case of a black/African heritage client will be reviewed.

I want to discuss the challenge of racism in the relationship between the therapist and the supervisor, and how they can go through this process for the benefit of the client. I will focus on practice and the reflective process, and on how situations of racism and challenge, inaction and terror can sometimes be evoked by recognition trauma. Recognition trauma can manifest in the therapeutic process and depends on the internalized impact of racism. Here are a few examples of how this can manifest:

- Clients not explicitly naming their experience of racism
- Therapists not taking issues of racism to their supervision
- Silence in response to the mention of racism
- Denial of racism
- Deflecting from a dialogue about racism
- Feelings of rage and guilt about processing racism.

Isabel Figueira (in Payne, 2008), when addressing supervision of dance movement psychotherapy, explains that:

'Sometimes we cannot nullify the real distance between personal experiences, we cannot cross the transcultural gap and it is better to acknowledge that there is a difference than trying to ignore it. Rita's worry about proving that she was not racist was actually preventing her from facing the real difference that existed between these boys. Rita was finally able, in the third term, to make interpretations where skin colour differences were recognised and, as Miguel (a white boy in a predominantly black class) heard his difference verbalised and accepted, he also found himself more capable of playing with the others, who eagerly integrated him into an improved band of rap. Their final sessions were spent dancing and making up songs, these words, in indirect and symbolic ways, talked about being isolated or being part of group, of being different and yet accepted.' (p. 86)

This supervisee's recognition trauma, manifest in a common fear about being called racist, was eventually worked through and the client made progress. There are several important concerns to be faced when exploring how the challenges of racism are played out in the therapeutic process and in the role of the supervisory process. First, we must take the risk to name racism and consider its pervasive role in damaging the psyche; otherwise, key areas of resolving and healing aspects of recognition trauma and the collective impact of racism may be missed. To assist reflection on this process, these questions can be asked:

- Am I, as a therapist, approaching in a responsible, supportive way the impact of trauma or ongoing intergenerational or contemporary racism?
- Do I consider the importance of my own ethnicity in communication with clients?
- How do I raise the challenges of racism in my clinical supervision?
- What responses do I get when I am able to present achievements or concerns about racism in practice, training or CPD?
- How does the supervisory process allow space for considering the challenges of racism?
- If my supervisor or I do not openly discuss the challenges of racism, what are we doing between us and towards our clients' self-esteem?
- What role does recognition trauma play in the process of self-discovery and understanding the dynamics of the therapeutic relationship?

In the process of answering these questions, therapists may be concerned about their own emotional welfare and their own mental health when examining an area that has generally been submerged and silenced. They may become concerned about focusing on one area of oppression, and they may also be concerned about harping on from the position of being a victim of racism.

To start this process, it is necessary to have an agreement that clinical supervision will enable a self-development and professional development process that addresses the challenges of racism in practice. Therapeutic practices without these considerations are colluding with racism and may block the relational process of therapist, supervisor and client in this area. This would be seen as counter to anti-oppressive practice and perpetrating the oppression of racism. The supervisory alliance should include openness and clarity about working with the impact of oppression and the silencing nature of racism.

It must be recognized that this commitment must also be considered in relation to black and Asian therapists who may have had less opportunity to be supported in this area, due to institutional racism and marginalization of their needs in training and therapeutic practice.

When facing the challenge of racism in therapeutic practice, we must primarily consider the role and experience of individuals within the oppressed group. In most cases, it would be clear that the individual with brown skin is more likely than not to have had experience of and internalized a degree of racism in their life, but we cannot take this position for granted. To what degree the individual may feel able to articulate their experience may not be apparent unless they feel safe enough to talk or express creatively their experience of racism. The therapist can only speculate that racism would be present in the client's life and that this would have influenced their mental and emotional disposition. Speculation is preparation in the context of racism. Without this, there may be collusion with racism.

At whatever level may be apparent, the therapist is placed in the role of therapeutically holding the impact of racism on the client, be it silently and internally, impactful or expressed openly. A student raises this question pertinent to therapeutic holding:

> Should I acknowledge diversity and sameness when initially setting up sessions with a client?

The answer to such a question always depends on the integrity of the therapist and the appropriateness of the situation on meeting the client for the first time. Of course, this question may be more relevant if a client has specifically requested to work with a therapist whose background and ethnicity are similar.

Many of my own clients specifically request to work with me because they want to work with a black woman. There is more to having a black identity than just skin colour and the experience of racism, and for this reason these clients are aware of their request to work with me. I ask these clients a question about this choice: 'Having chosen me as your therapist, what expectation do you have of me as a black woman?' The answers are varied. Some have said they 'want to explore particular aspects of their cultural and racialized identity'. Others have said they 'want to understand the intergenerational context of their current concerns about the impact of racism on their lives' – in other words, how internalized racism affects them. Others want some self understanding and healing from the impact of racism and marginalization within their life experience.

These are some examples: a very light-skinned black woman became aware of her black heritage when she was rejected by her white fiancé;

a black lesbian felt she was experiencing both racism and homophobia and she wanted somebody to help her make sense of and move on from these multidimensional oppressions. Some clients just want to sit with a black therapist and work on other areas of concern, knowing they do not have to explain their experiences of racism.

Some clients request a black-on-black approach because they have become aware of not being fully listened to or believed by white therapists or their peers in the workplace. The knowledge that some black clients may want initial familiarity with their therapist based on colour lines does not mean that a black therapist necessarily understands the impact of racism on themselves or their client. The situations identified above all relate in some way to recognition trauma, because they are all linked to the client's recognition of the impact of racism on their lived experiences. As in Jung's (1969) suggestion about exposing archetypes, I would see this as the beginnings of exposing black Western archetypes in order to heal the impact of racism on individuals.

Noticing the choices that they have made to work with the challenges of racism provides some context for black therapists in the initial stages. The approach that a black therapist may use will depend on how confident they feel about using a black empathic approach with the client. This will also be influenced by the black therapist's level of re-emergence from his or her own experiences of racism. In many situations, black therapists may not have had an opportunity during their training to engage with the challenges of racism and how they impact relationships between black people. For myself, I had to depend on my life experiences and reading about racism as CPD outside of my training. Support for working therapeutically between black people has not been forthcoming. We have had to support each other to draw on resources outside of training and make it up as we go along. We are developing more appropriate models for this work as we gain experience and confidence in the way we approach the challenge of racism.

We are not alone in this humongous task, but the feeling of isolation that a black empathic approach can evoke has at times made me question my own professional position and where my approach fits with the psychodynamic training that I received. Students continue to go through systems of training whilst doubting their ability to draw on knowledge gained from their experiences of racism and not hide from the impact on themselves and their clients. This position can create a particular kind of low self-esteem in black and Asian therapists, whatever their background experiences.

I have learned from this to develop a deeper level of trust in myself, because having integrated my approach and risked working in ways that support black clients' needs, the results have been rewarding. It boils down to giving permission to transcend the powerful influence of white Eurocentric power and traditional theories that underpin therapy training.

Alleyne (2005) explains the process of internalized racism:

A general finding in this study has indicated that although workplace oppression for black workers was not overtly about race and cultural differences, interpersonal conflict in black/white relations were frequently set off by subtle, silent and 'not so easy to pin down' incidents. Such incidents targeted a racial or cultural signifier of the black person's identity. These incidents ranged from those that were usually no more than minor annoyances, some unintentional and intentional, to more major incidents of racial assaults that were deeply painful and harmful. The unrelenting nature of these silent conflicts and the subsequent protective stances adopted by black workers to defend against further hurt, eventually wore them down. This particular observation was so common amongst the sample group I interviewed that it not only became clear that external oppressive forces were at work, but that there were other factors involved in this complex picture. Respondents' stories pointed to workplace cultures that covertly fostered collusive management structures when dealing with difficulties involving black workers. … Prejudices, projections, inter-generational wounds and the vicissitudes from our historical past are all aspects of this inner tyrant – the internal oppressor. They are kept alive through the transgenerational transmission of trauma.

I regularly witnessed black clients presenting with ill-health arising from prolonged and sustained workplace difficulties. These concerns were of a particular nature and frequently affected such things as physical health, self-esteem and opportunities for professional advancement. Such situations occurred mainly within predominantly white-managed structures and highlighted problematic relations within these setups. (pp. 5, 12)

In the review presented below, Carlana, a Jamaican woman who presents with workplace oppression, shows how she made use of her choice to work through her recognition trauma with a black therapist.

Isha: You chose to see me because I'm a black woman, so I would like to ask you how you felt helped in terms of a black woman exploring the challenge of racism in your life.

Carlana: Firstly, for me I needed to have a therapist that had an identity like myself, and that means a black woman that works in an environment that can be quite challenging. The majority of my counsellors have been white, but apart from you I did have one black woman. She evidently understood my needs as a black woman.

Isha: What was your age then?

Carlana: I was about 30.

Isha: And what was your age when you came to see me?

Carlana: 45, I think. The age would have been different for me and my problems.

Isha: When you came to see me, what were you looking for in me as a black woman?

Carlana: That's a difficult question – a mirror. The mirror, that mirrors me and mirrors you. So, therefore, you would have experienced some form of racism in your career. I think only another black individual could understand or recognize what I was going through. I do not want to generalize because I believe a foreigner could understand my problem. Someone who is non-British could recognize it, but I don't think they would have the confidence to understand in depth. They might understand in a different way but not as a black woman.

Isha: So you mean somebody from a different place but not necessarily a black person would understand to a degree, but they may not understand what it is like to be a black person in the UK. So when you came to me did you realize that you were actually experiencing racism?

Carlana: Yes, I think so, but I don't think I was able to pinpoint it; it may be denial – knowing it's there but needing someone to identify, and you were able to identify it. I don't like to identify something as being racist because it makes me feel that's a cop out, an excuse, that's what all black people do anyway – if they've got an issue, it has to be a racist being. So I was trying my hardest not to identify the situation as being racist. I think whether it's fear that black people are already always labelling an issue as racist.

Isha: At the time what did you fear might happen if you did acknowledge it was racism? If you had been able to name it, what would have happened?

Carlana: If I had named it, I would have been bullied more. That's my fear – if you speak out, your colleagues would then have more power to bully me because I was the only black woman in my team and I did not feel able to express as an individual how I felt. My fear was that I would be stigmatized and bullied even more and I would be pushed out slowly in terms of how they would identify me. They would have picked at my work in order to hide their cowardice.

Isha: When you came to me it seemed as though you were carrying that fear of challenging what was going on as racism. It sounded as though you felt you had nowhere to go with it in your daily work and when you were out with your colleagues. That was your daily experience.

Carlana: Yes, what happened here is really strange because if you go back into slavery, I had this discussion with one of my friends, where black people were called 'niggers' and 'house slaves' and they were fairly privileged. The outside slaves would know they had privileges. In all of us, genetically, to compensate what you tend to do is play with your colleagues. If I play it out, if I play the fool, if I play a plan, if I play stupid, if I play the clan, if I play as 'help me, please, master', they feel superior. Because I act stupid then they would ignore turning a job against me that I could not do, and if I choose to go out with them and act the fool and act stupid they felt that I was all right. An individual made a statement about being gay and she said if she went to Jamaica she would be killed. I was shocked because this person was stereotyping and suggesting that all black people don't like gay people.

Isha: So you were expected to collude with that stereotype because you are a black woman of Jamaican heritage; that must have been hurtful.

Carlana: Yeah, because it's annoying because you're generalizing.

Isha: And you challenged it.

Carlana: Yes.

Isha: When you challenged it, what happened?

Carlana: The individual was not happy and it got into an argument. To this individual, yeah, that's what black people do, yet, pardon me, you went to Jamaica and came back saying you had a good time. Did anyone gay-bash you? But you are standing here trying to make out that all black people are gay-bashers.

Isha: When you came to see me did I ever use the term internalized racism?

Carlana: Yes, you did.

Isha: I think you saw that as a new term because you seemed to be carrying a lot and you felt you had to hold on to it because you were not listened to and you did not feel safe enough to even talk to your manager about it. So I used that term and tried to explain and give you an idea of what had possibly happened to you. Was it useful for you?

Carlana: Yes. I went back home and looked it up to get a full understanding of what you meant at that time. So, in fact, that word was able to empower me because I did not know the existence of the word.

Isha: There were many times when you seemed to be relieved that I had named racism for you and that we were connecting on the challenges that you are experiencing. Then there were other things that you wanted to talk about in the therapy. You were having a home situation too. On top of that, there was a racism-at-work situation that was stressing you. Then you had your past that was coming up and the secret that you had not shared, and it was stressing you.

Carlana: Yeah, I didn't talk about it much and it did open up.

Isha: So what do you think about the work we've done together?

Carlana: For me, at that time, it felt like I was being bullied from every corner and abused in that triangle. I was being abused in every aspect.

Isha: You were feeling abused in your relationship and feeling abused at work. At times, it seemed to confuse you because it seemed so much that it was overwhelming.

Carlana: Yeah, and I guess that's me – I thought all that was normal. I suppose if you are brought up in an abusive situation, it becomes normal anyway because you internalize pain. What is very interesting, the pain of your soul and your spirit has not been identified and people see pain as someone who is suffering from pain, their body language of someone who is screaming from pain, but nobody sees your soul and your spirit. I was born in it, grown in it, nurtured in it and still am in it.

Isha: So there was a place where your internal pain was not seen, and you put on a mask. You put it on because it helped you to cope, and it also kept people at a distance from you. And you were carrying all that pain inside of you when you came to see me. We began to look at some of that, and what was also part of that was that within your family there were secrets, and you held on to the

*secrets and you were told by your family not to say anything. That also seemed
to be the way that you were coping with the pain in your life at that time. To
say nothing and to act clownish would help you because, in a way, that is what
you were taught.*

Carlana: Yeah, and to be an actress, you act out somebody else, and
I suppose I have lived that life often. (Laughs)

*Isha: So how do you feel about the work you have done since then, and has it
helped you with the challenges of racism you have faced?*

Carlana: I'll tell you something – it helped me to realize racism does
not exist just in white-on-black; it exists in black-on-black, white-on-
white, regardless. The only thing that is painful and still quite painful
is that it doesn't matter as a black woman how hard you train and you
study, you will always come up against institutional racism, and the
same happens for the black man. I think that we, as black people, as
a whole suffer internally a lot. And I think that growing up and coming from our families and ancestors, it appears that we are allowed to
express how we feel, but actually we are not. The poems I listen to,
doing my education, my counselling course, working, this appears that
we are allowed to speak as you feel and express, but it is not as easy as
it appears to be.

Isha: So what stops it if that is the case?

Carlana: I think ignorance, people's lack of understanding. Unless
people experience what we experience, they will not have any understanding. Some people who do experience what you experience, they
lash out and become bitter. If you become bitter, people ignore what
you have to say, and maybe that's why I try my best to have laughter. That's my way of survival, isn't it? Since I've had you as a therapist, I don't think I've ever cried – I've always laughed, and that's quite
interesting.

Isha: So you think that laughter is a form of crying?

Carlana: Yeah, because people are not used to it. In society, we are
used to tears, but laughter is also a stream of tears.

Isha: So where did you develop laughter instead of tears?

Carlana: As a little girl, I think. I think it's because my first abuser, I
remember at the age of five. I think when I told a member of my family
I laughed. It almost feels like a dream to me because I'm never sure

whether it's actually real. Because the other day I found that it was actually real and I had to ask how did I present that at the age of five? Did I present crying? Was I laughing? What was it? My aunt said I came in laughing and said, 'Aunti, Aunti, I just sucked this man's willie, ain't that funny?' I was shocked when she said, 'that is how you presented it, and you came in laughing. You were a very free-spirited child, so you did not see that was wrong. You came in and talked like it was normal, but to the adults obviously it was not normal.' Then as I got older, I had imaginary friends in my mind. My imaginary friends were angels and I believed in God. God is often unseen, isn't it? So growing up as a child you had to have an imagination to believe in God, because how can you believe in something that to my eyes was not there. So that means as a child growing up in a family that was heavy on believing in God, I had to have an imagination to believe in God. So that imagination kept me warm and kept me in laughter.

Isha: Laughter seems to be a feature of our heritage as well as in your family, and I wonder if you saw anyone in your family laughing instead of crying.

Carlana: Yeah, one of my uncles, actually; he was such a clown, always laughing a lot, and as a child I used to always wonder, are you really that happy? When I got older, I do the same thing. One of my friends said that man who died, Robin Williams, he reminded her of me because he laughed a lot (Laughs). As black people though, I grew up in Croydon and I was born in 1996. I was going to school and I wondered why teachers did not like people, and I remember getting my first whip because I did not eat the dinner. We were not allowed to refuse food, and I was sent to the head teacher. The teacher whipped me and I smiled, and he whipped me again and he said, 'How dare you smile.' Then I smiled till I went home and I told my mum and my family. I never forget because my uncle dragged me back at the school, and, because he was a man, he went to the school to fight. They called the police. All I remember is a lot of police.

Isha: So all that fuss happened because again you were being abused in school.

Carlana: Yeah, yeah, so I just think growing up in an area where you're not liked because of the colour of your skin. There are two ways: either you grow anger, OK, and I mean militant anger, or you kind of think, how am I going to get these people – you play the Masters game and you act stupid, and you laugh a lot, and when you laugh a lot people do not see the pain.

Isha: So you have talked about this as a family trait, but it is a conditioned habit of yours to keep you sane, really.

Carlana: Yeah, yeah.

Isha: So when you were laughing, were you aware that you were doing it to stop the pain?

Carlana: Yeah, yeah.

Isha: You were aware because you hurt at the same time; when you were laughing you are still hurting.

Carlana: I laugh a lot and people don't know, do they? You don't know what I'm thinking now, do you?

Isha: I am sure you are experiencing a great deal of pain going over this again.

Carlana: And I don't know if I feel pain; it becomes like the film.

Isha: Like a movie.

Carlana: You know, it doesn't really go away, does it; it's just something you play over and over again. So what is the point in me getting angry with it, if anything, the me now gets angry, not the past. It's me now trying to be real.

Isha: So through the therapy you have received, you are experiencing yourself differently – you said, 'the me now'.

Carlana: Yeah, in my last therapy the group one did not work for me. I think, if anything, it really made me realize, wow the mask was good, but the truth of my pain was there. It's easier for the therapist. It allowed the therapist to sit back and watch the dynamic of the group and allow the group to counsel each other. That is why I felt drained out of my energy because I do that every day in my job and in my home and in my family life. For me, coming there sorting other people's lives out was not what I needed. You could actually see yourself in the dynamic and I tried my best to keep my mask on and smile, and I couldn't do it any longer. I remember the therapist said to me as there was an argument in the group and it exploded like third world war to me. There were two black women, one black guy and one white woman, and it was too much of a mirror.

Isha: A mirror of what?

Carlana: I think the mirror of me in therapy was kind of different, but it was our culture and our cultures actually clashed. As calm as I tried to be, keep that mask, and I could not keep it. The therapist was very shocked. It was that I usually smiled, and suddenly she saw another side of me.

Isha: So it sounds like that group helped you to take the mask off, and you said it didn't work for you.

Carlana: It didn't work because I was too emotional. I had too much going on at home stuff, the racism was still there at work – so I came to the beginning of the triangle with you, and then I was stuck in a group. There was no longer a triangle; it was every angle. I could not contain no more, the true Carla actually reared her head and I think the therapists thought, 'Shit, this woman has done a lot of anger.' I wasn't angry in terms of 'F you'; it was logical and to the point.

Isha: Cool anger.

Carlana: Oh yeah, whereas the other woman she lashed out, she shouted, she swore, and the therapist looked at me like, 'you're the worst one, Carlana'. So I then thought, on reflection, I was not ready to release the real Carlana.

Isha: So then what happened?

Carlana: I was already seeing someone one-to-one. She was a white woman, actually; she reminded me a bit of you because I guess I was missing you, well, missing the therapy that we had. She reminded me of you because she was calmer and she helped me to identify things and I felt safe. I did not feel safe in the group, and I felt that with her support, she said give it a try and I thought, okay.

Isha: This time around you saw a white woman and initially you had asked for a black woman and you saw me, so after being in therapy with a white woman you then felt safe. What made you feel safe?

Carlana: At that point, I did not want to mirror the mirror in terms of my culture. Because we black women have a lot of challenge in our lives; it's not the person, it's the therapy. In the group, a black person felt like my bully cousin, and her attitude felt like that. I did not really look at the therapist's colour; I note that her personality reminded me of you. She was gentle and calm and she said, 'Let me name these identities for you.'

Isha: How did this help you with the racism in your life?

Carlana: I talked about it, and I said to her, 'I know you are a white woman, and as a black woman, I experience racism every day in my life.' I told her, but strangely enough, she has not made me feel that racism is in the room. She asked me how it felt. I said to her that when I was in the group I could feel that they were very judgemental – I sensed in the body language. With her, she named calmly, and I have learned over the past few years that it is not all about race. It is truly about people's background and their personality and character and their baggage and their grief. She helped me, like you, in terms of trying to put down the mask. But it is difficult because I cannot put down the mask one hundred per cent.

Isha: No, because you have had this mask since you were small. So how do you feel about the real Carlana that you are more in touch with now?

Carlana: I feel more safe. The real Carlana does not always have to agree to do things. I feel I am on a journey and I am able to say no. That may not mean nothing to anyone, but it means a lot to me.

Isha: Um, it sure does.

Carlana: Yes, I feel that I've had to say yes and be in agreement. I think I learned that from you in the beginning, especially with the particular situation about me and somebody I was seeing. With my therapist, I named it that he was one of my abusers in my past life. It made me sad, but how come I could have known it, felt it, but ignored it.

Isha: Because you were not fully conscious of it at the time.

Carlana: Yeah, that's what she was saying. So, if anything, that situation allowed Carlana to try and take off the mask.

Isha: Well done; you have come a long way.

Carlana: Yeah. I still have a long way to go.

Isha: It's been, what, four years now since you started therapy?

Is there anything else you would like to say about how that has been for you before we finish? The interview is really about how you have been supported to cope with racism. Your therapy started at that point – racism is what made you come.

Carlana: To be fair, therapy saved me – it gave me power. I was helped to reflect, look at it, bring it back, name it and try to find a way to get out of it.

Isha: I remember one of the things I first challenged you about was coming into the room and wanting to talk about me and take care of me.

Carlana: Yeah, yeah.

Isha: It was very hard for you not to do that. But you started to take yourself seriously at that point, and I saw how you grew through it. You have worked hard at this.

Carlana: Yeah, yeah, it was really hard.

Isha: It was hard for you, and I can see how you've grown through it and how different you are now, so well done. It seems as though it has been worth it for you.

Carlana: No, no, it has – it's a pity that you went off, but I had a foundation and you were my foundation, and that is why I came today.

Isha: Ah, thank you.

Carlana: I have spoken about you to my new therapist. She asked if I really want to see you for this review. I said 'yes' and she asked why. I said, 'She felt like a mother', so to me, if this enhances your book it makes sense to talk to you again.

In this review of my work with Carlana, many facets of recognition trauma were expressed. Carlana experienced early intergenerational trauma, humiliation, disassociation, multidimensional oppressions and institutional racism. I was reminded of the times where I struggled with my responses to her story. Outwardly she presented as jolly and sociable, with concern and care about me when she arrived at sessions. She would come bouncing into the room smiling and upbeat. On many occasions, her husband and father of her three children, who were now grown but living, had driven her to the venue. This confused me, as she had given me descriptions of her husband's drug-taking and emotional violence towards her. She would frequently inform me that she gives as good as she gets, and he has never hit her. Many of the early sessions were about her husband's erratic behaviour and the attitudes of colleagues towards her at work. I was also confused when she came into sessions joking around, as though she was having a lot of fun and things were okay in her world.

One of the first things I noticed was that her checking me when she arrived seemed to mean I had to be all right for her to share the load that she had been carrying for most of her early life. As we got to know each other, the impact of intergenerational scars and ancestral baggage became clear. When we started to build an alliance, I took the challenge to find out about what this meant for her because I was feeling uncomfortable that she couldn't settle before making comments about me and checking how I was feeling. It became clear that she felt a duty to take care of the adults to make it safe for her. These behavioural traits demanded some congruence from me, because I could feel the pull to politely respond to her enquiries as part of the alliance-building. The pull was to be flattered or assure her that I was fine.

The first turning point was when I named racism in helping her to clarify the stress that she was undergoing at work. Carlana expressed relief, as though she had been given permission to use the term racism. It appeared to me that she was aware that she was experiencing racism at work, but felt she had no power to challenge her experience of racist behaviour.

I became aware that Carlana's feelings about racism were sitting on top of other feelings about sexism, controlling behaviour towards her from her husband, and trauma from early sexual abuse.

It soon became clear that I was facing a woman who had pushed down inside of her a lot of pain and that she had created clowning behaviour patterns that she assumed would disguise the powerful feelings associated with her experiences. It felt very much to me as though she was on the edge of the cliff and I was hanging there with her. This metaphor that I described to Carlana became fundamental to the work of safely lowering her onto her feet, where at least she could notice how lost outside of herself she had become. I later became aware of a black Western archetype that was useful in understanding her behavioural mask as the jester-type entertainer, behaviour based on the role enacted by Africans in the master's presence during slavery – a way of coping with this brutality on a daily basis, whilst interacting with the household and overseers.

Once we had uncovered the masking behaviour, Carlana began sharing her story of sexual abuse and rape within the family and being silenced by her mother and grandmother. It became clear that at the heart of her pain about emotional abuse and racism from colleagues and abuse from her husband lay a deep intergenerational wound laced with taboo, and she had been silenced.

Carlana's recognition trauma was multidimensional, layered with recognition about early sexual experiences and silencing that had gagged her and forced unnatural behaviour patterns in order to cope with the trauma of her past. As a receiver of ongoing forms of abuse such as racism and domestic violence, she had drawn on the only coping skill she knew, that of controlling her despair and isolation by being the centre of attention and performing the role of an entertainer. In doing so, she could entertain me in a way of trying to gain some safety for what she wanted to heal and have witnessed and access her feelings.

The instability that I was experiencing seemed to be transference of her chaos and trauma into the consulting space. Although I became aware of this, it did not seem appropriate to talk analytically in Carlana's sessions. I took this approach because I felt interpretations might further distance her from the connections needed to create safety and address her trauma. I tentatively shifted from an alliance of friendship influenced by Carlana's approach to me, to one of showing her warmth and sincerity as a mother with open arms. This may have acted as a contradiction to the isolation, distancing and ignoring as collusion between her abusers that she had experienced as a young child within a black family, also being silenced by racism and the taboo of incest.

Working with the challenge of racism that Carlana experienced in her workplace was only one aspect of her recognition trauma. She knew that she was experiencing institutional racism, but within her workplace she had never felt able to name her awareness of this situation. She became the staff clown, joking at their comments, and she found herself unable to convey to her manager in a congruent manner what she was going through and the support she needed. This meant that any effort she made to draw attention to her difficulties at work was ignored. Consequently, she worked long hours without breaks, rarely took time off, and additional tasks were given to her because she seemed to be coping and clearly portrayed the strong black woman stereotype. Underneath all this, she was disintegrating and becoming exhausted and burned out, causing migraines that she tried to ignore whilst she was at work. Leaving work to recover from feeling unwell was unheard of, as she was afraid this would draw additional negative attention. At times, she arrived late to her sessions because she was being asked to take on tasks that overran the end of her working day.

I could see very clearly how she was impacted by institutional racism, and I was aware that these were my feelings and I needed to be a rock that she could cling to whilst noticing how fragile she had become. In summary, this was a fragile black woman trying to hold down past and present humiliation of abuse and racism, and 'don't discharge' messages.

In the above situation, clarity about my own level of assimilation into white Eurocentric theory acted as a mechanism for actively addressing the client's cultural diversity and recognizing the risk of misinterpretation about experiences of racism. The supervisory process needs to have an agreement that Eurocentric interpretation of African/Caribbean people's behaviour or experiences must not be the sole response, and that deeper reflection of the impact of racism and understanding of cultural connotations must be thought through. Overcoming the fears and limitations that recognition trauma can evoke is an essential element of this. One essential element of working black-on-black is to remember that whilst we are working with the impact of racism, we may also be working with diversity between us as black people.

Charura (in Lago, 2011) places an emphasis on understanding the transformational process and identity shifts for people of African/ Caribbean and Asian heritage adjusting to life in the UK. This awareness extends to a willingness to understand the power issues within these groups and the potential danger of being ostracized or rejected if individuals do not show conformity.

Recognition trauma can play a role in creating anxiety underlying the supervisory relationship. The fears and fantasies of both the supervisor and the supervisee can mask feelings of being scrutinized and inadequate about the challenge of racism in therapy. Racism also tends to influence how both parties view each other. The levels at which individuals experience racism can seem intolerable once they are on the surface, and there is a need to explore the process of feelings about this phenomenon.

Lago (2011) asserts that therapists have a number of varied responses, sensations, emotions, thoughts and fantasies that usually have meaning in relation to the client's material, no matter what therapeutic approach they are using. This is the reason why clinical supervision must be scrutinized. These responses cannot be seen as mere projections from the client to the therapist; they are integral to the relational process and the joint communication and therapeutic gaze. On the challenge of racism, Lago proposes: 'It is always good practice to consider whether one's being white has any bearing on these responses' (p. 101).

Exploring this process may test the commitment to the relationship of the supervisor and supervisee. This testing period will require both supervisor and supervisee to draw on their congruence and integrity about their own reflective process and the impact of racism. Both parties will be influenced by their levels of assimilation and how this part of their personal development can impact their willingness to scrutinize the challenge of racism in their work. Valuing each other's role in this process and their own process of recognition trauma is important to the evolution of this phase in therapeutic work.

Shohet and Wilmot (in Dryden and Thorne, 1991) clearly state that the priority for both therapist and supervisor should be to explore the process of their working together and that the issues become a welcome opportunity to work through this relationship. They take the view that anxiety in supervisory relationships can be hidden underneath the issues being discussed. They propose:

> So far we know that anxiety, power, assessment and history can impede the supervisory relationship. Ability and willingness to handle conflict is also a very important factor in this relationship. Again each side will bring a history of this from other relationships. In an interesting paper, Moskowitz and Rupert (1983) cite many studies on the importance of the relationship. In one study they quote, none of the trainees openly confronted their supervisor and discussed the difficulties in their relationship. The most common method of coping was through spurious compliance. Trainees often closely monitored their communication and concealed pertinent information such as their personal feelings. (p. 92)

Awareness of these blocks in supervisory relationships is vital to working with the challenge of racism. If there is an agreement about what the supervision process entails, then supervisees and supervisors can show willingness to explore the challenge of recognition trauma and the impact of racism in client work. The goals of supervisees and supervisors may be impacted by unconscious processes and internalized racism.

The essence of transcultural supervision

I believe that when scrutinizing the responses of the therapist in a situation where the client is black or Asian and the therapist and supervisor is black, Asian, or white, recognition trauma will be present. In addition, power relationships between white therapists and black clients may need to be considered. Guilt and shame, denial of the negative impact of racism, rupture in the therapeutic space and avoidance of the challenge may be facets of engaging with the process of recognition trauma. In addition, supervisors and supervisees may need to examine whether complicity or challenge is happening. If the supervisor is white or the therapist is white, their hierarchical position in the class system and dynamics of racism in relation to client work need to be considered.

Clinical supervision should be a place to contemplate black issues and the challenge of racism. It may be difficult to address racism without re-emergence from the trauma of racist experiences, and this is part of processing recognition trauma. A system of supervisory process is created by both supervisees and supervisors, and it is the responsibility of both to explore and recognize whether their responses to the challenge of racism create a safe, engaging platform for working through recognition trauma and associated fantasies and fears about racism.

If the therapist or supervisor is black or Asian, their assimilation processes will impact on how they respond to the challenge of racism in their work. This is an area of importance, because the developmental processes of black and Asian therapists often get missed when white therapists and supervisors inadvertently withdraw their support because of their own recognition trauma. Not being trained in this area is not an excuse to not engage with recognition trauma.

Ryde (in Lago, 2011), on the impact of whiteness within the intersubjective field of the therapy, suggests that

> maybe behind many of the therapist responses to black clients is a sense of guilt and shame. Guilt at our relative good fortune in being white and shame at our failure to really address the issues of any quality, both in our lives in general and in the therapy. We may also not want to be accused of this and be at pains not to appear at fault. (p. 101)

Ryde refers to a quote from Jacobs's 2005 paper 'For Whites Only', where Jacobs talks about wanting to be a 'nice therapist' who is 'not like the rest': 'Maybe to stave of guilt and accusations of not being able to understand our clients, we do what we can to show how sympathetic we can be but, in doing so, may find that we are chasing our own agenda rather than being present for the client.'

Ryde concluded that the above behaviours might cause avoidance of negative messages from black clients towards white therapists, therefore encouraging black clients to give predominantly positive feelings and gratitude. This can create a situation of over-compensation and compliance, rather than facing the challenge of racism.

Along with this, we must accept that there are differences between people of African and Asian heritage. There are dangers in the interpretation of cultural influences and intergenerational experiences.

Charura (in Lago, 2011) suggests a way of overcoming the dangers:

> I therefore advocate that it is important, through the therapeutic relationship when working with individuals of African heritage, to explore their thoughts and feelings and alternative ways of

understanding their experience. For example while I was working with a client with a diagnosis of schizophrenia, we explored her experience of hearing very distressing voices. A key question that enabled her to view her world differently was, 'if you were back home how would your elders explain what is happening to you?' Although the client was not in her home country this enabled her to explore her experiences within her worldview, including the effects of her African heritage. (p. 216)

In the above excerpt, we are presented with a challenge of considering a worldview. It matters that both parties will bring their life experiences, worldview and personal growth to the table during supervision. Power relationships in supervision can inhibit exploration about the challenge of racism in therapeutic practice. More often than not, the supervisor is seen as an educator and a guru in the profession, and this can sometimes lead to idealization. Both parties must become aware of this process and explore mutual responsibility for creating equality in the educative process.

Summary

We must remember that owning up to the dynamics of racism is not enough. Recognition trauma must be purposefully worked through for the benefit of clients both black and white. There is a lot to learn from what we know of how racism can cause psychological damage to black clients, and the anxiety that working with racism provokes for clients, therapists and their supervisors.

The ways in which supervisors and supervisees may differently experience recognition trauma need to be considered. There is no blueprint for what this may look like, but we do know that racism permeates the psyche in a number of inhibiting ways. We also know that recognition trauma, once acknowledged, opens a forum for feelings, experiences and the impact of racism to be made conscious and explored. Shame and guilt, hurt and rage are key elements of this process. Whilst the supervisor and supervisee begin to express and heal their own wounds from this challenge, a door will open for supporting clients with similar challenges.

If the supervisory relationship holds too much fear about addressing the challenge of racism in therapeutic practice, the supervisory relationship may fail the therapist's and client's personal development, and there will be a need to re-evaluate the impact of racism. We must consider whether we are brave enough to acknowledge our transcultural difficulties in this area. When racial difference is in the room, we can be sure that racism will impact the intersubjective space. Awareness of this means awareness of how racism can compound low self-esteem and evoke recognition trauma.

Supervisors' and supervisees' cultural frameworks and experiences of oppression will influence the manifestation of racism in the supervisory relationship, and also the role of internalized racism, splits, rupture, and gagging caused by the challenge of racism and recognition trauma. These crucial areas must be considered along with paralleling, interpretation and support. It is therefore important to make agreements about processing the challenge of racism in supervision.

Pointers:

- Whether the therapist is black, Asian or white, their relationship with the client is unique. In order to enhance their cultural competences, the history, cultural identity and experience of racism and racialized relationships of the client must be known and acknowledged.
- To work through recognition trauma, it may be necessary to have an agreement about reflecting on the impact of racism on the supervisory relationship.
- Be aware that recognition trauma is a process of working through the impact of racism.

9

Emerging from Recognition Trauma

Through dialogue and reflexivity, this chapter will explore ways of working with the conscious and unconscious impact of racism. Key questions about identifying and working with this challenge and responding therapeutically to the nature of the beast will be explored. Working with the apparent but unspoken in the therapist/supervisor dialogue and relational context of the theme will be supported. Using an interview with an experienced therapist, I will reflect on the key elements of exploring and working through the impact of racism and recognition trauma on the intersubjective space and relational process in clinical supervision. The impact of silencing and powerful emotions related to revealing racism and emerging from recognition trauma will be shared.

What does it mean to emerge from recognition trauma? To transform a gaze so that a black person, as in the quote from a client at the beginning of the book, may no longer frame their conscious thoughts within the impact of racism, assimilation and internalized racism. When a white person may no longer fear their role as a descendant of the perpetrator group, where their thoughts and actions may have been motivated by guilt and fear of retribution – a state that may seem untenable to some due to the hopelessness attached to trauma caused by racism.

When in my ancestral home of Tobago, I am not constantly alert to the responses of white individuals because I am not saturated by one culture presenting an overbearing bias due to skin colour. However, this does not mean that the effects of slavery and colonialism are absent. There are few signs of recognition trauma here, yet I am faced with the impact of intergenerational trauma and the intensity of how that gets played out between black people. I have heard comments from local people voicing their awareness that slavery and colonialism is still impacting the islanders. Although it is heartening to see many cultural elements that reinforce African heritage, there appears to be very little explicit challenge of the internalized racism.

Putting distance between a place of direct racism, I am more starkly aware of traits of humiliation, violence, and low economic status that appear to be accepted by the majority, who on this island are descendants of Tobago's original slave population. Dependent on their republican sister isle, many local people fiercely proclaim independence and concern about being dominated by Trinidad's Asian population. A heritage of indentured labour and proud resistance can be clearly seen through some behaviours. In this tiny part of the world, ancestral baggage and black Western archetypes are played out and recycled within a black and Asian population.

There is much work to be done to change attitudes to racism in therapeutic practice, and emerging from recognition trauma is one aspect of this. Bearing this in mind, and in view of therapeutic practice, several questions need to be considered:

> - How does recognition trauma present in the psychological development of individuals?
> - What does emerging from recognition trauma look like in the client's transformation process?
> - How can therapists, supervisors and trainers support personal development that involves the challenges of racism and process of recognition trauma?

The minute we encounter a new relationship, our unconscious stereotypes are challenged. In a situation when racism is the challenge, there are dangers of stereotyping. Therapist, supervisor and client may harbour unconscious stereotypes. We often think someone may be a certain way because of the way they look or talk. Even the clothes we wear play a part in stereotyping. Becoming aware of ancestral baggage and black Western archetypes as a source of some negative stereotypes that reinforce racism is a start to working through recognition trauma.

Carl Jung (1972) explained the phenomena of alchemy, that through metaphors and dreams and how when things come together, unconscious and conscious, past and present, there is potential to create something new. I see the process of emerging from recognition trauma as one that brings into focus old ways of coping with the challenge of racism and the opening of unconscious processes to bring a new voice that relieves both the oppressed and the oppressor. Emerging from recognition trauma may therefore come from an understanding of ancestral baggage, black Western archetypes and modern-day racist behaviour.

From this reflective process and challenge should emerge a more positive black gaze.

When visiting Ghana, I became aware of a gaze that reflected that local people were stereotyping me. On the one hand, I was welcomed home as a person of African heritage, and on the other, I was called 'white lady' and stereotyped due to the way I speak, my light skin and my European dress code. These stereotypes are practically unavoidable. They become the norm in white sociocultural interactions. Experiencing the other side of the coin was an eye opener for me. In the UK the gaze is different – I do not feel welcome in a genuine way, I am seen as black, though my skin is light brown, and I experience inappropriate reflection from the majority.

Things turn on their head in Africa and in the Caribbean, where the majority of citizens are dark-skinned. This stereotyping based on appearance runs deeper than words. There are whole communities in parts of Africa, Asia and the Caribbean where there are brown-skinned people whose presence may add to the pain and outrage of what we now know as shadism.

I hope that by now the use of concepts ancestral baggage and black Western archetypes may assist readers to find a vocabulary for the process of emerging from recognition trauma. So let's take a look at what gets re-enacted in the supervisory process when the challenge of racism is present and features of recognition trauma are manifesting.

I shall intermittently reflect on excerpts from an interview with Sadie, an integrative arts psychotherapist who is emerging from a fair share of racism, homophobia and recognition trauma in her training experience and supervision. You will notice that it is not a straightforward process. There are dips and peaks because the process needs to be mutually held between supervisor and supervisee.

Isha: In thinking about the challenge of racism in therapeutic practice, can you share with me your experience of being a black woman in supervision and some of the challenges that have arisen in your practice?

Sadie: First of all, when you say that, my gender identity is not binary. I have had many different supervisors, and I'm going to talk about supervision generically. I have a lot of experiences of supervision where I have been encouraged to discuss, expose, and explore issues around race, issues around gender, around class and racism. And there have definitely been some places where I have not been able to discuss those areas at all.

Isha: When you said your description of your identity is not binary, can you tell me how you would describe your identity?

Sadie: I would describe my gender identity as being gender-queer. I do not intend to transition; however, I would say my gender identity places me on the transgender spectrum.

Isha: And would you use the term black for yourself?

Sadie: I would describe myself as black mixed race because my racial identity incorporates all the different things that I am.

Isha: So what is your mixed heritage background?

Sadie: I was brought up knowing I was of African and European Asian heritage and all my grandparents were of mixed racial heritage.

Isha: You said that you had some good practice and supervision and also some that were not so good. Do you think that the not so good ones were influenced by racism?

Sadie: I think that they were not aware, particularly as a lot of my clients at that time were black children. I don't think they were aware of the impact at the time, whereas others were marginally aware, or maybe a lot more aware. And it [racism] came out as how they constructed my role as a therapist in relation to the client work or how they interpreted what was going on in the client work.

Where I have blatantly brought issues where I'm struggling with the client work and want to process issues around racism, the supervisor has not been able to hold that work, including even being unable to create or hold an understanding of what the client is saying. So, for me, it has meant that either I don't want to bring that to the supervision or the client doesn't get supervision of that area. The way I see it is that as I have become more mature as a psychotherapist, the supervisors have been able to understand it better. Early on in my career as a counsellor I was really lucky. I had two supervisors who were black women and they were able to do this work. So my experience of trying to bring race was not an issue. It was when I started to become a psychotherapist that it became quite difficult with some supervisors, particularly when I'm working with young people bringing issues of concern about racism and me working with that. They seem to have difficulty being told that young people have a perspective on racism. And they know what it is and they know how they are impacted by it, and they vocalize that. That's been one of the very interesting things to explore with different supervisors.

Supervisors displaying this resistance to accepting that black young people have a perspective on racism may be in denial about the occurrence and impact of racism. This is racism itself in operation. They may also be covertly responding from a perspective of the black Western archetype, that black people do not have feelings about how they are oppressed by racism. A modern sociocultural perspective on this projects the idea that we are a multicultural society and that younger generations are integrated and therefore do not experience racism first-hand. This approach may also perpetrate ideas that black people do not have the intelligence to understand, accept, or have their own perspective on racism.

This attitude perpetuates a one-size-fits-all response, influenced by white Eurocentric theories and black Western archetypes of how black people should be. It usually indicates denial and power issues of individuals who have tunnel vision about racism. Displaying an attitude that your version of racism is the only one can be detrimental to the psychological development of both black and white individuals. As part of working through recognition trauma, it is better to check this default position than blunder on not attending to the chaos that this may cause in the therapeutic process. In clinical supervision, the client's version of racism is the only true version, and this must be given attention and respect.

If this attitude is apparent, therapists can insist that they be listened to and that their supervisors work through their recognition trauma to free up attention for working with the process of racism. Emerging from recognition trauma will mean that therapists and supervisors can decolonize their approaches to working with the challenge of racism and unlearn their associated defences.

Sadie: **Things became more of a problem when my supervisors were not black. So I've found ways of bringing the client or I got better at picking supervisors. It was a sign because they don't get me, they could not understand me, they did not understand my clients, they had no concept of my client group. Early on in my career, I also had supervisors who did not want to go anywhere near black issues. They just did not focus with me on some issues of being black** [perpetuating racism]. **The focus would land in different places or they would ignore the presentation and what was happening in the process. They would plonk it over there, as though suggesting we ignore it, because they couldn't deal with it. It was like they were saying, don't talk about that part of it. And you feel that as a therapist when you are being supervised in that way. Where I feel I am being alienated, that's where I'm not comfortable, and that's where I have left supervisors.** [therapist's recognition trauma]

I can tell when people are fluid enough to be able to hold different issues that I am bringing, and I can tell when they are shut down because it was a subject that the supervisor doesn't feel it's something either to talk about or not knowing about [supervisor's recognition trauma]. It's almost like a butterfly landing on something and then it has to move away really quickly and they can't stay long enough with it. They will switch and I will be thinking, why have they done that?

Isha: Do you feel comfortable challenging your supervisors about this?

Sadie: It depends, because some of that behaviour is so distracting that I couldn't find it within myself [internalized racism]. It was problematic because not only was it about me and the supervisor, it was about a group. I noticed starkly how clients that I brought were being treated with suspicion almost and how at other times in the group supervisees bringing white clients were being treated well. You know something is being manifested there at that time.

Therapists and supervisors who shut down because they have difficulty addressing racism in the therapeutic process and in the supervisory relationship will have shifted their attention away from the relational process, and therefore they will have difficulty empathizing. This may cause a serious rupture in the therapeutic triad, a rupture that must be repaired for the benefit of the supervisory relationship and, ultimately, for the client.

Therapists and supervisors must train themselves to stay with, or 'hold' the complex nature of defences and powerful emotions that accompany recognition trauma. Just as we would expect to go into the client's world, or go alongside the client, we must find ways to hang in there and roll around in the dust, and wrestle with our emergence from this process until it is time to get up and brush ourselves off. It will then be possible to see the challenges and possibilities in a clearer light.

Isha: Did you find that this adversity related just to racism or to other areas of concern for minority groups?

Sadie: I think that my experience is that where a supervisor is able to own their own power within the supervisee relationship, it's not an affront to their identity, usually because they are already in a minority community. With some experience of discrimination, already they are more able to hear and move with a perspective where the client material brings up issues around cultural relations. So those supervisors who have had awareness and are clear about their own identity, who have had some connection and contact with a diverse community, are those who have not had difficulty in understanding or helping me to understand what is going on when I am struggling. [emerging from recognition trauma]

This is an indication of how experiences of multidimensional oppression can function to create an appropriate empathic response. A reflexive process develops from drawing on experiences of oppression and learning, and as a result, individuals move through recognition trauma to a more confident place. It may also show that a predisposition of recognized oppression makes the process of emerging from recognition trauma more accessible.

Sadie: I am not saying that middle- or upper-class people can't understand; I am saying I think it's a bigger stretch for some people who have not conceptualized these issues at all, who put themselves in a position of assisting me as supervisee to grapple with those issues as they come up. I am trying to understand and separate out what is happening in the therapy; what's happening with the supervisor I am with? What's happening to the client, and what is happening in the room between me and the supervisor?

Isha: And that is all to do with when you want to work out something that is about the challenge of racism.

Sadie: Yes, it can be about other forms of discrimination, but, quite frankly, the form of discrimination that is most difficult, not to bring but to think about, is when the client is bringing racial discrimination and the supervisor does not seem to have a clue what that might mean for the client. I can defend myself, let's put it that way. I can work with that if I feel it's happening in the relationship, but this is something that is compounded by the supervisor's lack of ability to empathically immerse themselves into the experience of the client that I am struggling with and what the client is bringing.

If I have a supervisor who is sitting there and can hold me, the client and my issues, then somewhere they understand and they can hold all the difference and it's not a problem. However, if there is an affront because I really think that is how it manifests itself when you are talking about racism, it gets played out by the supervisor minimizing it, avoiding it, denying it or acting it out in relation to it. [recognition trauma]

Isha: What are some of the ways that they act out?

Sadie: I am having to dig deep here. I know that I wouldn't say that if it were not part of my experience. I will say that I think that one of the ways is when the supervisor is not actually present. You turn up and they are not there, or they are late, or, hello, where have you gone?

Isha: So like a kind of rupture that they have induced by not being present.

Sadie: Yeah, it's like I have had different forms of supervision. I have had one-to-one supervision and group supervision, and I have seen that manifest in different ways. Sometimes my client has been black and that has compounded whatever the client's issues are, if I am bringing racism. Yeah, that kind of unconscious acting out in group settings. I know that is happening because having been a trainee where that has happened and I have breath in my body and in my response in relation to that, so I can see what's happening in the supervision context as well. Especially if I'm the only black person in the group. [recognition trauma]

Isha: Does being the only black person in a supervision group compound this?

Sadie: I am saying that sometimes what happens is that it is not named, and bringing issues of race is even sometimes seen as a racist attack, and I think it is unconscious that they think that only white people show their feelings. Yeah, experiencing it that way, I can reframe that as giving me more understanding of how clients might see me. It's quite hard when the group process is not aware of what is going on and the people involved in that process are not aware of what is going on. I think if I was really truthful about it, that has happened on a number of occasions. I was scared to say that, actually. Scared to say it, but that is my experience amongst people who are supposed to be aware of what they are doing. [recognition trauma]

Isha: What is the fear about saying that to me?

Sadie: It's not a fear about saying it to you – I know that you know.

Isha: About saying it out loud then.

Sadie: It's about saying it out loud; I think that is part of it because there you are in supervision trying to present your client, because you are trying to work with the process of what is going on and what it is supposed to be about. Sometimes I have caught myself in that place where I'm making excuses in my head about what is going on and then I think, is that what is going on? Did that just happen? That level of disbelief, when that happens, but a level of really knowing that it is going on. [recognition trauma]

Isha: Yes. So you are almost questioning yourself and what just happened – that is the point at which I see confusion, when that happens.

Sadie: Yeah, a kind of confusion, but it is not confusion because you really know that it is happening and you really know that that person just said that. And you really know that you have kind of like withdrawn, so it's like, wow! But you are being paid for your time. I think it's pretty hard when as a black person you are bringing a black client and you may be bringing something to do with racism or the way this person is acting out because you are a black therapist.

It's not so easy to put the client out there objectively. It's because part of that client's experience is your experience too. I am not talking about having some kind of merged identity with the client, I'm talking about there are ways that you also experience it as a therapist in the room. Your experience is first-hand and you have empathy for your client and how these people are not going to get it anyhow. You know you get it, but you can't check it out, because when you bring it to check it out there is denial or people feel affronted or they are not understanding or their defending all this, saying, 'I'm not racist', but they really actually don't know what you are bringing about how we are treating this time differently. So you end up taking the hero position, and you go in there expecting something because you need to make sure you bring in the client. [emerging from recognition trauma]

You go in there expecting somebody shutdown or burying their head in the sand and I don't want to see that. It's about your client, but it is not just about your client. You can create a number of different pictures of this, even though you can say, 'I know what is happening' and then ignore it all, or 'I know this is happening and I am going to challenge it' or 'I am going to forgive them for they know not what they do.' I don't know which of those positions is the most helpful because I don't think any of those positions are going to be helpful to the client. None of them is helpful to the supervisees or the supervisor and none of them is helpful to you because you end up in the position where you are educating them. [emerging from recognition trauma]

You end up carrying all of the subtleties, so what happens in relation to the client and you is that somehow, because you know about racism and people do not know how to deal with it, you end up having to process it yourself. Again, you are put in the position of a single parent, like, 'I am carrying this baby on my own'. The client group that I am thinking of is somewhere in the intergenerational trauma that you

have brought and this is perpetuated. So what options do you have?
You can't not bring it. [ancestral baggage]

*Isha: Some people do not bring their concerns about racism, and whether they
bring it or not, they are internalizing the pain of that situation that has been
marginalized. In addition to individual experiences that it brings up, all this is
not being held by the supervisor. So that is where the isolation happens, because
it gets turned back to you and it becomes solely your responsibility.*

Sadie: There is something about abandonment in that situation of
the supervision triad, but unlike a holding environment, the third parent required just walks away. They are just not there, so the mother/
therapist is left with the child as a single parent. So that is how it feels
in supervision of that kind. [Black Western archetypes]

There is something here that seems to connect with the concept of
ancestral baggage – when the black therapist's challenge of racism is
being brought into the supervision and they feel gagged and unable to
challenge the supervisor about their silence. The experience of internalizing pain and being marginalized and abandoned to cope with this
situation on your own plays a huge role in perpetuating racism. The
supervisee, in acknowledging that these responses are happening, is
thrust into their process of recognition trauma.

What can happen when someone is languishing in the silence? Is this
a moment of reflection, or has the therapist or supervisor disappeared?
We must analyse silence and know what it means in the context of therapeutic responsibility. Watson (2004) identifies silence as a means of survival. Silence may be an indication of the client's internalization of their
distress and ways of coping with racism. Silence of the therapist and
supervisor in supervision must be challenged, as they are not in a client
role during clinical supervision. Therefore, they must take responsibility
in their professional roles whilst processing and supporting the client.

Silence as a means of survival seems to be a common occurrence
when linked to the threat of oppression. I am aware that there are times
when I have silenced myself to preserve my ego and avoid the humiliation of making a mistake when addressing diversity or oppressive circumstances that I may not be too familiar with. This default position
of self-preservation does not mean I am a bad person; I am just a little
inadequate at that time. My belief that in the role of therapist or supervisor I need to be moving through this and not get stuck in this position is what helps shift my thinking from fear to action. To do this, I
must consider whether I am blocked and frozen in my fear of mistakes,

or still and in a reflective self-supporting position. Obviously, when with a client, this will be different than in supervision. All this is essential for emerging from recognition trauma.

Humans in the West are plied with suppressants and painkillers to ward off feelings. Self-medication is common, and we are encouraged to use alcohol, nicotine, caffeine and sugar to push down or numb powerful feelings that may seem uncontainable and can lead to depression or mental health problems. Unless the silence is meditative, it cannot aid individual self-esteem and build robustness against the cruel effect of racism.

According to Alleyne (2005; see Chapter 7), the internal oppressor tends to conflate with external oppressive situations (i.e. workplace oppression).

I believe that awareness of this process is paramount to working through recognition trauma. A space for processing the internalized pain and feelings about being marginalized and abandoned must be provided. If supervisors can recognize the need for this space, not only will it support the therapist and the client, it will be a breakthrough in the process of recognition trauma for the supervisor. This will provide a foundation on which to build a relational process that addresses the challenge of racism.

Therapists must be encouraged not to abandon their clients; therefore, supervisors need to hold their supervisees closer and tighter, to enable them to create safety to reveal their worst fears about working with the challenge of racism. Acceptance of whatever level a supervisor and therapist may be at in their journey through the terrain of addressing racism in therapeutic practice is a key area for emerging from recognition trauma. However, it is important to recognize a status of under-development when the supervisor is unwilling to acknowledge that unconscious processes may prevent their emotional and therapeutic progress in this area. It comes down to the status of the therapeutic and supervisory relationship, as Mearns (Mearns and Thorne, 1997) reiterates:

> In seeking to create a relationship which will foster the supervisee's professional growth, I need to be the kind of person with whom she can feel safe enough to express even her deepest fears and doubts. For me, this involves establishing a relationship where I am challenged to offer four basic conditions. The first is my commitment to the supervisee. Commitment is not simply the reliability afforded to regular meetings; it is an undertaking that I will be fully involved in our relationship no matter what difficulties we may encounter. Commitment to the relationship is an aspect of professionalism which forces me

as the supervisor to address the difficulties in the relationship even though my inclination may be to run away from them. (p. 116)

Although literature on supervision rarely alludes to what gets missed – such as the challenge of racism – supervisors and therapists must be ready to address this gap in their commitment to the client.

Following on from this, Mearns (1997) suggests, 'a related condition is my congruence as a supervisor; this is a technical term referring to the degree to which I am able and willing to be transparent in relation to the counsellor'.

The therapist and supervisor working with the challenge of racism may become incongruent whether they are conscious or unaware about their denial of racism. So, linking congruence with the emergence from recognition trauma can be a helpful way of exploring this challenge.

Mearns (1997) continues: 'The third condition which determines the health of the supervision relationship is the nature of my valuing of the supervisee' (p. 117).

Supervisors must reflect on the level at which they value their supervisees and how levels of valuing the supervisee may be influenced when racism is in the intersubjective space.

Mearns (1997) then confirms: 'Those familiar with the person-centered approach will not be surprised to find that empathy is my fourth condition. Empathy is the process by which I grasp the frame of reference of the supervisee and follow her personal meanings' (p. 118).

I would argue that there are times when it may be near impossible to empathize, when, as a result of racism, denial is functioning in a supervisory relationship. A black empathic approach can be helpful here (see Chapter 1). I have added this concept to the mix, but this does not require a strictly person-centred approach. When working through recognition trauma empathic qualities need to be based on knowledge of racism and cultural history, experience of actively engaging with racist concerns, and a belief that racism impacts individuals on a deep level. Thus, individuals respond to racism in a variety of ways, dependant on their exposure to racism, their levels of cultural capital and experience of multidimensional oppressions and learned coping behaviours. This context is transtheoretical and applies to all individuals. It is specific to black and Asian peoples, based on their heritages, historical backdrop, and personal experiences of racism. It is specific to white peoples with an additional inference of their membership in the perpetrator group. This difference means that therapists and supervisors need to be clear about not confusing prejudice with racism, if they are in a perpetrator group. Experiences of oppressive regimes backed by similar forms of hatred, for example holocaust and ethnic cleansing, are examples of this.

Mearns (1997) goes on to state that 'as a supervisor, one of the most important things for me to remember is that my supervisee is a different person from me: it is not my job to constrain my supervisee to model his work on myself' (p. 127).

Yes, of course it is vital to remember the diversity between therapist and supervisee and in a situation where racism may be apparent; it is also imperative that supervisors should expect to address the impact of racism, with clients and within their relationship with supervisees. Bearing this in mind as a key element of supervision, it is not about influencing the supervisee or enforcing assimilation processes, it is about anti-oppressive practice. Anti-oppressive practice is about actively working against oppression and perpetrating oppression within therapeutic practice and should be observed on all levels of personal development and clinical support.

This aspect of supervision may need scrutiny because it is easier said than done. Racism and assimilation are primarily about snuffing out difference in skin colour, so supervisors must do their personal work on the impact of racism on their lives.

Isha: How do you approach the challenge of racism with your own supervisees when that comes up in the supervision process?

Sadie: Because of my own experiences of supervision, I try to position myself relationally. If I find my internal supervisor is starting to sound like some of my external supervisors, and I know that is happening because I can recognize it, I try to stop it. So that's one thing. Where I find other interesting dynamics happening I can own that it feels like there is something going on that maybe we need to address in terms of how the supervisee is seeing me or what I am being asked to do in relation to something. (Coughing) [emerging from recognition trauma]

I don't know why I'm coughing, something in my throat.

Isha: Possibly because, as you mentioned earlier, this is something that is hard to voice and we do not often get the opportunity to do this and say things out loud about difficulty, challenge and marginalization in relation to racism.

Sadie: Yeah, it's like the stranglehold that psychotherapy has on issues to do with race are about shutting us up. I think that's part of it; you know, I feel that pressure to not talk about it.

Isha: So when you noticed in your supervision that some of that influence could be operating on you, is that what you are saying, that you have internalized some of that shutdown-ness of your profession, and when you begin to notice that happening you address it and you acknowledge it, you do something about it.

Sadie: I think it's harder to do that when you are tackling it at the time because you may not be able to process it as quickly as when you come away, and you think about it and you think, 'hang on a second'. I worry if people cannot raise it, reflect on that and look at it.

Like I say, there is more a lack of defensiveness in minority supervisors than there is in those who have more personal experience of any form of discrimination. They would look at that and question, 'did I do that?' 'Let's think about this' or 'let's try not to do that again'. I think that maybe if they can relate to it a bit more from their own experience in some way, there is more opportunity to look at how this feels for the supervisee, how this affects their work rather than, 'I didn't do that', 'I wouldn't say that', 'that didn't happen'. It's hard also to be able to stay in contact with the supervisor relationally when this defensiveness is happening. You are aware of carrying the baby on your own and you want something from them. It's not necessarily about reparation, it's about understanding; you want them to hear the baby crying. But I think they have got their fingers in their ears sometimes. They walked out of the room energetically. So rather than there being a triad, it's like, hang on, I am alone here with the weight of this.

Isha: So that supervisor needs to stay in the room.

Sadie: Yes, they do, regardless of how hard it is to be with you.

Isha: They need to stay in the room with you and the baby.

Sadie: Yes, no matter how difficult the baby or whatever the baby is triggering in you, as I understand it, that's useful information. It's like if you don't know what the supervisee is talking about, taking a defensive position is not helping the client. Taking a position of knee-jerk reactions does not help. I think there needs to be more reflection going on other than the supervisor being elevated to the position of 'I am only right'. My supervision training has really helped me understand what is required in terms of openness, humility to provide space for you, because, really, the role of the supervisor is support for the supervisee and the baby. It's not about how in charge you are or what you do know or about what you don't know at all. It's not about that at all, it makes a huge difference between those supervisors who can be open to a process of not knowing and non-defensive about it.

Isha: How did you feel whilst reflecting on these issues?

Sadie: Slightly overwhelmed by what it has brought up for me. Slightly fearful of what it is I am actually hearing myself say, because there is something realizing that some of my clients have not been safely held by the supervisor, really. Although I'm used to being a single parent and that's not such a bad thing, it would have been nice to have had this information and choice about my supervisor during training. When I started my work as a qualified psychotherapist, I very quickly chose a supervisor whom I felt I could trust, drawing on my experience of the one who had failed me. You cannot be a single parent all the time, and I do not believe that people want to do this on their own.

Summary

As in Sadie's experience of clinical supervision, I have known empathy to go out of the window when powerful feelings about racism are in the intersubjective space. It can sometimes feel like there is the battle going on internally, between both parties, and with the material that has caused an eruption of feeling. This situation is an essential component of recognition trauma. The supervisor must become aware of the need to clarify the relationship with their supervisee about how both parties may experience each other during this phase. Any assumptions or unvoiced and unexpressed responses to each other may need to be brought into the open so that a potential rupture in the relationship can be worked through. It is essential to remain aware of the mutual responsibility of both therapist and supervisor to work together for the benefit of their client.

As therapists, we must be aware of how the supervisor's denial can impact the supervisee and vice versa. Therefore, we may also notice that denial can cause clients to be denied the benefit of supervision in this area. This might be seen as a collective collusion and hindrance of moving black people's dilemma about racism on. Silencing and the intergenerational impact of gagging related to racism and recognition trauma requires therapists and supervisors to value the experiences and the perspectives that arise for clients engaging with the process. This requires therapists to be active in that they become aware that they may avoid taking black clients to supervision. Therapists and clients may feel the pain of racism and feel unable to express feelings about it because it is not being voiced in supervision.

Supervisors must be one step ahead in this process, so that they can utilize their role of holding both supervisees and clients through their emergence from recognition trauma. If this seems too much of a tall order, then supervision must engage in appropriate CPD to bring them to a place of confidence in this area. A transcultural anti-oppressive practice and the application of a black empathic approach is key to emergence from recognition trauma and must be recognized in therapeutic disciplines throughout the field.

I am unsure whether it is possible to completely emerge from recognition trauma, or any trauma, for that matter. Perhaps as therapists the least we can do is be hopeful in striving to emerge from our ancestral baggage and the influence of black Western archetypes, transcending the powerful negative responses that can get in the way of our practice and cause disconnection, giving us less opportunity to voice the impact of racism and greater opportunity to emerge less tarnished by our experiences. As Clarkson (in Bates and House, 2004, p. 61) suggests:

> There are three requirements for all associated helping professions that we be willing to move with our times, that we move with our art/science and that we move with each other.

Pointers:

- Identify aspects of recognition trauma and both clients' and supervisees' attempts to emerge from it.
- Allow and support the process of recognition trauma.
- The supervisee must have a space to process these elements of their client work and the impact that denial may have on themselves and their clients. This is working through recognition trauma.
- Be aware of where racism and internalized racism prevents discussion and exploration of racism and recognition trauma.
- Use the black empathic approach in discussing the impact of racism.
- Both supervisors and supervisees must expect and take responsibility for emerging from their own recognition trauma.

10

An Ethical Context

In this chapter, I will outline some of the ethical challenges that arise from reflection on the written text and its implications for practice. Some analysis of key ethical concerns presented by students and professionals during my study (Mckenzie-Mavinga, 2005) will be considered. The chapter will also encourage readers to try different approaches to acknowledging and addressing racism in the context of their discipline, service provision, and supervision settings. It is necessary to consider what 'ethical' means in the context of therapeutic practice and the challenge of racism. I will start with the knowledge that institutional racism is not ethical. This therefore means that individuals working within institutions and affiliated to organizations may need to rethink this context in relation to the challenge of racism in their practice and personal development processes.

Encouraging therapists and supervisors to break through rigid Eurocentric practice could be seen as an ethical concern. There is a lot of fear about transcending the traditional boundaries of taught therapeutic practice. This fear often creates resistance to trying out approaches that may complement work with individuals who themselves feel pushed outside of these boundaries and marginalized by their exclusion. I am aware that as a member of a marginalized group, my offering to a new discourse may be viewed as political rather than psychological and therapeutic. As an ethical backdrop to this book, I propose therefore that any organization or person who creates or perpetrates harm or disrespect to an individual or group because of the colour of their skin can be deemed to be acting unethically.

There is no need to be hyper-vigilant about racism, but there is great need for progress and transformation, and this may take time. Of course, our humanness means that we must recognize that it is near impossible to be completely ethical in any real context. However, as therapists, our work purports to support, validate, respect and guide individuals towards a healthy emotional state. I would therefore view an ethical approach as one that carefully considers the impact of racism on the personal and psychological state of individuals. This approach promotes healing and recovery from the damage of racism. A key question therefore remains: can we deem practice that does not consider or address the impact of racism unethical?

I was once challenged about my statement that 'racism cannot be eliminated'. I was thankful for the discussion that ensued, because my statement may have seemed provocative and closed, yet it created the promise of hope. I truly believe that racism towards black people has become so deeply embedded over centuries that it will take centuries to clear up the damage that it has caused. The consequences have also become an intergenerational feature of white people's personal development. Therefore, whilst to hope that we can eliminate racism may seem futile, we must not wallow in hopelessness or discouragement. It seems more rational to chip away at the damage that racism has caused. This is really no different to the process of eliminating trauma and how it is usually possible to find healthier ways of coping with its impact. It makes perfect sense to hope for an outcome that empowers individuals, raises their esteem and supports strategies to cope with the ongoing trauma and challenges of racism. Let's observe the following ethical concern from a student:

> Will engaging with the context of racism be viewed as educating the client or having an external agenda?

The main concern attached to this question was the implication that therapists might be making assumptions that might interrupt the therapeutic alliance. Acknowledging difference and sameness and exploring the impact of racism with the client appear to cause emotional turmoil. There is no wrong and right here, but I am proposing that a space to address concerns such as this in the supervision process will ensure ethical practice. Therapists need to ensure that their fears do not cause them to address racism in a patterned way that they apply towards black clients. Mindfulness, reflexivity and flexibility are important so long as therapists monitor their denial, naivety and levels of awareness about racism.

The list below indicates several ethical considerations that I shall briefly address:

1. Institutional racism
2. Terminology and homogeneity

3. Concepts
4. Assimilation and mythology
5. Silence
6. Rage

1. Institutional racism

If we are to start with training establishments, the trend towards essentialism in some of the more rigid psychological disciplines need to be challenged. This is a primary source for ethical consideration. The heart of institutional racism in therapeutic practice lies within therapy training organizations. In some of the transcultural workshops that I have facilitated, it never ceases to amaze me that there are still practising therapists who have never considered the implications of racism on some of their clients. This is the extent of institutional racism. In the psychoanalytical field, therapists may be more concerned with unconscious processes and lean towards interpreting experiences of racism, or cultural oppression. In this context, sociocultural dimensions of personal development might tend to be responded to through Eurocentric assimilative eyes that may be experienced as dismissal and/or lack of attention to the impact and historical context of racism. To redress this, therapists must think creatively and outside of the box. This approach is much like providing dolls with complexions other than white, or art materials that include black or brown paper to draw on.

If not addressed, a client who presents concerns about institutional racism may feel that they are not believed and viewed as having problems of fitting in or problems with authority, or with their learning. This then transfers the institutional racism into the therapeutic space and may condition the therapist's response if they are not aware or prepared to challenge their personal racism and institutional racism. The power of institutional racism should not be underestimated, and this is a starting point in a challenge of this type. The student's question below shows an ethical concern about power dynamics:

> As a white counsellor working with a black client, is it true to say that another dimension in terms of power and status comes into play, which may affect the relationship, or is this proposition racist in itself?

This is a really important question in terms of the white therapists working with a black client. Integral to institutional racism is white power, or in modern-day terminology, white privilege. Being aware of this level in terms of racism and diversity is confluent to the therapist's ability to empathize where racism is apparent. One could say it would be unethical not to consider this.

On the other hand, a rigidly 'person-centred' approach might not appear attentive enough to underlying cultural influences and oppressions if the client does not articulate their thoughts and feelings on this matter. In *Carl Rogers Counsels a Black Client*, (Moodley, Lago and Talahite, 2004) the writers seem to reflect a delayed response to the challenge of racism. This is shown in reluctance to address the term racism and the emotions of racism connected to the client's presentation until halfway through the book. As an onlooker, I became frustrated at the delay in addressing the racism in Rogers's reflective process and the parallel delay in addressing racism in the re-presentation of his work. I see this as the intergenerational context of institutional racism, where mistakes and omissions get passed on from one generation of trainees to the next. Once a model or example is regurgitated in literature and not challenged in the reading, the therapist is not encouraged to use an appropriate approach for their clients, and therefore a one-size-fits-all approach is perpetuated. This could be deemed as unethical in its contribution to marginalizing oppressed groups.

I view these problems as an unethical trail, because lack of acceptance and lack of attention to concerns about racism will inadvertently cause lack of empathy and ultimately non-maleficence to the client. An anti-oppressive approach will not be adhered to if these key aspects of ethical importance are not considered and acted upon.

2. Terminology and homogeneity

These aspects of ethical concern come into the context of using the term black and also the term racism, which are fundamental to the book. An openness and flexibility towards the use of the term black must be present in therapeutic relationships so that the client's identity development remains their own. By this, I am stressing that therapists and supervisors need to remain aware of how the term black might be associated as recognition of racialization and cultural alliances in the sociopolitical world. Professionals must also be aware how the term black might homogenize a client's identity or challenge the impact of shadism.

As I open up the possibility that terminology can produce an ethical concern, I am aware of the importance of connecting language with identity and my hope for greater reflection in this area. I maintain that my use of the term 'black issues' is to help designate a structural theme that incorporates a holistic view of the lives and lived experiences of people of African and Asian heritage who by nature of their skin colour may have experienced racism at some point throughout their lives. I do not think it is unethical to make this assumption. The term black in relation to individuals and their personal identity is subject to contradiction and political, sociological and artistic licence. As explained in Chapters 4 and 5, there are a variety of terms used to describe the identity of those with a darker skin than white Caucasian Europeans. Some people prefer to use the term people of colour, and this term usually incorporates the identities of those who do not wish to be identified as black. The influence of slavery, the apartheid system in South Africa and caste systems in India have played a significant role in the historical divisions between black and Asian people. These groupings and categorizations have also reinforced ideas about homogeneous groups. The language of multiculturalism gives us licence to use the term diversity, yet it is the divisions that have been inherited within different groupings that have caused sociological conflict and individual pain and oppression. This is not about the one-drop theory, which is a test as to who comes within the category of black, white or between. This is about the challenge of racism and different ways of approaching an intersubjective space where the influence of racism can be processed.

In my use of the term racism, I am referring to an oppression perpetrated by white people, backed by privilege and power, to the detriment of black people and people of colour. There is an ethical problem in using this term, because in some ways it is limiting, as racism is experienced in many ways. The concept of race, devised by racists to divide and rule and undermine difference, has many sides to it. Dalal (2002) uses the term racialization. This term seems to fit better with the doing to and dividing of humans into best, better than, not as good as, and worst, as commodities for economic gain. For want of a better word, and the more commonly associated word, I have used the term racism. In therapeutic work, breaking taboos about the use of the word racism is perhaps more important than arguing the semantics of this term. It is more important that our clients are given opportunities to explore their personal and institutional experiences of what racism means to them.

In writing this book, I am working with the oppressive factors that make up racism towards black people, hence my use of the term black as a divisive aspect of racism due to its negative attention to blackness. My introduction to the term black Western archetype draws attention to negative images imposed on the collective psyche that permeate both black and white psychology. This imposition of racism, where the shadow of institutional racism lurks, must be given equal attention to personal distresses caused by racism. Using the concept of black Western archetypes proposes that we consider the ways that physical features and cultural inferences are given negative connotations as they get exposed throughout society. Differences between African and Asian hair and the differences in skin tone are examples of this. It is not necessary for readers to agree with this terminology to use the concepts and suggestions that I have presented. The most important element in using the term black is to gain an understanding of racism and the challenges that it poses in the world of therapy.

Ethical concerns around using this term are likely to be exacerbated where this agreement is not upheld. Confusion about this context is down to individual relationships with the theme, and this in itself may create an identity crisis for the reader. Most importantly, we must be aware of the link between homogeneity and terminology. At every ethical corner, readers are encouraged to self-reflect, accept their personal challenges on this theme and take responsibility for how they inform others and affect their own progress when faced with the challenges of racism.

I have taken bold steps to address some of the concepts that are represented and form some of the contradictions that rarely get identified in therapeutic practice. One important ethical context that I want to emphasize is that not everybody describes himself or herself as black, and yet as the term is presented in the book some readers may think it is OK to address everyone in a homogeneous way, and that is not OK. By addressing some of these ethical contexts, readers will see that this is also a challenge for me whilst writing the book. However, we have to find a language to speak this speak, even if it does not please everybody.

3. Concepts

One ethical concern is the risk I have taken to propose concepts that have been created from my experience and from the need for us to have a language and some kind of framework within which to discuss racism. To confirm the value of proposing concepts, I have mainly relied on feedback, such as when people have said things like, 'We had this meeting and we discussed the term "recognition trauma" and it was very helpful'. I have received emails from a variety of people telling me they have discovered the term and they are using it. My intention is to nudge readers to add useful concepts to their vocabulary and develop new language so that we are not intrinsically repeating languages we have been taught that can be excluding and marginalizing concerns about racism. So, in some ways, it could be said that I am stretching the boundaries of theory and making them more flexible and applicable to the context of racism.

I have said to students, 'You can create your own language and your own theory; we are the makers of theory because it comes out of our practice.' This is how the great leaders of psychotherapy produced their theories. If we are willing to change our approaches and fill in the gaps, we may continue to develop theories about all areas of therapeutic practice and make therapeutic discourse accessible to people of all backgrounds.

These concepts I have proposed are created for training; using them can be tricky if we present them to clients, and I have demonstrated that it can work. On several occasions, I have shared the concept of internalized racism with clients, as described in the interview with Carlana. This appears to have been beneficial. Clients have reported having greater insights from this use of language. I would encourage therapists and supervisors to familiarize themselves with a language and concepts that they and their clients can use to challenge racism and work through recognition trauma. The student quoted below is curious about the ethics of exploring the language of racism:

> How appropriate is it, and when is it appropriate, to ask questions related to race and ethnicity?

This is a key ethical question because, really, it's about whether therapists make choices to ask questions about anything they feel might be useful to a client. Because there is a gap which means that more often than not a dialogue about race-related experiences gets missed in therapeutic practice and supervision, there is even more reason to be active in addressing this area. Otherwise, the oppression of racism is perpetuated. The second part of that question, asking when is it appropriate to ask questions related to race and ethnicity, bothers me. Again, therapists learn to use their knowledge of the client, their insights and intuition about parts of the client story and empathy and reflective process to assist the client's empowerment. The challenge of racism in therapy does not change any of this. It is the fears of therapists and their recognition trauma that may prevent them from taking risks in this area. It only takes a decision to be active in having a dialogue about race and ethnicity with the client. With appropriate supportive clinical supervision, the rest will follow.

Those places where we notice that we have feelings of embarrass-ment, shame, dread and numbness are the areas that we must pay atten-tion to, for the good of our clients. This is a bit like when someone is producing an essay and stating, 'I am not a writer', or someone drawing and stating, 'I am not an artist'. Most individuals are all these things, yet often we believe that we are none of them. This lack of trust in our creativity and flexibility makes many therapists approach their practice in a lopsided way that dismisses the importance of the cultural oppres-sion behind racism.

We have to get away from the constraints of the 'parental state', if you like. The pedagogy that we have been offered, and in some ways been encouraged to stick to in a one-dimensional way, is not really working for the groups that I'm talking about and some therapists that are working with those groups. Stepping further into areas that we may have avoided takes courage. Courage involves risk-taking, and so as not to remain stagnant, it is important to take whatever risks are needed to transform stagnant water into living water. In addressing these concerns, I don't doubt the risk of introducing new concepts, and I am encouraged to embrace the ethical implications of publishing my words. I hope that readers will be encouraged to do this too.

4. Assimilation and mythology

I will begin this section with a question from another student:

> Shouldn't non-white, African and Asian heritage people, as immigrants, strive to embrace the language, laws and traditions of their new home of choice rather than insist on sticking solely to their old traditions, at the state's expense?

This is a typical question about the process of assimilation in the UK and how this theme has an undertone of racism. The question in itself is political and has no real bearing on therapeutic discourse, except to show an unreasonable and ill-informed response to immigrants and Britishness. It is therefore unethical because it is biased towards assimilation and it generalizes and homogenizes. It shows the power structure of white privilege and, although enquiring, it is not helpful therapeutically. I do not believe it is true of the majority of immigrants arriving in the UK that they are unwilling to embrace language and culture in Britain. This in itself is a mythology and defensive ideology.

There may be a close link between assimilation and mythology. Unpicking the mythology of post-racism that appears when therapists fear the challenge of racism reinforces this link. We must ask these questions: is it unethical to behave as if racism is in the past? Would we say that about sexism or homophobia? In Chapter 1, I focused on the mythology of post-racism and unpicking this mythology because it is a concern for ethical consideration. I look at where this mythology has wound its way into the belief system of institutions and produced thinking that suggests we have done the work on racism, and therefore there is not really much to do – we can sit on our laurels and carry on as usual. If we are in the business of promoting good mental health, we must see this as an essential area for progress. Anything less than this is unethical.

5. Silence

I want to explore silence as an ethical issue in all its guises – silence in the therapeutic space, silence from the therapists who feel it is not kosher to mention racism, or try and explore the cultural frameworks of black people and people of colour in the context of racism. Silence in training, silences in not taking racism to supervision, or the silence of the supervisor. These are all ethical concerns. I want to outline and say a little bit about them so that readers will be clear that an ethical code of practice is not just about confidentiality or some of the areas outlined in the UKCP (United Kingdom Council for Psychotherapy) or BACP (British Association for Counselling and Psychotherapy) code of practice. There is a much wider berth of ethical consideration that comes with the challenges of racism in the context of therapy.

I have taken the risk to approach silence in a way that addresses speculation about its underlying causes. Silence as a common feature in therapeutic relationships may hold the key to an unshared dialogue. In the context of racism, silence usually holds elements of fear, hurt, anger, guilt and shame. This is why I have presented the concept of psychological gagging. This student's question pertains to silence:

> What if the client does not make concerns about racism explicit?

There is power in silence and there is fear in silence. In order to break through silences that may be caused by fear and denial, it is important to reflect on whether the benefits of naming the silence might be greater than the risks. This may raise the question of how do we know which might be greater? We may not know whether an individual benefits from a silence that is potentially protective or emotionally injurious, yet this does not need to prevent therapists from being curious. A dampened curiosity about the impact of racism means a lost opportunity to explore the challenge of racism in the therapeutic process. I would suggest that this is an ethical concern in the same way that therapists may want to explore over-identification and rupture with their supervisors. Maintaining an ethical approach means developing awareness of where lost curiosity remaining unchallenged may perpetuate racism.

It has been stated by students and professionals that the issue of racism is barely touched on in training, and that there are very few safe supervision places where therapists can unravel their silences about racism. I feel it is unethical to be silent about racism in therapy or supervision, and therefore there is a need to break through the silences. A process of ungagging must happen so that clients may benefit from greater connection about racism rather than resistance. With regards to the challenge of racism, therapists and their supervisors may at times be riding on resistance, and this therefore leads to collusion. If there were no problems about discussing collusion in supervision, it would be unethical not to discuss collusion linked to the challenge of racism. We must therefore remain aware that silence, as a resistance to the challenge of racism, may equal collusion if not explored in supervision. Silence can therefore be considered as an ethical concern in the context of racism and other oppressions. This is because the supervisor's silence may thwart the therapist's connected knowing and warp a relationship that should be open. In other words, the way we understand and empathize based on personal experience, knowledge of feelings and situations of racism can be highly influenced by a silence.

The therapist's unsupported silence may then silence the client or collude with the client's silence, meaning a lack of opportunity to repair unconscious or hidden pain about racism.

This could be seen as an intergenerational process of silence in relation to the theme of racism. If not interrupted, silence in this context may be deemed unethical because it will be dripping through the therapy bloodline and transferred into the client's well-being. In situations where this might happen, there may be clients who slip through the net without having had the opportunity to process the challenge of racism in their lives. It is vital that racism in the therapeutic relationship and in the client's material is not just acknowledged. There needs to be a period of processing the impact of the racism and its occurrence in the therapeutic relationship. This is why it would be unethical for supervisors and therapists not to prepare themselves for these discussions. In doing so, we may feel supported by knowing that this is a process, and although it may feel overwhelming at times, ultimately our knowledge base and wisdom will be expanded.

We have already identified situations where personal growth on all levels for client therapist and supervisor may occur. Clients who inhabit their unregistered silence may hold or withhold powerful feelings about racism. Whilst it may be considered unethical to break silence that may otherwise be reflective or protective, there is no excuse not to address the challenge of racism at an appropriate time, in a supportive way, which offers an opening for clients to share and recover from distresses caused by racism. Otherwise, a silence about racism should be addressed in supervision.

I would rather try to encourage a client to open a possibility that racism may be impacting their situation than miss an opportunity to engage with their internalized racism and recognition trauma, if it exists. If recognition trauma lies within the silence, or comes from opening a silence, therapists must be prepared to work with powerful feelings that have remained hidden. Fears about levels of rage that black people may have harboured because of centuries of silencing about racism have inhibited the process of working in-depth with the challenge of racism, and this in itself is an ethical concern that must be considered.

6. Rage

I also want to consider the issue of allowing rage and supporting rage in the context of racism, and I think that is a massive ethical issue, because it is a huge challenge for all of us. Your venting and where you are with this is OK. For some people, it will be really hard to listen to and accept that showing our rage is part of the change that needs to happen. Concerns about rage have been identified in this student question:

> In working in a mental health setting, why do I find it more difficult to make a connection to black males and find their violence more disturbing than white or Asian males? Could this be a huge justifiable anger existing from slavery and my white guilt?

In the Sainsbury review on mental health (2002, in Mental Health Act Report 2010/11), it was clear that many of the staff confused rage with violence, because they were afraid of violence. This inhibited their views of patient mental health. It is not about whether others accept our rage, it is about an opportunity to express it and noticing that it is one of the ways that we have been held back. Assimilation has caused many of us to sit on our rage and believe that it is too dangerous to rock the boat because of misinterpretations. It is unethical that rage has been suppressed in some people and that they cannot make a sound when they cry. Having been in that situation, I know what it is like. I cry inside when my clients cry in a voiceless way. I know what it is like to cry silently or hide when I am crying.

Fears about the expression of rage have caused unethical responses when individuals have not been able to contain strong feelings about racism. We only need to look at the over-representation of black people in the penal system and the mental health system in Britain to confirm that something has gone awry in the sociocultural nature of coping, both on institutional and personal levels. This shows us that the expression of rage about life issues and how these have been misunderstood or misinterpreted link to institutional racism.

I clearly remember a middle-aged Jamaican woman who lived in Brixton who was sectioned and sent into psychiatric care after being reported as singing hymns loudly from her balcony. This scenario had been repeated several times, because she found her religion was a way of expressing her grief and rage. She told me that she did not know why the police and doctors kept hauling her off to hospital. She was not given an opportunity to share her side of the story. She was one of several black mental health clients whom I worked with who did not know why they were taking medication. I offered the women some Reiki that she compared to 'laying of hands', and she began to talk for the first time in three years, since her first contact with the mental health system. I witnessed many stories of black mental health patients being shut down rather than listened to, and this was heartbreaking. I also worked for a short while with another black woman who felt that rather than sit and talk it was more helpful for her to sing. She stood up and without fear let out a powerful rendition, that I accepted as an expression of her rage.

In general, spaces for talking therapy are not set up to fully offer the time and attention that may be needed to encourage and allow powerful feelings of rage about anything, let alone racism. This in itself is unethical and perpetuates silence. Although I have never seen it documented anywhere, the cultural discourse of therapies in UK institutions suggest a limited period of time for each meeting, and, often, limited time for client contact with professionals.

Therapeutic practice in the white world is controlled by time and money. It has become normal practice to close down the session and the client's emotions within an hour. Many therapists, and I include myself, do not offer a therapeutic space that facilitates the expression of rage. We listen to our clients in cubbyholes virtually made of cardboard that reflect the stoic unnatural reserved culture in the UK. In short, we are boxed in and quietly listen and reflect when a space for loud voices may be needed. This means that clients are denied loud self-expression, and the expression of rage is viewed as abnormal rather than righteous indignation. I repeat, it is not ethical to have a space where clients feel restricted in expressing their rage and outrage about the experience of racism or any other ism. Think on this.

The perspective that rage is just scary prevents the idea that injustice, hurt and sadness attached to lifelong experiences of racism could be backing up on other intersecting oppressions. This is where the black Western archetype of the angry black person gets projected onto the rageful black individual and not taken for what it is. The hurt and intergenerational context of racism gets dismissed and replaced by blame and shaming. Closing down this as a perspective would be a defensive position and an unethical context of working with rage. In some ways, we could say that allowed expression of rage contradicts silent, inward, enclosed emotions that bind together in a network of guilt and shame.

I cannot stress enough the importance of therapists and supervisors working on their own silences and rage, and the ways that these powerful feelings may link to the challenge of racism in therapeutic practice. Allowing and supporting rage must therefore be considered as an ethical concern.

This email from Barua, an Asian interviewee, offers an insight into rageful feelings about racism and cultural marginalization:

Dear Isha,

Hope all is well.

I keep finding myself thinking about the last question you asked me: 'How did asking these questions make me feel?'

I would like to add just a little bit more. But I am really not sure what words to use. I keep finding myself getting knots of frustration and anger and soft rage and when I look inside to see what words are coming up for me, there's just really simple but strong ones, mainly ignorance, so I know it's an after-effect of answering your questions, and, really, by sharing it with you, it's a way of acknowledging it for me. How can such an experienced, long-standing supervisor who works at such great depth with a marvellous theory base just not know how to have a conversation about culture? (I am referring to my white British supervisor). Honestly, it baffles me. Colour and culture is everywhere? How can you avoid the conversation?

I have some relief, in the anger, that it's not just the therapeutic world this is happening in. An example of this is I am starting my little girl on solid foods soon and ordered a book to read about it. Yesterday I found myself wondering how I can follow the authors approach when it's all 100% totally British English recipes that incorporate her style. (It's not a recipe book as I would understand then but it's a theory approach of starting solids) there was no mention of any curry or Indian food. It summed things up for me really about how entrenched this ignorance is – so entrenched that people just don't even know they are blind to it or what they are missing.

I just cannot blame anybody for carrying the wounds of the past into the present over the years, through generation after generation; what other option did they have? It's mind-blowing how deep the issue goes, to the point that people of colour themselves are not even aware that that's the reason why they have blockages in their lives until somebody talks to them about it. It really makes me sad and angry and that's why when I visited places like apartheid museums in South Africa, aboriginal museums of the stolen generations in Australia and

British Indian marked places of shootings I cried like a baby every time. It abso-
lutely broke my heart to see what people have been through, and for what? The
colour of their skin. Gosh it makes me mad! And yet helpless too. When I left uni
to go travelling, the biggest and most interesting wake-up call I had was that
each and every country I visited were at war with each other because of skin
colour. white South African versus black South African. Aborigines versus white
Australians, Muslims versus Hindus. It's everywhere!

Summary

Consideration of ethics when reflecting on the challenge of racism in therapeutic practice may seem a huge task. It is an essential task, however, primarily because our job is to expose where this has not happened and make it happen. I have briefly covered six key areas for consideration and used these as examples of ways to look at making practice more specifically geared towards working with this marginalized area.

Reflecting on an ethical context that considers multidimensional oppressions, and for the purpose of this book, the specifics of racism, provides a key to language, attitude and behaviour. My aim was to generate thinking about taken-for-granted areas. It is not enough to use guidelines on ethical practice without considering the gaps and thinking politically about necessary changes. No therapist will deliberately harm their client, but all therapists who ignore the challenge of racism contribute to the perpetuation of racism and inadvertently contribute to the client's pain about oppression. In this chapter, I have taken the lid off a steaming pot, which is still simmering. This is my hope for taking seriously the impact of racism and the challenges of working with this area in therapeutic practice.

Conclusion

Transcultural clinical supervision must be set up to facilitate the cultural dimensions of the therapeutic relationship. In addition, there must be space for therapists to share their vulnerability and personal challenges when working with diversity and oppression. This is where the concept of recognition trauma is relevant. An important element of this process is freedom for a supervisee to develop his or her own style and invest in the expertise of the supervisor to support this.

Developing integrity as a therapist means that a parallel with cultural diversity can be created. Allowing this to evolve means facing recognition trauma in its many guises. This does not need to be a harmful or frightening process. It is a learning process that can also be supported by the therapist's personal development and their own therapy. Being attuned to intergenerational influences and ancestral baggage during supervision is a key area of this process. This is where both parties must be open to the challenge of racism and multidimensional oppressions and evaluate defensiveness. The use of a black empathic approach and constructive criticism is important here and will benefit this process.

Often, there is a layer of racism that we must get through before we can get to some of the everyday experiences. This presents as a gap between experiences of being really concerned about racism and facing the challenge of racism. There must be some kind of parallel with the counter-transference towards racism that happens on training and racism being singled out as a theme that can be perpetuated with our clients if we do not put this challenge on the agenda.

There are often isolation and blocks within the organizational context of support for the challenge of racism. The quote from a client at the start of this book ('When will I be able to live my life without having to think about being black?') must be paid attention to in a variety of ways that include what being black means to the client and the client's early experience of their cultural identity and racism. These aspects can be explored in terms of the client's coping skills when faced with multidimensional oppressions.

Evidence of ancestral baggage and black Western archetypes that impact shadism, identity development and internalized racism are key areas of this process. Support to understand and work through manifestation of recognition trauma is key to the challenge of racism in the therapeutic process. Therapists' and supervisors' abilities to reflect on the challenge of racism as it impacts on the client and the supervisory relationship are important. Strategies of empowerment that include openness to transcending racism and internalized racism must be considered.

The therapist carries around with them their own diversity and different elements of internalized oppression, depending on what adversity they have faced in their lives. When holding a space for the challenge of racism, it is important that the needs of white individuals are not permitted to distract from the impact of racism, on black and Asian clients or therapists. In itself, this is a challenge, and it is the only way that therapeutic and supervisory needs in this area can be met. It is necessary to have a dialogue about this dynamic if it becomes apparent.

In this book, I focused more deeply on the occurrence and impact of racism within the context of the therapeutic relationship. My intention was to open a dialogue where there may have been silence that can ultimately impact the client. The threads that link a client's experience and the challenge of racism are finely woven into what occurs in clinical supervision and the reflexive process. This concern may be more challenging for some than others. It depends on whether the individual locates themselves within the survivor or perpetrator group. All individuals are perpetrators and victims of oppression, and this can be a motivator for responding ethically to the challenge of racism. Akin to this is the individual context of intersecting identities and identity development, cultural collateral and multidimensional oppressions.

I have challenged readers to consider the impact of internalized racism and the process of assimilation that makes up the challenge of racism. The first challenge is about complacency underpinned by a post-racism ideology. I point out that choosing to be silent and therefore inactive is not an option, as it supports this mythology. In order to do this, we must reflect on our ways of coping with the powerful feelings associated with racism. Every time therapists, supervisors and clients experience these powerful feelings, they are going through the process of recognition trauma. Shame is one such powerful feeling that can hold individuals in a silent, voiceless place that perpetuates the mythology of post-racism. I have explained how homogeneity, stereo-typing and taboo can also contribute to this mythology. Therapists and supervisors can identify these problems and open a dialogue to ease restriction and psychological gagging.

Exploring the internationalization process that upholds taboo and informs therapists' responses is a key aspect of breaking through silences and creating safety on all levels of therapeutic practice. I have encouraged readers to link this process with an intergenerational context and trauma related to ancestral baggage and oppression.

In Chapter 2 I began to disclose the unspoken cultural nuances of sexuality and the impact of racism on families and individuals where there has been sexual abuse. I have described how the multi-dimensional context of racism, minority sexuality and sexual abuse can reinforce taboo and the responses of professionals. The concept 'cognitive dissonance' is introduced to assist with thinking about the impact of silencing reinforced by taboo and mythology. I placed an emphasis on therapists and supervisors not making assumptions about black sexuality and therefore being aware of how racism impacts on the hiddenness of these experiences. I have addressed black rage as a form of expression and coping with the way racism can compound other hurts.

Therapists and supervisors are encouraged to reflect on their own association with rage, and their anxieties about rage connected to rac-ism, and the ways that this can be internalized. Stereotyping and men-tal health labelling have been identified as key elements of this process. The concept of black Western archetypes and ancestral baggage were linked to this process, and I emphasized the importance of considering black rage as a challenge to racism and a feature of recognition trauma.

Part II took a peek into the juxtaposition of assimilation and rac-ism and how one of these inferences can impact on the other. I have outlined the role of the therapist and supervisor in not perpetuating institutional racism. They are also encouraged to be aware of their own assimilation processes and how these can either support or perpetuate internalizing of cultural messages.

Professionals are encouraged to explore the hidden nuances of racism that create defences and be willing to explore internalized racism. In Chapter 5, I opened a dialogue about black diversity and the internali-zation of whiteness, blackness and mixedness as aspects of black diver-sity. Stereotyping of physical features has played a significant role in the hurt of racism and lowering the self-esteem of black people who lack sufficient cultural collateral. Therapists and supervisors are encouraged to be concerned about how they listen to and respond to these aspects of cultural diversity.

I highlighted the additional dimension of gender, and I have encouraged readers to focus attention on intersecting identities and the intrusive nature of multidimensional oppressions. Attending to inclusion rather than one identity at the risk of marginalizing another is highlighted. Racism and gender oppression are what I call everyday oppressions that frequently emerge and rarely get addressed in the complexity of their mutual influences.

Acknowledging the intergenerational context of black Western archetypes and ancestral baggage is key to working with this challenge. I have shown that the challenge of racism clearly indicates the need to accept that racism gets internalized into the psyche and impacts from an early age. To encourage attention to this area, I have focused on the impact of history and heritage and ancestral baggage. The therapist's and supervisor's dilemma portrayed by Alleyne in Chapter 7 is a stark reminder of this challenge. The book culminates in sharing ideas about working with and working through the process of recognition trauma.

Trying to get my head around the ethical importance of my writing and addressing racism has been a challenge in itself, and I hope it has been as useful to readers as it has to my own learning process. Embarking on this challenge has enlightened me about my own personal challenges in this area, lest I, myself, remain gagged.

All transtheoretical theory is relevant and linked intersectionally to the ethics of challenging racism in therapeutic practice. Both black and white people are fascinated and intrigued by each other, which is why we want to be with each other. Assimilation helps this process along. 'Many black people live in the "Bush of ghosts" and do not know themselves separate from whiteness' (hooks, 1995, p. 32). Internalizing representations of whiteness creates a confused gaze; this is what I call cultural schizophrenia (Mckenzie-Mavinga, 2009). We must remain aware that all black people in the UK, irrespective of their class, will experience the imposition of whiteness. We are reminded of this on a daily basis by murders of innocent people. Stephen Lawrence was one example of this. We sometimes forget that many Africans took their own lives rather than face the terror of white domination and violence. In some ways, subverting black identities could be seen as killing a part of ourselves.

Therapists may inadvertently affirm whiteness and Eurocentric qualities of their clients without addressing blackness. Black Western archetypes arise from the negative bits that whites have projected onto black people. Black people, Asians and women and men alike interject negative stereotypes. This decreases our levels of self-love. Therapists must be aware of this impact and its racialized context. It is clear from present-day responses to the theme of racism that it still remains almost untouchable as a sociocultural phenomenon.

When referring to the training of counsellors, a white colleague stated, 'Everything we learn is white.' This statement confirms the inevitability of Eurocentric domination on both black and white therapists. It is clear that therapists need to be vigilant in our approach to unlearning, or to colouring in the theories that back therapeutic practice; otherwise, we are in danger of perpetuating the status quo. Then there is the issue of challenging assumptions about who people are and about their experiences of racism. Looking at boundaries and support in terms of the challenge of working with racism is an important ethical concern. It is unethical not to consult those involved in matters of racism. Alongside all this goes fear of offending the institutions and traditions of psychotherapy and counselling. These are just some of the ethical concerns that I have identified.

Realizations about these challenges offer a great opportunity to use our own therapeutic forums to process feelings about our identities and oppressions. Once these challenges become apparent, we are usually faced with the effect of multidimensional oppressions. An incident of racism may have occurred out there or with the client, and we may feel bad about ourselves, but this feeling is likely to be linked somehow to something that happened in the past in terms of our experiences of racism, gender or another oppression.

This quote from Junte, a Zimbabwean student, concludes the process of finding a voice:

> I remember a colleague who left the course because she was a black lesbian and she was challenging that you don't understand what it's like for me. I can never understand what it is like to see another person I can only understand these issues of being a black woman. When it comes to doing things it means I have to perform many times more than my white counterparts and at this age, besides being black and being too mature some people think she can't learn any more. Taking the point of black on black, I also understand that not acknowledging what I am doing and black oppression is different. Sometimes even being a foreigner and trying to fit into the new system, a new culture also brings to me black issues which are 'ubiquitous' as Franz Fanon said everywhere.

You cannot take a hammer to racism every day, but when you become aware of yourself in this situation, you may feel as though you are in a minefield. Perhaps you attempted to deal with it and then the challenge felt huge and you shut it down. It is never too late to get some support with what it has left you with, so that when the next challenge comes it is not backed up on the last one, and you may feel more supported. It is a normal thing to talk about these challenges and get support, even if it's five minutes on the phone to someone you trust who can remind you of your worth.

References

Alleyne, A. (2005). *Invisible Injuries and Silent Witness:* The Shadow of Racial Oppression in Workplace Contexts. *Psychodynamic Practice* 11(3), 283–99.

Alleyne, A. Tuckwell, G. Shears, J. and Wheeler, S. (2008). *Working With Diversity in Counselling.* Leicester: University of Leicester.

Anderson, D. S. (2015). *Emmett Till: The Murder That Shocked the World and Propelled the Civil Rights Movement.* Jackson, MS: University Press of Mississippi.

Arie, I. (2006). *Testimony:* Vol. 1, Life & Relationship. US: Motown Records [album].

Barnard. C. (2001). *Constructing Lived Experiences: Representations of Black Mothers in Child Sexual Abuse Discourses.* Ashgate: Surrey and Burlington VT.

Basu, N. (2013). *Honour Killings: India's Crying Shame. Aljazeera.* 28 November.

Bates, Y. and House, R. (2004). *Ethically Challenged Professions.* Llangarron: PCC Books.

Berger, P. (1993). *The Social Construction of Reality.* New York: Penguin.

Briscoe, C. (2006). *Ugly.* London: Hodder & Stoughton.

Briscoe, C. (2008). *Beyond Ugly.* London: Hodder & Stoughton.

Butler, L. and Homer, U. (2010). *Listen My Son: Wisdom to Help African American Fathers.* US: Abingdon Press.

Byfield, C. (2008). *Black Boys Can Make It.* Stoke-on-Trent: Trentham Books.

Campbell, T. (2011). Interview with British Director Topher Campbell. *Guardian Professional.* 30 March.

Carroll, M. and Tholstrup, M. (2004). *Integrative Approaches to Supervision.* London: Jessica Kingsley.

Carson, C. and Shephard, C. Eds (2002). *A Call to Conscience. Landmark speeches of Dr Martin Luther King, Jnr.* New York: Warner Books.

Cartwright, S. (1851). Report on the Diseases and Physical Peculiarities of the Negro Race. *The New Orleans Medical and Surgical Journal,* May, 691–715.

Constantine-Simms, D. (ed.) (2001). *The Greatest Taboo.* California: Alyson.

Dalal, F. (2002). *Race, Color and the Process of Racialization.* London: Brunner-Routledge.

d'Ardenne, P. and Mahtani, A. (1989). *Transcultural Counselling in Action.* London: Sage.

Davids, M. F. (2011). *Internal Racism.* Basingstoke: Palgrave Macmillan.

Davis, A. Y. (1990). *Women, Culture & Politics.* US: Knopf Doubleday Publishing Group.

DeGruy, J. (2005). *Post Traumatic Slave Syndrome.* US: Joy DeGruy.

Dhillon-Stevens, H. (2004). Anti-Oppressive Practice in the Supervisory Relationship. In Carroll, M. and Tholstrup, M. (eds.), *Integrative Approaches to Supervision.* London: Jessica Kingsley.

Dhillon-Stevens, H. (2005). Personal and Professional Integration of Anti-oppressive Practice and the Multiple Oppression Model in Psychotherapeutic Education. *The British Journal of Psychotherapy Integration*, 1(2), 47–62.

Dryden, W. and Thorne, B. (eds.) (1991). *Training and Supervision for Counselling in Action*. London: Sage.

Ina-Egbe, E. (2010). *Developing a Positive Racial Identity. The Psychotherapist*, 44 (Spring), 10–12.

Eleftheriadou, Z. (1994). *Transcultural Counselling*. London: Central Book Publishing.

Elliot, J. (1968). Jane Elliot's *Blue Eyes Brown Eyes Exercise*. www.JaneElliot.com.

Ethnic Health Initiative. (2010). Ethnicity and Use of the Mental Health Act. 24 May 2010. London. http://bmehealth.org/.

Fanon, F. (1986). *Black Skin White Mask*. London: Pluto.

Fernando, S. (ed.) (1995). *Mental Health in a Multi-Ethnic Society*. London: Routledge.

Fletchman Smith, B. (2000). *Mental Slavery*. London: Rebus.

Gilman, S. (1985). *Difference and Pathology: Stereotypes of Sexuality, Race, and Madness*. Ithaca: Cornell University Press.

Grier, W. Price, M. and Cobbs, P. (1992). *Black Rage*. New York: Basic Books.

Hernton, C. (1973). *Sex and Racism*. Hertfordshire: Granada Publishing.

Hill, L. (2012). *Black Rage* [song by Lauryn Hill].

hooks, B. (1984). *Feminist Theory From Margin to Centre*. New York: South End Press.

hooks, B. (1992). *Black Looks*. New York: South End Press.

hooks, B. (1993). *Sisters of the Yam*. London: Turnaround Press.

hooks, B. (1995). *Killing Rage: Ending Racism*. Middlesex: Penguin.

hooks, B. (2001). *Salvation*. London: Women's Press.

Howitt, D. and Owusu-Bempah, J. (1994). *The Racism of Psychology*. Hemel Hempstead, UK: Harvester Wheatsheaf.

Hughes, L. (1955). *Not Without Laughter*. St. Louis, MO: Turtleback.

Hussain, Y. and Bagguley, P. (2007). *Moving on Up*. Stoke-on-Trent and Sterling, USA: Trentham.

Jackson, V. (1996). *Racism and Child Protection: The Black Experience of Child Sexual Abuse*. London: Cassell. Used with permission of Bloomsbury Publishing PLC.

Jung, C. (1969). *The Archetypes and the Collective Unconscious*. London: Routledge & Kegan Paul.

Klein, M. (1946). *Envy and Gratitude and Other Works 1946–1963*. London: The Melanie Klein Trust and Virago.

Klein, M. (1975). *Love, Guilt and Reparation and Other Works 1821–1945*. London: Hogarth.

Lago, C. (2006). *Race, Culture and Counselling*. Maidenhead and New York: Open University Press.

Lago, C. (ed) (2011). *The Handbook of Transcultural Counselling and Psychotherapy*. Maidenhead and New York: Open University Press.

Lynch, W. Willie Lynch letter: *The Making of a Slave* (1712). *Finalcall.com News*. Last updated 22 May 2009. This speech was said to have been delivered by Willie Lynch on the bank of the James River in the colony of Virginia.

Mckenzie-Mavinga, I. (2009). *Black Issues in the Therapeutic Process*. Basingstoke: Palgrave Macmillan.

Mckenzie-Mavinga, I. (2010). The Myth of Post Racism. Paper. www.Baatn.co.uk.

Mahmud, H. (2008). How Sharia Law Punishes Raped Women. *FrontPageMagazine. com.* 17 November.

Mason-John, V. and Khambatta, A. (1993). *Lesbians Talk, Making Black Waves.* London: Scarlet.

Mearns, D. and Thorne, B. (1997). *On Being a Supervisor: Person-Centred Counselling in Action.* London: Sage.

Moodley, R. Lago, C. and Talahite, A. (2004). *Carl Rogers Counsels a Black Client: Race and Culture in Person-Centred Counselling.* Llangarron: PCCS.

Moodley, R. (2003). *Matrices in Black and White:* Implications of Cultural Multiplicity for Research in Counselling and Psychotherapy. *Counselling and Psychotherapy Research,* 3(2), 115–121.

Ocheing, B. and Hylton, C. (2010), *Black Families in Britain as the Site of Struggle.* Manchester: Manchester University Press.

Payne, H. (ed.) (2008). *Supervision of Dance Movement and Psychotherapy.* London: Routledge.

Powell, D. (October 2013). Unpublished journal.

Roberts, Y. (2012). Campaign calls for open investigations into deaths of mental health patients. *The Observer.* 26 May.

Rycroft, C. (1968). *A Critical Dictionary of Psychoanalyisis.* New York: Penguin.

Sainsbury Centre for Mental Health (2002). *Review in Health Mental Health Act Report* 2010/11.

Scheurich, J. and Young, M. (1997). *Colouring Epistemologies:* Are Our Research Epistemologies Racially Biased? *Educational Researcher* 26(4), 4–16.

Sewell, H. (2009). *Working with Ethnicity, Race and Culture in Mental Health.* London and Philadelphia: Jessica Kingsley.

Solomon, S. (2014) *Far from the Tree.* London: Vintage Books.

Tuckwell, G. (2002). *Racial Identity, White Counsellors & Therapists.* Buckingham and Philadelphia: Open University Press.

Watson, V.V.V. (2004). *The Training Experiences of Black Counsellors.* Unpublished PhD thesis, University of Nottingham.

Wheeler, S. (ed.) (2006). *Difference and Diversity in Counselling.* Basingstoke: Palgrave Macmillan. Reproduced with permission of Palgrave Macmillan.

Supportive reading

Berthoud, R. (2006). *National Survey of Ethnic Minorities: 6. Family Formation in Multicultural Britain.* Research, Essex Institute for Social and Economic Research, University of Essex.

BME Pilot Campaign. *A Report on Mental Health Problems in the South Asian Community. (2010).* Report. Harrow, North West London. Research carried out March and May 2010.

Boggan, S. (2006). Interview with Constance Briscoe. *Guardian.* 14 October.

Caligor, L., Bromberg, P. and Meltzer, J. (1984). *Clinical Perspectives on the Supervision of Psychoanalysis and Psychotherapy.* New York: Plenum Press.

Costigan, L. (2004). *Social Awareness in Counselling.* New York: Universe.

Cress Welsing, C. (1991). *The Isis Papers*. Chicago: Third World.

Francis, E. and Sashidharan, S. (1993). *Epidemiology, Ethnicity and Schizophrenia*. In W.I.U. Ahmad (ed.), *Race and Health in Contemporary Britain*. Buckingham: Open University Press.

Holmes, J. (1993). *John Bowlby and Attachment Theory*. London: Routledge.

Meeston, C. M. Trapnell, P. D. and Gorzalka, B. B. (1996). Ethnic and Gender Differences in Sexuality: Variations in Sexual Behaviour Between Asian and non-Asian University Students. *Archives of Sexual Behaviour* 25(1), 33–72.

Pinkola Estes, C. (1996). *Women Who Run With the Wolves*. New York and Toronto: Ballantine/Random House.

Poston, W. (1990). *The Biracial Identity Development Model. Journal of Counseling & Development* 69, 152–5.

Prins, H. Backer-Hoist, T. Francis, E. et al. (eds.) (1993). Report of the Committee of Inquiry into the Death in Broadmoor Hospital of Orville Blackwood and a Review of the Deaths of Two Other Afro-Caribbean Patients: *Big, Black and Dangerous?* London: Special Hospitals Service Authority (SHSA).

Samuels, A. Shorter, B. and Plant, F. (1986). *A Critical Dictionary of Jungian Analysis*. London: Routledge.

Index